Group Homes for People
with Intellectual Disabilities

Group Homes for People with Intellectual Disabilities

Encouraging Inclusion and Participation

Tim Clement and Christine Bigby

Foreword by Professor Jim Mansell

Jessica Kingsley Publishers
London and Philadelphia

First published in 2010
by Jessica Kingsley Publishers
116 Pentonville Road
London N1 9JB, UK
and
400 Market Street, Suite 400
Philadelphia, PA 19106, USA

www.jkp.com

Library of Congress Cataloging in Publication Data

Clement, Tim.
Group homes for people with intellectual disabilities : encouraging inclusion and participation / Tim Clement and Christine Bigby ; foreword by Jim Mansell.
p. cm.
Includes bibliographical references and index.
ISBN 978-1-84310-645-6 (pb : alk. paper) 1. Group homes for people with mental disabilities.
2. People with mental disabilities--Housing. I. Bigby, Christine. II. Title.
HV3004.C54 2009
362.3'85--dc22
2009014496

British Library Cataloguing in Publication Data
A CIP catalogue record for this book is available from the British Library

ISBN 978 1 84310 645 6

Printed and bound in Great Britain by
Athenaeum Press, Gateshead, Tyne and Wear

From Tim... To Cathy, for her encouragement at home; and to Chris, for her persistence at work.
From Chris... To Alma, for seeing the closure to the very end; and to Tim, for an always challenging research partnership.

Acknowledgements

The original research project, *Making Life Good in the Community*, upon which this book is based was funded by the Victorian Department of Human Services (DHS). That the Department supported such an innovative design based on ethnography and action research was due to the vision of Alma Adams and John Leatherland that such a project was worth the risk and could contribute significant knowledge about community living for people with severe intellectual disability. We thank John and Alma for their foresight and their continued support throughout the project. The research was made possible by the willingness of the Department's staff members to participate. We also thank the residents with intellectual disabilities whose lives we shared for three years, their supportive family members and the members of an enthusiastic research steering committee. The specific contributions of Patsie Frawley, Kelley Johnson, Alan Robertson and Silvia Warren who participated in parts of the original research are also gratefully acknowledged.

Contents

List of figures and tables

Figures

Tables

Foreword

The 'Implementation Gap' in Supported Accommodation for People with Intellectual Disabilities

Almost since the beginning, there has been concern that the opportunities inherent in community living for people with intellectual disabilities were not being realised in practice. The strong, consistent policy narrative in many Western countries, that community living arrangements are better than care in long-stay institutions, has been accompanied by a counterpointed theme, that these services are not as good as they should be. Just as results showing exemplary outcomes from demonstration projects were being published, others were publishing results showing that 'second-generation' housing projects were not doing as well. Reviews of research have highlighted variation in these results and pointed to programmatic and organisational variables as the key source of this variation, along with the characteristics of the people served (Emerson and Hatton 1994; Kozma, Mansell and Beadle-Brown 2009; Mansell 2006).

One attempt to understand the reasons for the gap between what has been shown to be possible and what is routinely achieved in supported accommodation has been to argue that group homes – the most widespread form of community living – are themselves necessarily institutional. The argument is that because group homes are organised by service agencies they inevitably recreate the institutional care practices of larger congregate care settings. The key intervention to overcome this is to support people to attain their own homes in their own right as citizens, and to require service agencies to provide support on terms dictated by the disabled person. Thus the problem is which category the person and their home are placed in. If the person is a resident in supported accommodation run by a service agency, it is argued that it will be a constant battle to overcome the pressures of economy, management and regulation to adopt institutional practices, and that eventually the setting will be just a smaller-scale version of the large residential institutions of the past. The solution is to re-classify the person as a private citizen living in their own home, so that service agencies have to treat them as they would treat other members of the public (Ericsson 1996; Kinsella 1993). This has been a popular policy initiative and there is some evidence that people who receive support in their own apartments or houses, live with people they choose to, and control the kind of service they receive, experience a better quality of life, at least in some respects (Emerson *et al.* 2001; Howe, Horner and Newton 1998; Stancliffe and Keane 2000). The implication is that a second wave of deinstitutionalisation from group homes to supported living is now required.

The first important contribution this book makes is to examine this position in some detail. The authors point out that a great many people now live in group homes and that it may be difficult to resource and organise a second wave of service development to move people into their own homes. They also make a more fundamental point: people with the most severe intellectual disabilities are never in the position to make informed choices themselves about where they live, who they live with, or how they are supported to live their life. The nature of their impairments means that other people – family members, advocates, service agency staff – have to make decisions about these things on behalf of the person with intellectual disabilities. Using language to describe the person as a 'private citizen' or 'sovereign of their own home', may be helpful in cueing services and society to respond to people with intellectual disabilities in certain ways but it is not an accurate account of what really happens.

In practice, many people with severe and profound intellectual disabilities will continue to live in circumstances largely dictated by other people. For these people, 'supported living' is not likely to be a guarantee of a better life. The task therefore remains, to understand why the quality of life people experience in community settings is often not as good as it could be.

There have been several attempts to suggest answers to this question. Landesman (1988) and Mansell *et al.* (1987) have suggested that sustaining quality over time is difficult given factors such as staff turnover and shifting management interest, and have pointed to self-evaluation against resident quality of life as a key intervention. Commenting at a broader, service-system level, Mansell (1996) cites unclear goals and lack of direction, insufficient help and preparation for staff, and the absence of monitoring and accountability as the causes of poor performance. At an even broader level, Felce *et al.* (1998) and Castellani (2005) identify the impact of competing and conflicting policy requirements on the development of community-based services, and illustrate how these cut across laudable aims to support people with intellectual disabilities.

What this book does, for the first time, is to show how these factors play out in the lives of people with intellectual disabilities and the staff who support them. Starting with detailed descriptions of daily life, Clement and Bigby show how staff struggle to find a way through the lofty goals of community living, the substantial impairments of the individuals they support and the context provided by the organisations that employ them. They show how apparently trivial decisions made by officials far removed from the lives of the people served cut right across the aims and philosophy of the service that staff are trying to provide. The picture that emerges is not only of a difficult task made harder, but of an organisation demonstrating over and over again that it does not understand, nor seemingly care very much, what it is doing to people with intellectual disabilities and the staff it employs to support them. It is an important contribution to the literature on supported accommodation for people with intellectual disabilities to trace the relationship between how decisions made elsewhere affect the reality of daily life. The rise of general management in human services has been accompanied by an assumed separation between management decisions and care practice, so that senior managers claim that their actions do not interfere with the delivery of good support by staff to the people they serve. This book shows that this is not true – the actions of senior managers directly affect the quality of life of people with intellectual disabilities in many practical ways.

In a sense, then, this book is about a failure of management and leadership. The development of community living to replace institutional care at Kew in Melbourne could be regarded as a case study of the wrong buildings, in the wrong places, with the wrong furnishings, staffed by people with the wrong training, managed according to the wrong rules, with the wrong policies, the wrong leadership and the wrong purposes. The good that is being achieved is too often in spite of, rather than because of, the organisations that set up and run the services.

But it is not as simple as this. The description given by Clement and Bigby could apply to many services in many countries. So this is not just a case study of the poor implementation of the ideal of community living, but an example of a common problem. Nor is the problem simply that these services were set up by Government agencies rather than by non-profit providers. Some of the best examples of community living were set up by Government agencies (Felce and Toogood 1988; Lowe and de Paiva 1991; Mansell *et al.* 1987; Mansell, McGill and Emerson 2001), and the efforts of the Victorian Department of Human Services to introduce active support show that they are trying to improve service quality.

Rather, this example illustrates how difficult it is to retain a focus on what really matters in providing services for people with severe and profound intellectual disabilities – the quality of life of the individuals concerned. Thus the fundamental issue to address is how important the quality of life of people with severe and profound intellectual disabilities is deemed to be when judged against other criteria such as regulations for worker health and safety, public building standards, operating procedures for financial or personnel matters; or, at a broader level, when judged against organisational principles such as uniformity, reputation and dependence. At present, these demands seem more potent than the quality of life of the individual and whenever they are in conflict with that quality of life they win through.

Switching the balance of power so that the individual's quality of life trumps other considerations requires action on more than one front. First, legislative action to enshrine individual rights is important. For example, if health and safety regulations are being used to reduce the risk of staff being injured due to challenging behaviour by preventing the person with intellectual disabilities from taking part in everyday activities at home and in the community, human rights and disability discrimination legislation can provide an important counter-balance. Second, evidence of the gap between policy and practice, and evidence about what helps and what hinders achieving a better quality of life for disabled people provides a narrative about how things could be different. As Clement and Bigby point out, the rhetoric of evidence-based policymaking provides an important opportunity to debate the impact of decision-making on the quality of life of individual people. Third, political processes have to be used to give priority to the issue. Ultimately, what gets noticed and dealt with is what has a lobby putting its case. Service users (as far as they can), families, advocates and staff have to work together to build and sustain that lobby as a collective force protecting the vision of community living for everyone, and advocating the practical steps needed to make it a reality.

Jim Mansell
Tizard Centre
University of Kent, Canturbury
July 2009

Chapter 1

Introduction

Adults with intellectual disabilities who have left their family home live in various 'types' of accommodation. Depending on the location, it may be called a boarding home, community residential unit, core and cluster housing, dispersed supported living, group home, hostel, nursing home, registered care home or village community (Braddock *et al.* 2001). The use of different terminology and the range of accommodation models are related to factors such as the history of social policies and the associated development of services, available money, alternative service philosophies and the preferences of different service providers (Mulvany, Barron and McConkey 2007).

This book is concerned with one of these service models, the group home, which Jan Tøssebro (2005) had suggested is the emblem of 'community care'. Since a 'group' can be defined as 'two or more people', it is no surprise to find that the term 'group home' has been applied to architecturally diverse residences that vary both in the number of people who live in a setting and the amount of support that people receive to live there.

For the purpose of this book, we want to rescue 'group home' from being a generic term that is applied to a variety of settings, by putting some boundaries around it. These boundaries reflect the context for the research findings that we present and also provide some criteria for describing and managing group homes in the future.

We define a group home as accommodation for between four and six people, where *extensive* or *pervasive* paid staff support is provided to the residents, both in the home and when leaving it to use community-based settings.

At a general level there is no 'one best way' for this housing and support to be organised. It would be unusual for a group home to be owned by the people who live in it, although there is nothing that precludes this. In practice, there are a wide range of organisations, including statutory authorities, housing associations and not-for-profit or private (for profit) agencies, that provide either the housing and support or both the housing and support. Current thinking suggests that the housing and support elements should be separate, i.e. provided by different agencies, as this offers particular benefits to the residents. For example, we know of a situation where an organisation providing poor support was replaced by a new agency, which allowed the residents to remain in their home and receive improved support. In another case, ageing residents moved from a house that had become unsuitable to a fully accessible bungalow. The staff group who had supported the residents for a number of years were able to move with them to their new home.

The notions of extensive and pervasive support are taken from the American Association on Intellectual and Developmental Disabilities' (AAIDD) work on support intensities (Luckasson *et al.* 2002). Extensive supports are characterised by 'regular involvement (e.g., daily) in at least some environments (e.g., school, work, or home) and not time limited nature (e.g., long-term support and long-term home living support)', whilst pervasive supports are characterised by 'their constancy, high intensity, provision across environments, potentially life-sustaining nature. Pervasive supports typically involve more staff members and intrusiveness than do extensive or time-limited supports' (p.152).

What follows from our definition of a group home is that the residents are more likely to be people with severe or profound intellectual disabilities. We are not advocating that people with severe or profound intellectual disabilities should only live in group homes, or that people with moderate or mild intellectual disabilities should be excluded from living in them. We are simply noting that this is increasingly the outcome of current policies. Our interest in group homes for people with severe and profound intellectual disabilities is based on a number of pragmatic realities that are developed during the course of the chapter:

- Group homes have been, and will continue to be, part of the landscape of intellectual disability services. They are perceived to be the practical implementation of the relevant social policy for people with intellectual disabilities.

- The 'best' group homes can realise 'quality of life' outcomes for people with severe and profound intellectual disabilities that are superior to larger residential settings.

- Although well-managed, highly individualised services are likely to achieve even better outcomes, supporting all people with severe and profound intellectual disabilities in this way is likely to be perceived as being too costly. Group homes are therefore a means of meeting the housing and support needs of people with severe and profound intellectual disabilities in a pragmatic way.

A note on terminology

The language used to label and categorise people with intellectual disabilities changes over time and place. The American Association on Mental Retardation (now AAIDD) dropped the distinction between mild, moderate, severe and profound levels of intellectual disabilities in 1992 and replaced them with intensities of supports. The four support intensities (intermittent, limited, extensive and pervasive) are yet to establish themselves in everyday language. People still use terms which suggest that they distinguish between levels of intellectual disability and level of support, e.g. mild intellectual disability, complex needs, high support and so on.

The British Psychological Society (2000) distinguishes between two categories of intellectual disability, significant and severe impairment of intellectual functioning. A problem with this categorisation is that there are significant differences between people at extreme ends of each category (see Cleland 1979). In the absence of 'better' terms we use severe and profound intellectual disability to try and suggest notional differences, which we will show to have practical consequences for how services are delivered.

Throughout the book we use the term 'intellectual disability', which has greater international recognition, rather than more localised terms, such as 'learning disability' and 'learning difficulty' in the United Kingdom, and the disappearing 'mental retardation' in the United States. Although not the choice of some self-advocates in the UK, 'intellectual disability' helps to avoid any confusion that might arise by using terms that have different meanings in other countries, such as 'learning disability'.

What are group homes supposed to achieve?

Providing group homes is more than a way of meeting the perceived housing 'needs' of people with intellectual disabilities. They are also intended to realise a number of other broad policy goals, which are usually stated as abstract concepts. Although there may be minor variations in the way different countries, states or human service organisations select or espouse their goals, there is a good deal of continuity about the outcomes that a group home is expected to achieve. This has changed little in the last 25 years.

In England, for example, *Valuing People*, the strategy for people with intellectual disabilities, is based on four key principles: legal and civil rights; independence; choice; and inclusion (Department of Health 2001). Staff in a group home are expected to support people with intellectual disabilities in a way that is consistent with these principles, perhaps supporting residents to vote, to wash their clothes, to select a programme on the television and to go swimming at the local pool.

On the other side of the world in Victoria, Australia, a similar set of guiding principles can be found in the State Government's *Disability Plan* (DHS 2002b, pp. 1–30):

- People with a disability should be able to live and participate in the life of the Victorian community, with the same *rights*, responsibilities and opportunities as all other citizens of Victoria.

- The Government will assist people with a disability to be more *independent* and have maximum control over their own lives.

- People with a disability will be supported to make *choices* about their lives and be enabled to live the life they want to live.

- The Government want to *build inclusive communities* so that the Victorian community is more welcoming and accessible, so that people with a disability can fully and equally participate in the life of the Victorian community.

In Massachusetts, Alternatives Unlimited Inc., a provider of services to people with intellectual disabilities, uses similar words and phrases to proclaim goals related to choice, independence and inclusion:

Each of our community residences provides a safe, nurturing home environment for between four and six people. In these small, intimate groups, people learn how to apply the practical skills of daily living in real life settings. (2008a)

Our caring staff work hard to help people realize their hopes and dreams and reach their potential. To do this, we take a practical approach that includes: assisting people to set goals based on their *preferences* [choice] and needs; *teaching and reinforcing critical life skills* [independence]; creating challenging, yet balanced program structures and activities that encourage personal growth; and by creating multiple opportunities for *community involvement and relationship building* [inclusion]. (2008b, emphasis added)

One of the more eloquent and comprehensive expressions of these broad policy goals was put forward in the 'Ordinary Life' series of publications in the United Kingdom. *An Ordinary Life* (King's Fund Centre 1980) was the principal title of the first publication that came to symbolise a philosophy to guide the provision of services for people with intellectual disabilities in the UK (Towell 1980/1982). Linda Ward (1992) summarised the key message in these publications concisely, stating that people with intellectual disabilities should live their lives in the community like anyone else. She suggested that the means of achieving this was also simple: ordinary houses in ordinary streets; ordinary jobs in ordinary workplaces; ordinary friends, neighbours, social and leisure opportunities, with whatever support is needed to enable this to happen (King's Fund Centre 1988; King's Fund Centre 1984). The recent history of community-based services shows that realising simple ideas is not only hard work but exceptionally difficult to achieve.

In a later publication the authors expounded on the notion of 'ordinariness', in order to make sure that people did not interpret it as meaning dull, standard, average or exactly like everyone else.

'Ordinary' simply means having the opportunities and options which most people have. We live in a world where it is ordinary to have variety and opportunity and choice. It is ordinary to be special, at least to someone. It is ordinary to have opportunities for parts of our lives to be special and also to be different in ways which other people value very highly. (King's Fund Centre 1988, p.2)

A person's home provides the place where these things happen, or is the base from where they start. Paul Williams (1993, p.11) imagined what 'an ordinary life' might look like in a home for two or three people:

With an ordinary house in an ordinary street, with a well-kept garden and only one car parked outside, at least it is possible that the building will not be identified as a service establishment. The two or three people who live there can become well known to the neighbours, the milkman, the postman, the local shopkeepers, the post office and the library. They can each have a front door key and come and go individually.

Their families, friends and neighbours can call and sit with a small number of people at the table or on the sofa. There can be a domestic hallway uncluttered with the staff notice boards and fire hoses. There need be no 'office'. Everyone can use the one or two toilets in the building. The kitchen can be the main thoroughfare to which everyone can have access to make a meal, a snack or a drink, wash up or have a chat.

The people who live there can answer the front door and the phone. They can choose what TV programmes to watch, whether to open the window or turn the heating up, and what food to buy and eat. They can do their own shopping, have their own routines and enjoy a real sense of having their own home. They can have the opportunity to provide hospitality to visitors. Everyone could have a friend in at once without the house being swamped.

This vision of 'an ordinary life' applies to *all* people with intellectual disabilities, regardless of whether they have severe or profound intellectual disabilities, challenging behaviour (Blunden and Allen 1987), sensory disabilities, dual diagnosis and so on. However, the extent to which some or all of these ideas have been implemented, and are still adhered to, have varied from place to place. Of all the 'ordinary life' aspirations, this is most noticeable when it comes to work. Although work has retained a central place in the lives of most people, 'an ordinary working life' has been hard to realise for many people with intellectual disabilities, especially those with severe and profound impairments. Consequently adults with intellectual disabilities spend their days in a range of ways: in full- or part-time employment, in sheltered workshops, in day programmes, pursuing leisure activities, or at home, retired or unemployed. Having a proper separation of home, work and recreation was a principle advocated more than 30 years ago (Committee of Enquiry into Mental Handicap Nursing and Care 1979), and so leaving home during the weekdays was strongly encouraged. This principle has not endured, and although people living in contemporary group homes may still leave the house to go to work or a day programme, it is not unusual for 'day programme staff' to come to a person's house, or for the residential staff to be responsible for supporting people during the notional working day too.

In addition to this vision of 'an ordinary life', services have used a number of theories, frameworks and models to guide their endeavours. 'An ordinary life' drew heavily on the Scandinavian and North American versions of 'normalisation' (Nirje 1969/1976; Wolfensberger 1972) and its later manifestation of 'social role valorisation' (Wolfensberger 1983), which has had a profound influence on deinstitutionalisation and the growth of community-based services. A derivative of these 'guiding principles' is John O'Brien's (1987) Five Accomplishments, which are more easily understood than social role valorisation, and have endured as a guiding framework (Table 1.1).

Table 1.1 The Five Accomplishments
(adapted from O'Brien 1987, pp.177–8)

Accomplishment	Definition and rationale
Community presence	*Community presence* is the sharing of ordinary places that define community life.
Choice	*Choice* is the experience of autonomy both in small, everyday matters (e.g. what to eat or what to wear) and in large, life defining matters (e.g, with whom to live or what sort of work to do).
Competence	*Competence* is the opportunity to perform functional and meaningful activities with whatever level or type of assistance is required.
Respect	*Respect* is having a valued place among a network of people and valued roles in community life.
Community participation	*Community participation* is the experience of being part of a growing network of personal relationships that includes close friends. Without focused effort, people with severe intellectual disabilities will have unusually small social networks whose membership is restricted to clients and staff of the services they use, and perhaps immediate family members. Many of these contacts will be impersonal and temporary. As a means to increased community participation, it is important to provide opportunities for non-disabled community members to meet people with severe intellectual disabilities as individuals.

Paul Williams' imagined home life both promotes and reflects the Five Accomplishments. For example, the residents achieve *community presence* by living in 'an ordinary house in an ordinary street' and by using the local shops; they exercise *choice* by coming and going when they want to and selecting what food to buy and eat; they display *competence* by having a well-kept garden, doing their own shopping and making a meal; they gain *respect* by 'having their own home' and being able to 'provide' hospitality to friends; and *community participation* is enhanced by becoming well known to neighbours, the postman and so on.

Group homes are therefore an important vehicle for realising a society's social policy goals for people with intellectual disabilities. Human service organisations are guided by these goals and, as we will show, are more or less successful at translating them into outcomes.

The growth of group homes

The advent and growth of group homes is closely related to the closure of institutional settings. Figure 1.1 shows that as the institutional population declined in the USA there was a corresponding increase of all types of 'community settings'.[1]

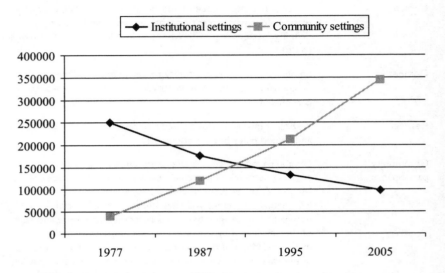

Figure 1.1 Numbers of people with intellectual disabilities living in institutional and community residential settings from 1977 to 2005. Data from Lakin and Stancliffe (2007)

There has been a similar reduction in the 'institutional population' in England. In 1976 51,000 people with intellectual disabilities lived in state-operated institutions, which fell to just over 3500 in 2002, a drop of 93 per cent (Emerson *et al.* 2005b).

The group home was not the first community residential service model to be developed. Institutions were initially replaced by large residential homes, for example the Locally Based Hospital Units (LBHUs) for 20–25 people in the English county of Hampshire (Felce, Smith and Kushlick 1981), which were in turn replaced by group homes. Although group homes have not been replaced, they have been supplemented by a model known as 'supported living'. In addition to the UK and the USA a number of other countries, such as Australia, Canada, Norway and Sweden, have followed this pattern of service development.

Size of community-based residential services

There is a strongly held belief that the number of people living in a residence is related to outcomes, with smaller numbers of residents being necessary to achieve good outcomes. Perceptions of 'small' have changed over time (Felce and Emerson 2005). The LBHUs that were developed in Hampshire in the 1960s came to be seen as being too large and were initially superseded by eight-place 'staffed housing' in the 1970s (Felce 1989). Although the term 'institution' will forever be associated with large hospitals, colonies, training centres and state schools, more recent definitions include much smaller settings. Lakin and Stancliffe (2007), for example, define an institutional setting as housing 16 people or more.

Figure 1.2 shows how the size of community residential settings has changed in the USA between 1977 and 2005. There was a 696 per cent increase in community settings housing six or fewer people between 1982 and 2002. Just over 50 per cent of people receiving a residential service were supported in settings of one to three people in 2002 (Stancliffe and Lakin 2005).

A survey of 2898 people with intellectual disabilities in England showed a similar broad range of community living arrangements (Emerson *et al.* 2005b). Sixty-nine per cent of the total sample were living in private households, that is either living alone, with a partner, or with their parents or relatives. The remaining 31 per cent were living in some form of 'supported accommodation'. Figure 1.3 shows the number of other people with intellectual disabilities that were sharing each participant's home. Of the people living in supported accommodation, 58 per cent were living in houses for six or fewer people; 25 per cent were living in houses for between one and three people. So, although people with intellectual disabilities live in a variety of residential settings, a significant proportion live in group homes, and they are more likely to be people with severe or profound intellectual disabilities (Emerson *et al.* 2005b).

In the USA in 2005, 107,118 people with intellectual disabilities were living in accommodation that meets one of our criteria, that of being a home for between four and six people (Lakin and Stancliffe 2007). In a survey of 7129 people with intellectual disabilities in the Republic of Ireland, 43 per cent (3077) lived in 'group homes', which were reported as being typically for 'four residents along with support staff as needed' (Mulvany *et al.* 2007, p.72). In the aforementioned English survey 33 per cent of those people living in supported accommodation were living in settings for between four and six people (Emerson *et al.* 2005b).

Figure 1.4 shows the number of people living in 'accommodation support services' in Australia, and more specifically in the state of Victoria, where we

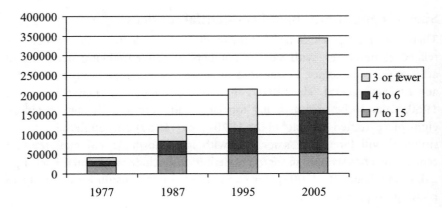

Figure 1.2 Changing sizes of homes among community residential settings on 30 June 1977, 1987, 1995 and 2005 in the USA. Data from Lakin and Stancliffe (2007) Reprinted with permission of John Wiley and Sons, Inc.

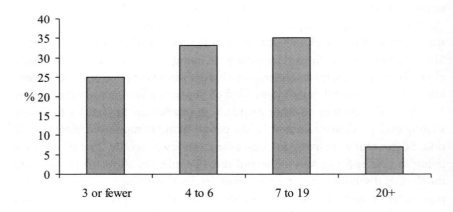

Figure 1.3 Number of people with intellectual disabilities who share a person's home. Data from Emerson et al. (2005b)

carried out our research. In 2005–6, 11,414 people with disabilities were living in group homes across Australia, of which 3398 were in Victoria (AIHW 2007).

Given the number of people with intellectual disabilities who live in group homes, it seems important that we should not only know the kinds of outcomes they produce, but also to understand how they should be managed to consistently realise the best possible outcomes.

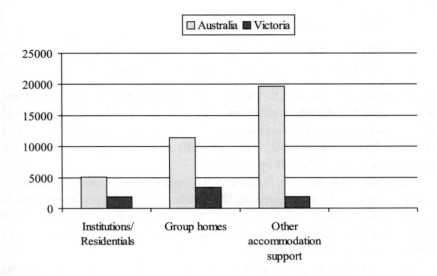

Figure 1.4 Number of service-users for Commonwealth State / Territory Disability Agreement-funded accommodation support services 2005–06. Data from AIHW (2007)

Outcomes in group homes

The failure of the old, large institutions to realise the important features of human well-being has been explored extensively (see Manning 2008 or Potts and Fido 1991 for examples). A large body of research compares the 'quality of life' of people living in community and institutional settings and establishes a relatively clear picture that community-based services are better than institutions (Mansell 2005). In their review of 71 published research studies, Emerson and Hatton (1994) reported that residents in community settings had:

• increased satisfaction from people with intellectual disabilities

• increased choice over day-to-day matters

• increased participation in community-based activities

• increased engagement in ongoing domestic and personal activities

• increased support from staff.

More recently Lakin and Stancliffe (2007) reported that in contrast to institutional settings people with intellectual disabilities living in community settings experience:

- greater personal freedom
- more participation in social activities
- more frequent associations with family and friends.

However, we are not able to state unequivocally that all community-based services are better than the institutions they replaced. This is because there is significant variation in the performance of different types of service models (Mansell 2006). For example, when group homes are compared on the same measures there are widely differing results.

One common outcome measure is 'engagement in meaningful activity', which Mansell *et al.* (2004) define as, 'Doing something constructive with materials; interacting with people; or taking part in a group activity.' Figure 1.5 shows the mean and range scores of 'engagement' compiled from Emerson and Hatton's (1994) review of 46 British studies.[2]

Although on average staffed houses achieve higher levels of engagement than hostels and units, which, on average, achieve better outcomes than large institutions, when we consider the range scores, the best institution outperformed the worst staffed house significantly.

It is helpful to attach some more concrete figures to these percentage scores. On average, residents in institutions were engaged in meaningful activity for just over eight minutes in each hour. In the worst performing institution this figure fell to just over one minute. In staffed housing the residents were engaged in meaningful activity for nearly 29 minutes in each hour, and the best house recorded engagement levels of 44 minutes. Although no large institution, hostel

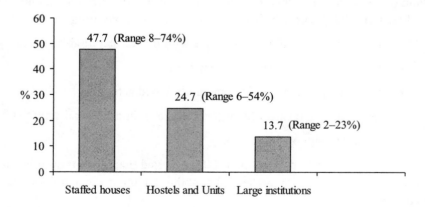

Figure 1.5 Mean percentage of time residents are engaged in meaningful activities in large institutions, hostels and units, and staffed houses. Data from Emerson and Hatton (1994)

or unit came close to exceeding the best performing staffed house, there was very little difference between the worst performing settings in each category. It is important to ask questions about the participants' levels of intellectual disabilities when looking at research data like this. Research consistently shows a negative association between 'ordinary life' outcomes and severity of impairment, despite evidence from demonstration projects that such outcomes are possible (Felce 1989). The levels of engagement in meaningful activities are therefore usually lower for people with severe and profound intellectual disabilities. This is because they rely on the paid staff to provide the necessary support to engage in meaningful activities. Without this support they can be disengaged for a majority of the day (Mansell *et al.* 2008). This alerts us to the critical relationship between staff performance and the 'quality of life' of people with severe and profound intellectual disabilities living in group homes (Mansell 2005).

'Engagement' is acknowledged as a particularly important concept because it is associated with many other 'quality of life' outcomes. High levels of inactivity should therefore be a source of concern for both the funders and providers of group homes. If residents are disengaged they are likely to:

- be bored and express dissatisfaction with the service, if they can

- have fewer opportunities to exercise choices

- have fewer opportunities to participate in social activities

- receive fewer visits from family members or friends, and so on.

Although the move from institutions to community-based services has brought many improvements to the lives of people with intellectual disabilities, certain areas have not changed in line with expectation (Felce *et al.* 2008). In a country like Norway, where the debate over institutional versus community-based accommodation has been laid to rest, we agree with Tøssebro that, 'It is time to stop talking about institutions and community, and just focus on the lives of people living in the community and how they can be made better' (2005, p.187).

The growth of supported living and semi-independent accommodation

The variable outcomes found in group homes have left the model vulnerable to criticism, initially on ideological grounds, but more recently from research evidence that shows that even smaller housing arrangements are associated with better outcomes (Lakin and Stancliffe 2007). The appropriateness of the group home model has been particularly called into question by advocates of 'supported living' (Kinsella 1993a; Simons 1995), which Mary Ann Allard describes as both a 'philosophy' and an 'approach', and defines as, 'Enabling people, regardless of their disabilities, to live in the community where they want, with whom they want, for as long as they want, and with whatever supports they need to do that' (1996, p.102).

Although supported living does not preclude groups of people living together, it is seen as an improvement on the group home model, where more often than not the residents have had limited choice about who they live with or where they live. 'Functional groupings' are a common way of deciding which residents live together in a group home (Simons 1995), i.e. there are homes for people with severe intellectual disabilities or challenging behaviour, and so on. In the Emerson *et al.* (2005b) survey, 67 per cent of the people living in supported accommodation said they had no choice, or were reported to have no choice, over who they lived with. Fifty-four per cent had no choice over where they lived.

Peter Kinsella (1993b) lists five principles of supported living (Table 1.2). Anyone who has direct experience of people with profound intellectual disabilities will acknowledge that some of these principles are not easily applied to individuals with this level of impairment. Indeed, difficulties related to the application of abstract concepts in broad social policy goals to people with severe and profound intellectual disabilities were a recurring theme in our research.

The reality is that someone who has a profound intellectual disability cannot choose their own lifestyle. Even drawing the conclusion that a person with this level of impairment 'enjoyed' a trip to the supermarket requires guesswork and inference on the part of the supporter. It is even more unlikely that we can reliably ascertain that person's views about where she wants to live and with whom (if anyone). Nor is she going to choose who supports her, state how that support should be given, or control her own money. By using a high degree of inference, other people may, with a good deal of effort, do a reasonable job in deciding the solutions to these issues, based on what they think they know about the person (Ware 2004). They may subsequently organise the housing and support in a way that enables the person to have a good 'quality of life' according to some objective measure. Yet, 'choice and control' and the shaping of that person's lifestyle remains in the hands of that person's immediate social network.

More recent research suggests that semi-independent living and supported living are associated with some better outcomes when compared to group

Table 1.2 Principles of supported living (adapted from Kinsella 1993b, pp.16–17)

Separating housing and support	The agency that provides or coordinates supports is not the landlord, nor does it have any organisational connection to the property owner.
Focusing on one person at a time	A process of person-centred planning is used to find out what each individual person wants, and then to plan individually and assist them to secure the accommodation and supports that are right for them.
Full user choice and control	Individuals choose where they live, who they live with (if anyone), who supports them and how. Individuals hold their own tenancy or mortgage and are in control of their own money and household.
Rejecting no one	There is an implicit assumption that everyone can live in the community. The fact that someone has complex needs does not mean they should be denied the opportunity to choose their own lifestyle. Attention is given to environmental adaptations and personally designed supports.
Focusing on relationships; making use of informal supports and community resources	The starting point is to build on a person's existing relationships and connections. Paid help is only used when natural and informal supports are not available. Paid supporters work to develop a person's social network alongside other activities.

homes, although the current available evidence still paints a mixed picture (Lakin and Stancliffe 2007; Stancliffe 2005). For example, Felce *et al.* (2008) found that residents in semi-independent settings did worse than people in group homes on certain measures, such as money management, the frequency of sight tests and health care.

In reality, semi-independent living based on less intense 'drop-in' staffing is not suitable for people with severe or profound intellectual disabilities who require pervasive support. Rather than accrue any of the benefits identified by Stancliffe (2005), such as better outcomes on autonomy, choice, independence and self-determination, people with severe and profound intellectual disabilities would be put at risk in a semi-independent environment. As we have suggested, this group requires support from other people in order to achieve good outcomes in the areas we have highlighted, such as community presence, community participation, engagement in meaningful activities and personal well-being.

Economic considerations

As well as being motivated by a desire to improve outcomes for people with intellectual disabilities, the expansion of semi-independent living is also driven by an economic imperative. As Felce *et al.* state, 'The perennial scarcity of resources always implies a need to pursue cost-effectiveness alongside other goals' (2008, p.88). Rehousing people with moderate or mild intellectual disabilities who are living in group homes with greater levels of staff support than they need in semi-independent settings may allow them to have a better 'quality of life' in some domains. It also reduces the cost of supporting them, and potentially allows any savings to be used to expand service availability. As a consequence, the growth in the number of people with intellectual disabilities living in settings with three or fewer people, as Figure 1.2 shows in the USA, is likely to continue. It is to be hoped that more people with intellectual disabilities will live in homes that they own or rent.

Economies of scale

Although there are some excellent examples of people with severe and profound intellectual disabilities living in settings that are smaller than group homes (see Fitton, O'Brien and Wilson 1995, for example), it is the scarcity of resources that makes it unlikely that this will become the norm for people with these levels of impairment. Although we agree in principle that no one should be rejected from 'supported living' on the basis of level of disability, it is likely that such highly individualised living arrangements will be prioritised for people with moderate and mild intellectual disabilities because the support needs of people with severe and profound intellectual disabilities are too costly to support in this way (Stancliffe and Lakin 2005).

Diseconomies of scale set in within very small settings when the level of support to residents needs to be pervasive. The need for pervasive support implies that residents living in group homes require either a sleep-in or waking night-staff. If all six residents in a group home require the presence of either 'type' of night-staff, then six night-staff would be required in six individualised supported-living arrangements. Activities where 'good practice' suggests 1:1 support is required, such as a trip to the doctor or an individualised leisure pursuit, call for the same amount of staff time regardless of the size of the setting. Two people with profound intellectual disabilities living together would require the presence of two staff if one of the residents were to be supported to go shopping whilst the other remained at home. In a group home, two members of staff could similarly support six residents. One staff member could provide general support to five residents in the group home, whilst the sixth resident was supported 1:1 in the community. It is the utilisation of staff for this 'general supervision' that allows economies of scale to be realised in group settings.

Value for money

Contemporary services are driven by a moral imperative to realise good 'ordinary life' outcomes for people with intellectual disabilities. Certainly, the adoption and promotion of a rights-based social policy agenda demands that people with intellectual disabilities enjoy 'quality of life' outcomes that are comparable with what is available to other citizens. A focus on economics brings another important financial dimension into play, value for money. Governments and taxpayers should expect that the money spent on group homes will deliver quality outcomes. For without good outcomes the 'quality of life' of a significant minority is compromised by residence in 'poor' group homes and the money spent on services represents a poor return on a considerable investment of limited social resources (Stancliffe and Lakin 2005).

In the UK, Lesley Curtis (2007) estimated that an annual 'care package' for one resident living in a group home is £70,512. In Australia in 2005–6, A\$1.92 billion funded 'accommodation support services' for 35,566 service-users. One third of these people lived in group homes (AIHW 2006). This expenditure is small when compared with the US\$35 billion spent in the USA in the 2002 financial year on non-educational services for people with intellectual disabilities by the federal, state and local governments (Stancliffe and Lakin 2005).

If societies are serious that people with intellectual disabilities should have lifestyles that are comparable to other citizens', it is important that utilitarian arguments are not used to justify larger community-based accommodation. 'Ordinary life' outcomes cannot be realised in anything other than 'ordinary houses'. The larger 'supported accommodation' becomes, the more it moves away from being 'an ordinary house in an ordinary street'. More importantly, there is no research evidence to suggest that larger or more institutional settings are associated with better outcomes on any 'quality of life' domain (Walsh et al. 2007). On the contrary, larger living environments, such as hostels, provide poorer outcomes than domestic scale settings (Felce and Emerson 2005). In Figure 1.5, neither the best institution, nor the best performing hostel or unit, achieved engagement levels approaching those of the best staffed house. In addition, larger group homes are associated with poorer outcomes than small group homes (Emerson et al. 2005b). In their review of 86 research papers published between 1995 and 2005, Patricia Walsh *et al.* (2007) reported that residents in larger facilities have:

- less choice and self-determination than group homes
- less frequent contact with people in their social networks than group homes
- less participation in community-based activities.

If research shows that adequately resourced group homes for four to six people are more expensive than larger accommodation, then this extra expenditure can be justified on the basis of the greater benefits these services can offer (Stancliffe and Lakin 2005), but *only* if these benefits can be consistently realised. As things currently stand the relationship between domestic scale community residences (one to six residents) and outcomes shows considerable variation (Felce and Emerson 2005). How can this be explained?

A problem of weak implementation

It is naïve to think, as some people did in the early years of institutional closure, that changing people's living environment from institutions to small homes would be enough to ensure that all the 'hoped-for' outcomes would follow (Felce *et al.* 1998). Outcomes do not just 'happen', but are a consequence of the things that people do. Mansell posits the 'problem of weak implementation' (2006, p.70) as an explanation for why poor outcomes are found in some group homes, when they have been shown to be capable of realising good outcomes.

'Weak implementation' is related to the notion of 'implementation failure', a term from the evaluation literature (Rossi, Lipsey and Freeman 2004). In order to have a chance of achieving the outcomes that the group home has been 'designed' to meet, a service has to function in the way that it is intended to. 'Weak implementation' or 'implementation failure' means that 'programmes' (i.e. group homes) are not being put into practice according to their intended design. Thus, a group home for four residents may have the advantage of being of smaller size than a hostel, but if the staff undertake most of the household activities themselves, i.e. without involving the residents, then the residents are likely to spend long periods being disengaged. In order to take advantage of its size, and the inherent opportunities that a group home offers, staff need to understand that their role is to engage people in household activities and structure the delivery of support accordingly (Felce *et al.* 1998), i.e. implemented as designed.

Assuming that a service is adequately resourced, poor outcomes arise through ineffective 'organisation', which inhibits or makes it impossible to develop and maintain a high-quality service. We are using 'organisation' in a very broad way here, to refer to the systematic way in which a group home, typically embedded in a larger organisation, is organised to deliver its intended outcomes. Research shows that significant improvements in outcomes can be realised without additional resources, through changes in management practices (Felce and Emerson 2005). So, how should services be organised?

What factors lead to high-quality outcomes?

Felce *et al.* (1998) proposed that services need to structure the delivery of support in a way that the evidence suggests is associated with positive outcomes. Over the last 20 years researchers have identified a range of factors that are associated with good 'ordinary life' outcomes, and there have been attempts to organise factors into conceptual frameworks (Felce 1996; Felce, Lowe and Jones 2002; Hastings, Remington and Hatton 1995; Mansell *et al.* 2008; Parmenter and Arnold 2008). However, these frameworks remain underdeveloped, have not been tested empirically, and none have been consistently identified as predicting high-quality outcomes. The framework in Figure 1.6 shows one attempt to illustrate the *possible* associations between factors identified by past research and resident outcomes (Felce *et al.* 2002).

Given the variety of factors that impact on outcomes, it is not that surprising to find that group homes which superficially look very similar can produce very different results. Research has arrived at a point where the variables shown in Figure 1.6 are understood to be important but are not precisely linked to outcomes. Understanding the individual factors and explaining the combinations that work together to produce high-quality outcomes in group homes remains a significant research issue, especially, as we have argued, because a large number of people with intellectual disabilities live in these settings and they account for substantial financial resources.

Much of the published research has used a similar methodology and small number of research methods to investigate the relationship between these factors and outcomes. For want of a better term, we have labelled these studies as adopting a 'quasi-experimental' approach. Researchers have attempted to maintain a positivistic, experimental stance, and have primarily relied on statistical procedures to demonstrate the degree of association between factors and outcomes.

Although such research has contributed much to our understanding of the workings of group homes, there are still gaps in our knowledge. In their review,

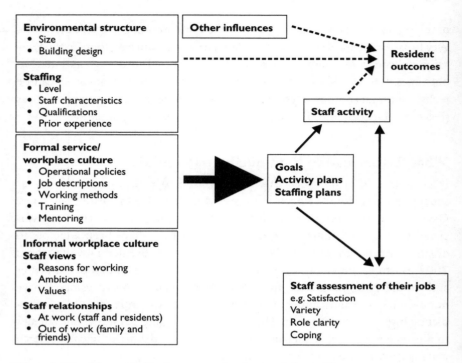

Figure 1.6 Possible associations between service characteristics, staffing, processes and outcomes. From Felce et al. (2002, p.391)

Walsh *et al.* (2007) identified a number of methodological issues with the past research:

- an absence of a clear conceptual framework to guide the selection of outcome indicators

- no consensus regarding what outcomes should be measured

- no consensus regarding the use of specific measures to operationalise the collection of data relevant to the outcomes.

They also noted three factors that have been little researched to date and suggested that attention should be given to them in the future: poverty and income, organisational culture and geographical variation.

The contribution of our research

In this book we present findings from a three-and-a-half-year research project called *Making Life Good in the Community* that primarily used ethnographic and action research methodologies to investigate five group homes. These approaches have rarely been used to investigate group homes.[3] Our findings complement the existing research and we hope will influence any future research programme to incorporate a range of methodological approaches and a broad assortment of methods to research group homes. There are some specific advantages of the approaches we used:

- Ethnography looks to describe and interpret a cultural or social group (Creswell 1998). This focus on 'culture' begins to fill-in the gap on 'organisational culture' identified by Walsh *et al.* (2007), the 'informal service culture' by Hastings *et al.* (1995) and 'informal workplace culture' by Felce *et al.* (2002).[4]

- Participant observation allowed the examination of phenomena that are less accessible to 'quasi-experimental' research. The day-to-day contexts of group homes were explored, revealing the specific situations, circumstances and problems facing the people who lived and worked in these settings and the processes by which they responded to them.

- Action research, which attempts to change practice in line with predetermined aims, revealed a great deal about the day-to-day working of the group homes in the study (Hart and Bond 1995; Wolcott 1994). An emphasis on 'process' allowed us to interrogate the 'weak implementation' thesis, as we were able to evaluate the activities and operations of both the group homes and the broader organisation. The relatively poor outcomes we describe lend support to the idea of 'implementation failure'; that is, the intended or necessary structures, resources and/or services were not provided and consequently the hoped-for outcomes could not occur.

- The longitudinal nature of the research allowed the group homes to be investigated over an extended time-frame.

Structure and aims of the book

In this chapter we have defined a group home and argued that this type of residential service will be part of the future landscape of intellectual disability services for people with severe and profound intellectual disabilities. The research evidence informs us that well-managed group homes can realise good outcomes for residents, but many settings are underperforming.

A book of this length cannot address outcomes related to every 'quality of life' domain. Our research focused on the more 'ambitious' or 'higher-order' social policy goals, such as assisting people to develop relationships and friendships. In doing so we are not denying that the more basic needs, such as quality health care (Birenbaum 2009), are important issues. The lives of people with severe and profound intellectual disabilities are more likely to be understood by a medical discourse, and consequently there are many other useful resources that are oriented to 'nursing' or 'care' (see Pawlyn and Carnaby 2009, for example). Whether we conceptualise the hoped-for outcomes of social policy as residents having 'an ordinary life', leading their lives as full citizens or having access to the good things of life (Wolfensberger 1998), this will only be achieved if we look towards the higher-order goals.

Our research findings, rooted in actual practice, add to the extant knowledge about how to manage for quality outcomes. Our aim has been to write a book that is useful for practitioners who are struggling to make headway with these higher-order goals. There are a number of orientations that run throughout the book:

- Human service organisations are complex systems, which we must seek to understand as a whole. As Charles Handy writes, 'Everything affects everything else, everything is part of something bigger and nothing can stand on its own or be understood on its own' (1993, pp.22–3).

- Outcomes do not just 'happen', but are a consequence of the things that people do. Thus the outcomes for residents we describe are a consequence of the way that the system was designed and enacted.

- Many social policy goals are what Michael Patton calls 'big hairy audacious goals' (2008, p.267). As a consequence they are often fuzzy and conceptually weak, which makes them hard to implement.

- People with intellectual disabilities are not a homogeneous group and organisations supporting individuals with severe and profound intellectual disabilities face some specific challenges. Not least of which is interpreting the meaning that fuzzy social policy goals should have for their everyday lives.

As context is so important, realising social policy aspirations will not be accomplished by simply ticking all the boxes in a checklist or following a series of steps in a 'magic recipe'. A more 'experimental' approach is required and all human service employees, but managers in particular, will have to work hard to relate the research findings to their specific situation. In order to help people focus on important topics, relevant issues are listed for consideration at the end of the related chapter.

In Chapter 2 we provide an account of what it is like to live and work in a group home for people with severe and profound intellectual disabilities. We present data that we gathered using participant observation in three group homes, which is structured as a chronological day. We contrast this account with the notion of 'an ordinary life', which we outlined in this chapter, and argue that when measured against this standard, the lives of many people with intellectual disabilities compare poorly.

In Chapter 3 the concept of 'home' is discussed and ways in which a group home is unlike a 'typical' home are examined. A model of 'home experience' is presented, which provides a framework for thinking about homeliness, direction for creating a homely environment, and an interpretative framework for understanding a specific setting. One aspect of homeliness is 'the personal home', and in Chapter 4 we highlight the planning and action that is necessary to realise individual lifestyles. The very nature of group homes means that some activities will inevitably have to be undertaken in groups, but this does not mean that residents have to lead the same life as everyone else. Issues related to the implementation of a keyworking system, designed to achieve individualised outcomes, are discussed.

Chapter 5 focuses on a particularly important outcome for service-users, 'engagement in meaningful activity'. 'Engagement' is linked to a number of other concepts and a technology known as 'Active Support' is outlined. Active Support has been empirically shown to increase levels of engagement for people with severe and profound intellectual disabilities. We discuss a number of issues related to its implementation and sustainability. Although 'meaningful activity' can take place in any setting, Chapter 5 is specifically concerned with activities that take place in 'the home'.

Chapter 6 discusses 'inclusion'; an ambiguous goal that has shaped social policy for more than 30 years. We use the concept of 'social space' to discuss the 'social inclusion' of people with intellectual disabilities and make links to other ideas that have been used to discuss this concept. As well as a lack of clarity about the goal of inclusion, we suggest that the factors leading to *community presence* are stronger than those leading to *community participation*, which helps to explain why the social exclusion of people with intellectual disabilities remains an enduring social problem.

The house supervisor[5] shoulders a disproportionate responsibility for achieving high-quality outcomes for a group home's residents. Chapter 7 outlines the knowledge, skills and abilities required by house supervisors. We discuss the notion of 'practice leadership', a term that is gaining greater currency in intellectual disability services. The 'everyday' language of house supervisors and managers is used as a way of explicating the concept, which we link to more theoretical frameworks. Practice leadership takes place in a broader organisational context, bolstered by organisational structures and resources. In Chapter 8 we emphasise the need to understand the organisational system. We discuss how the organisation of the service system influences the outcomes in a group home.

Chapter 9 contains some final thoughts about the practical task of supporting people with severe and profound intellectual disabilities to have good lifestyles in group homes. We provide a summary of the book's contribution towards this end and highlight some key points for the future management of group homes.

Notes

1   The data for state and private institutions and nursing facilities is merged to form one category, 'Institutional settings'.

2   Emerson and Hatton (1994) used the term 'staffed house' rather than group home to refer to 'ordinary' domestic-scale housing in which 24-hour staff support was provided. We have retained their term in Figure 1.5 as some of the staffed housing in their sample was larger (i.e. had more than six residents) than our definition of a group home.

3   See Finlay, Antaki, Walton and Stribling (2008) and Finlay, Walton and Antaki (2008) for some recent studies that have used ethnographic approaches in residential settings.

4   Both 'culture' and 'organisational culture' are problematic terms. Joanne Martin's (2002) book, *Organizational Culture: Mapping the Terrain*, provides an excellent overview of the debates and issues related to the application of 'culture' to organisations.

5   We use house supervisor to refer to the manager of a group home. There are a number of other terms that can substitute, such as front-line manager or front-line supervisor.

Chapter 2

Living and Working
in Group Homes

On 20 April 1988 a British advocacy organisation collected stories about what people with intellectual disabilities were doing on that particular day. The aim was not to present details of special events, but to provide glimpses into the lives of people with intellectual disabilities as they went about a typical day. The accounts were published as *An Ordinary Day* (Dowson 1988).

In a similar vein, this chapter aims to provide a picture of life for people with (predominantly) severe and profound intellectual disabilities living in group homes in Victoria some 20 years later. Rather than accounts from a single day, what follows is a composite picture of life for the residents of three group homes derived from observations that we made towards the end of 2005 and the beginning of 2006. We do, however, present our fieldnotes in chronological order, from morning to night, to give the sense of 'an ordinary day'.

As disheartening as we find some of the descriptions that follow, our research did not expose the worst living conditions experienced by people with intellectual disabilities. A survey in England showed people living in supported accommodation with high support needs were relatively well off in comparison to people with mild and moderate intellectual disabilities living in other types of accommodation (Emerson *et al.* 2005a). Group homes are reasonably well resourced, and the residents were more likely to be able to afford many of the things that we think people should be able to have, such as new clothes, pursuing hobbies, and going on holiday.

The descriptions are snapshots of the lives of 16 men and women, which we believe to be typical for many more people with intellectual disabilities living in group homes; particularly those with severe and profound levels of intellectual disability. These descriptions tell us little about the best lives being led by people with intellectual disabilities. They show that these residents were leading a life-style that fails to measure up to the 'ordinary life' standard, which was generally the case for those individuals with intellectual disabilities whose stories were told in 1988.

This type of comparison is a common way of undertaking analysis; comparing what you are looking at with a standard (Wolcott 1994). In Chapter 1 we outlined an overarching standard that we can use to judge the lives of the people with intellectual disabilities: 'an ordinary life'. The idea that any person with intellectual disabilities should be living his or her life in the community like anyone else was broken down into a number of subsidiary goals: ordinary houses in ordinary streets; ordinary jobs in ordinary workplaces; ordinary friends and neighbours, with social and leisure opportunities. We also introduced a number of ideological frameworks that have been used to guide and evaluate intellectual disability services: normalisation (Nirje 1969/1976), social role valorisation (Wolfensberger 1998) and the Five Accomplishments (O'Brien 1987). We outlined some abstract concepts that appear in social policy documents, which are more contemporary benchmarks, such as choice, inclusion, independence and rights.

As you read this chapter you will no doubt have a view about the lives of the residents, the practices of the staff supporting them, and the employing organisation. Our experience has been that when our fieldnotes were read by staff, self-advocates and family members who were unrelated to these particular houses, the descriptions resonated with their experiences of similar settings. In this chapter we introduce a number of additional simple concepts that we also used to discuss our observations with employees of the organisation where we conducted our research. It is inevitable that some readers will use supplementary interpretive frameworks to understand the descriptions that follow. However you understand the descriptions, our aim is to use the concepts we present as a means of improving the way in which we support people with intellectual disabilities.

It is worth reiterating a point we made in Chapter 1, that our research focused on the more 'ambitious' social policy goals. Therefore what follows is necessarily a 'partial' account of life in three group homes, not only in the sense that all descriptions are incomplete (Spradley 1980), but also in that we have marginalised some issues, such as health care. Our goal has been to give as much detail as we can within the constraints of the chapter, which will give readers a sense of the residents' lives and support they received, prior to embarking on action research projects in the respective group homes.

The context

The broader background to our research project was the closure of Australia's oldest and largest institution for people with intellectual disabilities, Kew Residential Services (KRS). As part of the final phase of the institution's redevelopment some of the last residents moved into 93 new group homes situated across metropolitan Melbourne and regional Victoria. Rather than use 'ordinary' housing stock, these group homes were purpose built. In designing these houses, the architects took account of broad disability standards and additional criteria determined by the Disability Services Division of the Victorian Department of Human Services. Although the group homes were built in ordinary streets, they were not really 'ordinary' housing. Chapter 3 discusses the design of these buildings and the consequences for their 'homeliness'.

In this chapter we present data from three of the five group homes where we were participant-observers: 96 High Street, 64 Penny Lane and 16 Temple Court. Table 2.1 gives some broad information about our initial contact with these houses and the data we collected there.

Table 2.1 General information about the data collected in the three group homes

Domain	64 Penny Lane	96 High Street	16 Temple Court
Hours of participant observation	46	36	59
No. of days on which data was collected	9	9	11
No. of interviews	9	0	1
Data set (no. of words)	58,000	20,000	29,000

The residents

Given the research context, it goes without saying that all of the residents had spent a significant amount of time living in that institution (Mean = 41 years; Range 28–62 years).[1] Twenty of the 26 residents who were living in all five group homes at the start of our research had been assessed as having either a severe or profound intellectual disability. These individuals were more likely to have secondary disabilities and a significant number of health-related needs (Hutchinson 1998). By definition, one would also expect these individuals to have low levels of expressive and receptive communication, which was borne out by results of a communication assessment designed for adults with severe intellectual disabilities, the Triple C (Bloomberg and West 1999).[2] Basic demographic details of the 16 residents in the three group homes we are concentrating on are shown in Table 2.2.

Although a number of criteria had been used to determine which residents should live in each group home, Table 2.2 hints at the notion of 'functional grouping' that we highlighted in Chapter 1. In general, the 'average' level of

Table 2.2 Demographic information for the 16 residents of 96 High Street, 64 Penny Lane and 16 Temple Court

Group home	Sex N=16	Pseudonym	Age when moved to group home	Years lived at KRS	Level of intellectual disability	Communication level (Triple C – Bloomberg and West 1999)
	M	Brian	42	42	Moderate	Stage 5
	F	Aphrodite	64	42	Severe	Stage 6
96 High Street	M	Alberto	43	32	Moderate	Stage 6
	F	Rose	55	50	Severe	Stage 6
	M	Simon	51	40	Moderate	Not available
	F	Sarah	55	47	Moderate	Stage 6
	M	Dan	57	53	Severe	Stage 4
	M	Franco	51	41	Profound	Stage 4
64 Penny Lane	M	Joseph	51	47	Severe	Stage 5
	M	Milan	53	53	Severe	Stage 4
	M	Wally	48	31	Severe	Stage 4
	M	Charles	70	62	Severe	Stage 3
	M	Christos	57	48	Severe	Not available
16 Temple Court	M	Mathew	50	38	Profound	Stage 2
	M	David	52	49	Severe	Not available
	M	Shane	35	28	Severe	Stage 1/2

intellectual disability changes as we move from 16 Temple Court to 64 Penny Lane, to 96 High Street, with 16 Temple Court being a home for people with the highest support needs. Although Table 2.2 shows similar levels of intellectual disability for the residents at 16 Temple Court and 64 Penny Lane, four of the five residents at the former used wheelchairs, whilst all of the residents at 64 Penny Lane were ambulant.

The staff

Of the 30 staff whom we met close to the opening of the five group homes, about 75 per cent had transferred to the houses from Kew Residential Services (the range within respective staff teams was between 33 and 100 per cent). Many of these employees had worked at the institution for a significant number of years (from less than one year to 31 years). The house supervisors at 96 High Street, 64 Penny Lane and 16 Temple Court had all qualified as a Mental Retardation Nurse (MRN). The direct support staff were either unqualified or had a Certificate IV qualification in disability work, acknowledged as the minimum competency requirement for working with people with disabilities.

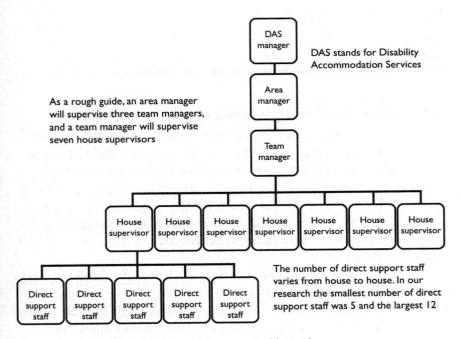

Figure 2.1 Schematic representation of the managerial hierarchy

Allen, Pahl and Quine (1990) made the point that it is absurd to blanket all staff who worked in an institution as unsuitable employees for community-based services because they are 'too institutionalised'. Some of the aforementioned employees embraced their new role with enthusiasm; others struggled to make the adjustment.[3] Figure 2.1 shows a generalised schematic representation of the managerial hierarchy within Disability Accommodation Services.

Table 2.3 gives an overview of the staffing resources available in each of the three group homes. Each group home was established to provide the residents with an *extensive* support intensity (Luckasson *et al.* 2002).

Table 2.3 Overview of staff hours at 96 High Street, 64 Penny Lane and 16 Temple Court

Group home	Total number of rostered hours per 28 days	Total number of staff	House supervisor (full-time)	Direct support staff		Night-time staff
				Full-time	Part-time	
96 High Street	791	6	1	3	2	Sleep-in by staff team
64 Penny Lane	1182	8	1	2	3	2 active night staff
16 Temple Court	1158	10	1	2	5	2 active night staff

Focusing on severe and profound intellectual disability

Diagnosing people with a severe or profound intellectual disability is an inaccurate science. In some of people's historical records we noticed that their diagnostic label changed over time. We have used the most recent diagnosis in Table 2.2. As we highlighted in Chapter 1, the label or diagnosis is important, not only because an orientation of the book is towards people at the more severe/profound end of the intellectual disability continuum, but also because of the significant differences between people at extreme ends of severe and profound categories (Cleland 1979).

In order to give a sense of how the personal restrictions of profound intellectual disability impact on an individual, we are going to give a description of Christos, adapted from the written information that was made available to staff at 'resident familiarisation sessions' during the move from the institution to the new group home. In a small number of words it is hard to present a person as a rounded human being. Burton Blatt reminds us that, 'Some stories enhance life; others degrade it. So we must be careful about the stories we tell, about the ways we define ourselves and other people' (quoted in O'Brien and Mount 1991, p.1). The description presents a limited view of Christos, but brings to the fore the type of support required by a person with profound intellectual disability who has additional impairments and major health concerns. As a reader, it may also help to think about an individual you are familiar with who has a similar level of disability.

Christos (57, a resident at 16 Temple Court) has severe intellectual disability, epilepsy and spastic quadriplegia. He is a thin man who weighs 31 kg. He needs full staff assistance to wash, dress, undress and attend to his personal grooming. Christos is showered and dressed on a shower trolley. A hoist is recommended for all transfers. Christos uses incontinence pads both day and night. He sleeps in an electric bed with cot sides and uses a v-shaped pillow to maintain an upright sleeping position. Christos uses a manual wheelchair and is unable to manoeuvre himself without staff assistance. He has limited protective behaviour and no stranger danger awareness. He would be vulnerable if exposed to aggression as he would not vocalise if injured. Christos is non-verbal and has limited means of communicating his needs. He reacts to touch, looks at people momentarily and begins to show anticipation. His meals are vitamised and his drinks are thickened due to having aspiration pneumonia two years ago. He has a history of reflux oesophagitis, dysphagia, gastric ulcer and chronic constipation.[4] Christos is a very slow eater. He enjoys eating all types of food, particularly chocolate, pureed fruit and custard. Christos likes monthly visits from his mother, bus trips, spas, back rubs, massage and listening to soft music.

It is perhaps understandable that people with severe and profound intellectual disabilities are seen through a medical lens. As we stated above, they are more likely to have additional disabilities and a higher number of health-related needs. It is also understandable that attending to these needs, or anxieties about medical issues, should preoccupy staff. Anxieties about managing people's health needs and managing health crises featured strongly in the data we collected from 16 Temple Court. Yet, if staff only attend to these aspects of a person's life, then 'an ordinary life' is unlikely to be realised. Providing high-quality services to people with profound intellectual disabilities that embrace all the 'quality of life' domains is certainly a challenge, but it is not impossible.

Interactions and styles of support in the house: A day in the life

The fieldnotes that appear below sketch out a chronological day. As for many people, the residents' day is structured around relatively fixed times for food and drink. The excerpts reflect patterns of behaviours that we noticed in the group homes. Each passage is therefore part of a much larger data-set that represents how things typically happened in the houses. We are not suggesting that what is described was the only way that people behaved. However, we propose that the extracts illustrate the dominant patterns of behaviours within the house. There is very little analysis in this chapter, as our primary aim is to provide a picture of people's lives. We do introduce a number of 'light' analytic terms that suggest that staff are the major players in the group homes. As you read the extracts it is worth considering this overarching question: To what extent are the residents leading 'an ordinary life'? You may want to consider some subsidiary questions, such as: Who appears to be making the decisions? Who is in control? How involved are the residents in the running of the homes? And so on.

The names of the residents are given in Table 2.2. All of the other named persons are staff, except when a researcher is mentioned. We have tried to make it clear who the staff are in the extracts. A researcher is usually referred to in the first person. As participant-observers, we moved between different roles. For example, sometimes a researcher was merely trying to watch what was going on in the house but on another occasion was involved in supporting or interacting with the residents.

Beginning the day

In the group homes with an active night staff, a weekday morning begins for two day staff at seven o'clock.[5] The roster allows for a 20-minute overlap with the outgoing night staff; a period of time for a 'handover'. Officially, this is an opportunity for the outgoing staff member to pass on brief highlights of his shift and flag any important information. The time can also be used by the incoming staff to plan their shift together, which may mean looking at the house diary, reading past entries in the communication book and so on. A staff member who has not been at work for a day or two may take this time to scan all the entries since she was last at work.

During the week at 16 Temple Court there is considerable pressure on the day staff to support the residents to shower, dress and eat breakfast, so that the minibus can leave for the day programmes at 08.45. A decision had been made by the staff team that as far as possible two of the men would shower in the mornings and the others at night to make the mornings a little easier.

Elizabeth [staff] commented that it was necessary to shower Christos first as he took a long time eating breakfast. Elizabeth woke Christos gently. He was curled up in bed. He stayed huddled-up, with his eyes shut, and then opened them to have a look at us before closing them again. Elizabeth chose clothes carefully for him. She said that she had organised the wardrobes of two of the residents and intended to do the same for the others in the near future. We took the clothes, towels and a face-washer into the bathroom. Christos is washed lying down on a shower-trolley. Elizabeth and I wheeled it into his bedroom and adjusted the height so that it was level with his bed. She then rolled him from the bed onto the trolley and said that it had taken her a while to learn how to do this. I wondered about the feeling of being in a warm bed and then on cold vinyl. It is not the way that I would want to start the day. We talked with Christos as we moved him, explaining what was happening. We then wheeled the trolley back into the bathroom. Elizabeth put on plastic gloves and we talked about wearing these. I commented that I thought it would not be very pleasant to be washed by people in gloves and she agreed, but she added that sometimes she had to wash faeces from people and then thought that she needed them. She removed Christos's pyjama-bottom and the nappy and found that he had had a bowel movement. She washed him with the shower hose and faeces floated in the shallow water, which she quickly washed away down the plug hole. Before beginning to wash Christos properly, Elizabeth shaved him with an electric shaver. She said she found this quite difficult and it needed to be done before his skin was wet. Then we washed Christos gently, talking to him as we did it. I supported Christos's head and upper body as he showered lying down. I then washed his hair and found it hard to do this without getting soap in his eyes. Clearly I failed in this as he rubbed furiously at his eyes. I quickly wiped them. I managed to wash his hair but also filled one ear with water, which seemed uncomfortable for him. I apologised for this. Christos was then dressed and lifted into his wheelchair and pushed down to the dining area for breakfast. I felt sensitive about moving his arms and legs which are locked as I was afraid of hurting him. He wore socks but no shoes.

Breakfast can be a time-consuming activity. All of the plates of cereal are organised by the staff member who is not involved in supporting the residents in the showers. The bowls are placed in front of the men on the table. The dining table is typically covered by a tablecloth, which is removed at mealtimes. All of the men wear bibs for breakfast although David always takes his off immediately. David is blind and requires some help with meals, but he can eat his toast alone if it is placed in his hand.

Meena [house supervisor] said that David could once feed himself, but had for some years refused to do it. He simply puts his hand behind his back if asked. She said people lost skills very quickly if they didn't use them. As usual David ate neatly. He had been very vocal this morning with lots of humming noises and twisting of his head as he waited for breakfast. Meena gave him some bread and jam and he ate that himself.

Mathew needs support to eat. He wears a helmet, which is put on after his shower. The staff expressed anxiety about him injuring himself, should he have a seizure. However, his head in its helmet tips forward and staff feed him with a little difficulty. Christos takes a very long time to have breakfast. He is given a spoonful and holds it in his mouth for a long time before being ready for the next. The staff commented that this is in part because he has problems with swallowing. Shane eats very quickly and staff try to slow him down by feeding him. If he eats alone then much of the food falls off the spoon onto his bib or clothes. Charles is able to eat and drink independently and usually sits at the head of the table.

After breakfast the residents who are in wheelchairs are pushed so that they are in front of the TV, which is usually on, sometimes without sound. Mathew sits in a big armchair, usually curled in a ball with his knees under his chin and his T-shirt pulled down over them. His head rests on his knees. The other men do not seem to be engaged in watching the TV. Shane sits on the couch or wanders around the living area playing endlessly with a cord that has been attached by staff to his jacket. Having the cord to play with makes Shane less likely to tear his clothes.

The residents who are going to day programmes take packed lunches with them, which have been prepared overnight by the night staff. This means that there is one less task to do in the morning, but as a consequence the men are not involved in preparing this meal. The lunches are packed into knapsacks by staff, with changes of clothing.

At 64 Penny Lane it is common practice for some of the men to have a shower before the day staff arrive. John, the active night staff, explains that this is a way in which the staff help one another.

I think here you do a bit in the morning to help [the day staff], and they appreciate it, because they're coming in and they've only just got up. Everybody does their bit in the morning, especially when the five [residents] are going to programmes. If they're getting up at six [o'clock], it's not you turfing them out of bed. As the guys get up, because they do a lot of things themselves, you're not rushed, you can do three showers. It means that they can take their time with breakfast and the guys can just sit down. It's like me coming on at night. You may have only been up for a couple of hours when you come in. They do things at night and the place is tidy, the dishwasher will be empty and things like that.

The five men who live at 64 Penny Lane have virtually no spoken language. They have found other ways of making some of their wants known.

I ring the door bell at 06.55 and April [night staff] answers the door. Joseph and Franco have had a shower and are sitting on the same settee. Franco is lying curled up with his head on the arm. Dan grabs my arm and leads me to the shower. I try to explain to him that I would like him to wait, because I want to be clear with the staff about what I am to do. I go back and sit in the lounge and talk to April. Keith [house supervisor] arrives a couple of minutes later. Shelagh [staff] arrives at 07.10. Keith tells us that the bus has to go in for a service today. No alternative arrangements have been put in place to get the residents to their day programmes. Usually it is only Wally who stays at home for the entire day on Wednesday as his mother visits in the afternoon. Milan goes to the day programme for the afternoon only. Keith decides that Franco will go to the day programme and Joseph and Dan will stay at home. There is some talk between us about yesterday's Melbourne Cup. April won nearly $300.00 on the winner, Makybe Diva. Shelagh makes herself a hot drink and a slice of toast. Keith supports Dan to have a shower. April leaves at 07.20.

Although the five men can do some tasks themselves, all of them need support to get washed and dressed. One of the staff will begin to serve breakfast to the residents who have been helped to shower by the night staff, whilst the other staff member supports the remaining residents to get washed and dressed.

Breakfast is 'served' to the residents. People are given the cereal selected by the staff member. People are given a drink. People are given toast. Keith sits down with Wally and feeds him the cereal with a spoon. He says that he is doing this because Wally has not been eating his food. Franco pushes his cereal away. Keith stands by him and feeds him with a spoon. He tells Franco to sit firmly. After being given three or four mouthfuls Franco finishes the cereal by himself. Keith says that Franco will regurgitate his food after breakfast. He likes Franco to have very hot coffee as this slows down his drinking. Franco picks up Milan's drink and I intervene to stop him drinking it. Joseph is sitting at the end of the table. His drink is on the mat in front of him.

Plates, mugs and mats are taken away by the staff. The cork place mats are very shoddy. Some are curled up at the edge; another has a piece broken off at the corner. Shelagh comes over to Joseph and asks him to lift his drink up so she can take the mat away. She asks him again. She lifts the drink up and takes the mat away herself. Shelagh loads the dishwasher. She wipes the kitchen surface down. Dirty laundry is put in the machine. Shelagh remakes Wally's bed, which he wet during the night.

At 96 High Street, the staff member who had 'slept over' had woken prior to 07.00 and prepared the breakfast.

Six bowls were laid out on the kitchen counter. Some had [the Australian breakfast cereal] Weetbix in and others a mixed cereal. A plastic container had a tinned fruit salad in it. Mugs were laid out on the counter. By the toaster were peanut butter, Vegemite [a yeast extract spread] and marmalade.

Andrew [staff member] told me that the residents would be woken up at seven o'clock. At two minutes to seven he asked if I would go and knock on Simon's door. I did, said, 'Good morning', told him the time and left him to his own devices. He came to the dining area in his blue striped pyjamas. Then I went to Brian's room. He appeared to be asleep. I tapped him on his shoulder, as Andrew had suggested, as he uses hearing aids. He got up and came to the dining area in his pyjamas. Sarah was sitting up in her bed with the door open. She put on a dressing gown and came to the dining area.

Andrew spooned the fruit salad over the cereal and called people up to the counter to 'choose' a bowl. The residents could choose between Weetbix/fruit and the cereal/fruit combination until three bowls of one type of cereal were exhausted, then there was no choice.

Julie [staff member] arrived just after seven o'clock. She shouted 'hello' to everyone and went to Aphrodite's bedroom. Aphrodite appeared in a dressing gown, gaping open, carrying her wet bed linen, which she placed in the laundry. She then came and sat down at the table. Just as Simon had put a spoonful of cereal in his mouth Andrew asked him to come and be weighed. He apologised for interrupting his meal.

Andrew made everyone coffee in a big plastic jug. He poured it out at the counter and gave people the mugs. Brian's drink had been thickened. Andrew gave out the medication. Some people got their medication in their hand; Alberto's tablets were put on his spoon. People took their cereal dishes back to the kitchen. Julie was standing by the toaster. She spread butter on the toast and people were given the option of the three spreads. Julie made an effort to get people to apply the spreads. Then Julie cut the toast in half and people took their toast back to the table. Rose only got one slice. Aphrodite was asked to point to the preferred spread from her place at the dining table.

Ownership

As we move from house to house there is evidence of residents doing more for themselves, with individuals at 96 High Street making some minor decisions and exercising a larger degree of choice. This is probably to be expected, as we have ordered our fieldnotes so that they move from 16 Temple Court to settings where the residents have more adaptive skills. Yet in each group home, the extracts suggest that the staff have the dominant role in the house, i.e. they have greater control over the day-to-day running of each house. They take the lead in waking people, preparing food and drink, weighing people and administering medication. They have determined the parameters of resident participation at breakfast by the way that the meal has been set up. In our discussions with the respective staff teams we used a number of concepts to discuss these fieldnotes, such as: principal and minor actors, active and passive roles and the notion of ownership. Ownership in particular has a number of meanings that seem relevant to understanding the dominant staff role: the state of being or feeling responsible for solving a problem; to have or hold as one's own; to have control over or direction of a person or thing; to be or feel responsible for considering or solving a problem, issue or task, etc. (Simpson and Weiner 1989).

As we move through the day, space limits us from visiting each house. Our aim is to present enough excerpts from each house to give a sense of the patterns of behaviours that we noticed in each group home.

Going to the day programmes

All three group homes had their own minibus, and it was the responsibility of the staff to drive the residents to and from their day programmes. In each group home there was significant variation in the way that residents attended day programmes. Some people had full-time day programmes; others attended on a part-time basis. At the start of the project Charles had no formal day programme. At 70 years old, other people had decided that he had 'retired'. Residents not attending a day programme were supported during the day by the group home staff.

At 16 Temple Court getting to the day programmes was both time consuming and complex, especially when more residents attended. All the staff talked about the difficulties of 'parking' the minibus, especially on trips to the city centre or when reversing out of the drive when the neighbours were parked opposite. Filling the bus with petrol is often left to Ray, the one man on regular day duty in the house. Four of the five residents use wheelchairs, which are raised on to the minibus by a tail-lift and then locked into place. The staff have learned to do this efficiently, but it still takes time. Shane gets on to the bus unaided and sits in one of the chairs in the back. Usually one staff member takes the men to the day programmes.

Shane and David sat in the back of the van in wheelchairs. It was not possible to sit with them as there were no chairs so I sat in the front with Ray. The drive to the first day programme took about 10–15 minutes and we got there just after nine. Ray commented that the people at the day centre did not seem to like working with Shane as he was very active and liked moving around a lot. He had two changes of clothes with him and Ray said that if he didn't like what was happening he peed. Shane got out of the bus with no seeming reluctance and went into the day programme. He disappeared down the passage with a staff member whom we had met on the way in. Ray told me that staff in the house did not know what happened in the day programme. There were no opportunities to visit with the men.

This lack of connection between the day programmes and the house became a strong theme during the field work at 16 Temple Court. A further two staff commented that it would be good to know what happened during the day and similar remarks were made by the day programme staff who said it was frustrating not to know if the things the men were doing at the day programmes were carried over into their lives at home. There were no regular communications between the two groups of staff and each time we dropped someone off there was a sense of rush and busyness as the day programme staff began the day.

Shane attends a different day programme to David, Christos and Mathew. He is usually dropped off first and then the van continues to the second day programme, which is a further 15-minute drive. It takes about an hour to drop people at the day programmes and return to the house. The staff organised a network with other houses so that people are picked up and taken to the day programme by staff at one house, while staff at another house do an alternate trip.

At 64 Penny Lane the residents leave for day programmes at the same time.

We leave for the day programmes at 08.45. Franco, Dan and Joseph are going to the day centre this morning. They are helped to pick up their knapsacks, which have their lunches in. These have been made by the night staff. Wally comes along for the ride. Before we leave, Keith [staff] gets Franco out of the bus, and takes him inside the house. When they come outside again Franco rushes to get in the bus, trying to squeeze past the seat, which needs to be tipped forward, and then past Wally. In his hurry, Franco hits his head on the doorway.

Dan sits in the front seat. I sit in the back next to Joseph. It takes 20 minutes to drive to the first day programme. Keith sees someone that he recognises. After he has taken the men in, he talks to the acquaintance for a while.

At 09.15 we arrive at Franco's day programme. Franco gets out of the bus and his trousers and the seat are soaked in urine. Keith says 'I'm going to be a little bit longer' and goes with Franco into the building. I suggest to Wally that he moves into the bench seat in front to avoid the urine. He does. He says 'piss the bed' a number of times. He makes an 'eeee' sound, and puts his hand to his face. I don't know what it means. Keith comes out of the building 15 minutes later. He asks whether I want to move to the front seat, but I stay with Wally in the back. We arrive back at the home at 09.45, a 60-minute round trip.

Back at the house

All of the houses placed a strong emphasis on cleanliness. This may have reflected a desire to look after the new properties, but it may equally have reflected an institutional perspective that emphasised order, cleanliness and safety (Egli *et al.* 2002). The period of time following breakfast and when arriving back from the 'bus-run' is when housework and laundry are done. If any residents are at home, these tasks may or may not involve them.

When residents are incontinent, then washing laundry is a constant process. At 16 Temple Court several loads are washed each day, hung out and retrieved. If the residents are at home they are generally sitting in the living area in front of the TV, whilst housework activities are undertaken by the staff.

Similarly at 64 Penny Lane, once the bus has returned to the house there are domestic jobs to do. The house supervisor stated that he has tried to encourage resident participation in household activities, but this imperative has only been taken on board by some of the staff group. Making sure that the house is clean and tidy may be privileged over resident participation. The house supervisor said:

We need to make the home itself homely, clean and tidy, because the fellas haven't got the capability of doing that or in one case Milan doesn't want to be involved. We need to make sure that that's done. That's an expectation they have of us as well.

If no residents are at home, the jobs will still be done by the staff members. On this particular morning a number of the men were in the house.

It was time to do some housework, clean the bathrooms and toilets and mop the kitchen/dining area and bedrooms. I offered to do the kitchen/dining area and bedrooms. I offered the broom to Milan, who was sitting in the lounge. He got up from his chair and went and stood in the corner of the room.

Joseph had pushed all the chairs to the side wall. Wally had taken himself to the middle lounge, where he was sitting on a couch. Dan had come in from the garden. He seemed agitated, grinding his teeth and vocalising. Joseph started to vacuum the carpet. Susan [staff] cleaned the toilets and bathrooms.

I offered Milan the mop, but he walked away from me. He did this three times. So I mopped the kitchen and then went to Franco's bedroom, who was at the day programme. When I came to Joseph's bedroom I went to see if I could get him to mop his bedroom. He was sitting down on a chair, pushing the vacuum-cleaner over the space in front of him repeatedly. I turned the vacuum off and had to pull him to his feet to show him what I wanted him to do. He took the mop and cleaned a third of his floor, and then did a bit outside the bathrooms and front door.

The fact that resident participation had not been incorporated into staff practice at any of the houses as a matter of routine, together with the pressure felt by the staff groups to complete the tasks, means that the residents are sometimes unoccupied and disengaged.

I had asked earlier what the plan for the morning would be as Wally and Milan were at home. I got the impression that there may be a trip outside somewhere. This never materialised. Wally is asleep on a chair in the middle lounge. Keith comes out of the office and rubs Wally's leg and turns the radio on. Keith tells me that Wally's preferred choice of music is classical; his mother's influence. He says that Wally is comfortable in any area of the house. He will sit or sleep in any area of the house and go into other people's bedrooms. This is not the case for all the other men. Keith spent most of the morning in the office. He apologised when it was time for me to go, saying that when he has been off for a few days there are usually a number of things that he needs to address.

Some of the men at 64 Penny Lane can find things to do for themselves.

At 09.30 Dan came out of his bedroom, holding a basketball. He paused in the lounge, as if looking for someone to say that he could go out to the backyard. Linda [staff] told him that he could go. A little later Dan was jumping up and down in the backyard and grinding his teeth. It was very windy outside. He did not seem interested in shooting baskets. He seemed to want to get to the shed, so I opened the security gate and he walked over to the shed and touched the padlock. He did exactly the same about ten minutes later, so I fetched the key and opened the shed. There were some paint cans and some tiles in the shed. Dan peered inside and then shut the door.

The hotel model

A term that had common currency amongst the organisation's middle-managers was the 'hotel model'. Although it was rarely defined by middle-managers, the metaphor was used to evoke an image of what services should not be like. In a hotel, you expect the staff to wait on you, as in this example from 96 High Street.

'Morning tea' is served at 10.30. A cloth has been put on the table in the back yard. Cathy [staff member] has made the drinks and a snack. The residents go outside and sit around the table. Cathy serves people their drinks. There are two individual tea pots. The milk has been put in the pots. There is a plastic jug of coffee. People are given little bowls and Cathy serves crackers that have been spread with a topping. She serves them with barbeque tongs. Some people dip them in their drinks. Rose drinks and eats quickly and leaves the table. Brian stacks up the bowls. Simon wants to take a plate with some mugs on it into the kitchen. Cathy tells him that she thinks it will be too heavy.

It is easy to understand how this event might be considered an illustration of the hotel model in operation. A number of earlier fieldnote excerpts also contain examples where the staff wait on the residents, do their laundry, clean the house and so on. Although the concept has some resonance, it is an oversimplification of what we observed, for staff do not always act like hotel staff and residents do not always act like guests, as can be seen from reading the fieldnote extracts. Nonetheless, it is quite a useful orienting concept that can help people to judge the extent that residents are involved in the running of their household. When staff perform in this way, it sends a message to the residents that the staff have control over the day-to-day running of the house. One of the researchers was observing at 96 High Street one morning.

After the bus had gone I started to quiz Frank [the house supervisor] about the morning routine, how the jobs were decided, and what would happen now. He said that he was going to make himself a coffee. He said I could make myself a drink. I asked Simon, who was staying at home, if he wanted a tea or coffee. He did not answer, so I asked again. Simon said that he'd just had breakfast. Then he said that he would have to ask Frank.

This is a vivid example, which suggests that Simon believes that Frank should decide whether he can have a drink or not. If Simon felt that 96 High Street was his home, then perhaps he would have said that he wanted a drink, been hospitable and offered to make the researcher one.

A mid-morning drink was part of every group home's routine. At 16 Temple Court the residents and staff might sit together at the dining table or on the patio having a morning drink that has been made by the staff. Although the men were physically present at the table the conversation between staff went on around them. Sometimes a comment was made directly to one of them, particularly Charles. Occasionally there was a physical interaction: a mock boxing match with Charles, or a head massage for Mathew, or a gentle touch on Christos's hand.

Mathew, Christos and Charles were sitting outside on the patio with two staff members, Penny and Neil. Neil works on the night shift but does one day shift on the 28-day roster. I sat down and Maria [staff] joined us. There was some discussion about Charles and his health. He looks very frail and Maria commented that he had lost 9kg since his illness, which had required hospitalisation. The staff all agreed that he was settling back home well.

Activity and inactivity

The fact that staff have the most active roles in the group homes has significant consequences for the residents.

After morning tea I sit back on the settee again between Sarah and Rose. The horse racing is on the TV. No one is particularly watching it. Aphrodite is sitting in an armchair that is not facing the television. She shuts her eyes. Sarah, who is sitting on the couch, spends much of the time trying to look at what a staff member is doing behind her in the kitchen and dining area. After a while Simon comes and sits down next to Brian. They do watch the TV for a little while, but Simon too shuts his eyes. The horse-racing commentary competes with the sound of 'Dancing Queen' coming from the other lounge, where Alberto is watching his ABBA DVD. Rose sings along to 'Dancing Queen'. Once, during the morning, she appeared to tell another resident off for touching the tablecloth; 'Don't touch that, it's not yours,' she said.

If we think of our own lives at home, a significant amount of time is taken up with domestic activities, cooking, washing-up, tidying, cleaning, decorating, washing and ironing clothes and gardening. If staff take the lead role in completing these tasks, and the residents do not have other activities to fill their time, then their time at home is likely to be characterised by disengagement and boredom. There were very few organised activities in the house that were not domestic ones. At 96 High Street there is one resident who seems to do more activities than the other residents.

Simon is vacuuming the hallway. Alberto is standing in the middle lounge. Brian, Aphrodite and Rose are sitting on the settees in the other lounge. Sarah comes out of the toilet and sits down. The TV is on.

Simon was the most articulate resident, with the most adaptive skills. He seemed to do more activities than the other residents and was more willing to do jobs around the house. It is typically the case that people with intellectual disabilities with the relevant adaptive skills are given, or make their own opportunities to be involved in, domestic activities while staff do the same tasks for people with profound and severe intellectual disabilities (Felce *et al.* 1998). In such circumstances the most able residents are likely to receive attention and support, rather than those who need it more.

Lunch

Lunches tended to be less substantial than the evening meal. The preparation of mealtimes at 16 Temple Court, where some of the residents required a vitamised diet, was often a time-consuming process. Decisions about what people should eat were made by staff, and were typically based on their understanding of the residents' likes and dislikes.

Penny commented that the men really liked pumpkin soup and she provided this on several occasions while I was at the house. When she was on duty, Penny was usually the cook and clearly enjoyed this part of the job. She said that the meals had to be cooked for a long time because they needed to be soft so that the men could eat them. She felt this made it more difficult to go out in the afternoons. By early afternoon there was usually a very homely smell of the evening meal being cooked.

In the absence of any trips out, the afternoon continues in a similar vein to the morning.

There was very little interaction with Milan for the 50 minutes that I had been in the house. When I was sitting on the settee next to him he reached out to grab my hand, which he raised to rub his head. I saw him do this gesture a few times during the day. Linda [staff] put some water in a blue plastic mug and put it on the dining table and told him it was there. Martin [staff] reminded him that it was there a little while later. Later, he stood up and walked to the toilet doorway where he paused. A staff member told him to go to the toilet, and said, 'He feels like he needs permission.' Wally is slumped over on a settee in the lounge. The TV is showing a children's programme.

After lunch at 16 Temple Court some of the men had a formal 'rest'. Christos, who was often awake during the night, sometimes became tired. It is difficult to know whether the men actually slept but they did spend an hour or two in bed.

The residents had varying amounts of contact with family members. Wally, a resident at 64 Penny Lane, received a visit from his mother twice a week.

Mrs Smith puts a towelling bib around Wally. She refers to herself as 'Mummy' when she talks to her son. She sits at the table whilst he eats a sandwich. For most of the afternoon Wally and his mother are shut in his bedroom, where Wally sits on his bean bag. They listen to music.

Community-based activities

Time spent in the group homes was broken if a trip was organised. This could be to supermarkets, cafés and restaurants, visits to other group homes or taking part in a leisure activity. The house supervisor at 64 Penny Lane saw such activities as important. He stated that, 'Our role and responsibility is to ensure that the fellas are given every opportunity to experience what community life is all about, like you and I.'

Chapter 6 discusses the Victorian social policy goal of *building inclusive communities*. As we shall see, the residents made use of a variety of ordinary community facilities. During the period of participant observation, community-based activities took the form of group activities, with very few occurring during the weekday evenings. The evening schedule at 64 Penny Lane was simply listed as 'TV/music'. Community-based activities may have taken place during the day for people not attending day programmes, or else they happened at the weekend. The extract that follows, of an outing to a nearby shopping mall, is a good example of how the staff facilitate *community presence* for the residents. We present a description of the outing without comment, as it is discussed at length in Chapter 6.

It is a hot day. The top temperature is forecast to be 31 degrees. Keith [house supervisor] changes some of the men's clothes. Milan is wearing blue shorts, a blue and green Diadora T-shirt, white Nike pumps and white socks. Wally is wearing a pastel green short sleeved shirt, putty-coloured shorts, blue and white trainers and socks. Dan has a Slazenger T-shirt which has cranberry, black and white stripes, blue jeans and brown boots with three Velcro fasteners.

The house supervisor places a strong emphasis on making sure that the residents are dressed in a manner that is valued by other people in the community when they go out.

The presentation of the residents flows on to everything we do. There are times where you can be a little bit relaxed, once the fellas are active in the community. Whether at the day programme or going out to have a coffee around the corner it's all about their presentation and about their grooming. I think that's important to us as carers because that says if we take a little bit of extra time and care about the individual's grooming we care about them. That's been one of the things that I've been focused on. We still haven't got it right but we're getting there. I think it's important to make sure that we do that because when an individual goes into the community and they're not well dressed they could be standing next to somebody who looks just the same as them but because they have a disability that's homed in on very quickly. This is my view and people look at them and say, 'Look how shabby they are.' That's how I look at things, we have to be quite conservative about how our residents dress.

Shelagh carries some money for the men; $5.00 each. Seven of us set out from the house at about 11.30. Shelagh walks in front holding Milan's hand. Keith suggests that I go in the middle as he is walking with Dan, who is the slowest. Wally walks by himself. Joseph wants to hold my hand. I let him do this some of the way, but as I have seen him walk around the block on his own previously, I know that he can walk on his own.

We turn left into High Street. At the pace we are walking it would be at least 30 minutes to the bus stop. After ten minutes Keith decides we will catch the tram, which will take us to the Woodhouse shopping centre. It is very hot in the full sun. None of us have any sun cream on or sunglasses. No one has a hat. We cross the busy High Street. This takes quite a while to do as there is no pedestrian crossing. The road up to the tram stop is steep. Twice on the journey Milan sits down on the pavement.

After another ten minutes we near the tram stop. We miss a tram by a minute, which means that we have ten minutes to wait for the next one. There is a shelter that we can sit in. The tram is busy when it arrives. We do not need to purchase tickets as we are 'companions' to the residents who themselves meet the eligibility criteria for free travel on Victorian public transport services. A man gets up for the residents and goes to the other end of the tram. Keith sits with three of the men. Milan sits next to a man who greets him and opposite two other people. Shelagh stands up. When someone moves Shelagh sits opposite Milan and the man and woman talk to her.

When we get to the shopping centre we are taken to a café/juice bar. The four men are seated around a table and Keith and Shelagh go to the counter. They come back with four identical orange drinks and doughnuts. I go and order my drink.

The seating area is quite tight, so Shelagh sits at a different table. Joseph clutches his trousers in the groin area. I confirm with Shelagh that this is his sign for wanting to go to the toilet. I take him to the toilet. We use the parent and child/disabled toilet.

Linda, who is working later that afternoon, passes the table where we are sitting and talks to Shelagh. Shelagh goes and buys herself a sandwich.

Keith and Milan go into the supermarket and come out with the trolley containing half-a-dozen plastic bags, containing mainly milk and bread. People are given a bag to carry. Milan refuses.

We go into K-Mart [Australian department store]. Wally and later Dan take it in turn to push the trolley. The seven of us head off to the men's shoe department. Keith wants to buy Dan some shoes. After trying on some shoes we head off to the clothes. A number of items are put in the trolley, but I have no idea who they are for. They are mainly T-shirts and shorts. The four men are not closely involved in any decisions about what to buy. Joseph gestures at all the clothes as we pass them in the aisle. Caps are placed on Dan's head. Shelagh and Keith debate whether a Holden or Jim Beam logo is preferable. Neither of these caps is eventually chosen. Hats are placed on Milan's head, but he takes them off and pulls a face. He does not like wearing hats. Wally wanders off several times and people raise their voice to get him to come back.

In the queue at the checkout Keith pays for the items in the trolley. Wally has wandered out of the store and is making his way onto the pavement. I hurry to him as he wanders out into the car park.

Keith has decided that we are all going to get taxis back to the house as Wally's mother is arriving at about 13.00. She has been given her own key to get into the house. We wait by two bench chairs for the taxis to come. The men are sitting on the chair, next to an older man and woman.

Return from the day programmes

The staff at 16 Temple Court saw the afternoon 'bus-run' to the day programmes as another reason why it was difficult to do external activities during the day with the residents who had stayed at home. The minibus needs to leave the house to pick the men up by about two o'clock in the afternoon. When the men returned from the day programmes they were usually placed on the toilet, then they had a drink, and then sat in front of the TV until dinner. If the weather was mild they sometimes sat outside on the patio with a staff member.

Shane was often restless at this time and wandered around the house. A staff member would follow him if he went out of the living area although there seemed to be nothing that he did in the rest of the house that might be a concern for his safety. On one occasion Maria discussed Shane's behaviour on the afternoon before:

Maria said that after I had left Shane had gone outside and stripped off and 'done a dirty thing' near the window of the house. She was concerned that the neighbours might see. Although there are high fences around the garden she said that she had seen a neighbour on a nearby roof a few weeks ago and they might see in by accident. I asked what she had done and she said she had sent Shane to his room as that is where he should do things like that.

The residents at 64 Penny Lane who are at day programmes also need to be picked up by the house staff.

Martin was nominated to do the 'bus-run', picking up four men from three different day programmes. At 14.20 Martin told me it was time to go. In the bus, Martin filled in details of the journey in a file. This has to be done on every trip. It is part of the lease agreement and helps identify staff for speeding and parking fines. We got back to the house at just before 16.00, so the round trip had taken about 90 minutes. Keith and Linda obviously thought the journey had taken a long time because they joked with us that they were beginning to get worried and were going to send out a search party.

A 'snack' had been prepared for the men. All the residents were sat at the dining table and they were given a plastic bowl that contained lollies [sweets], crisps and cheese balls. Dan pushed his bowl away, and he was offered a cereal bar. He took one bite of it and put it down on the table. Wally picked it up and put it in his bowl. Keith had stated that he was going to make 'the boys' a coffee. Linda gave one person an orange drink, which was then given to everyone.

Afterwards a staff member may support Franco to go for a short walk in the local neighbourhood. Dan would entertain himself by playing with his basketball.

I went into the garden, where Dan was playing with a ball and the basketball net. He would bounce the ball two or three times and then shoot. More often than not he would find the basket. I would have a go and throw the ball to him, which he would catch. After we had played basketball for about five minutes he hurled the ball over the rear garden fence into the garden next door. The fence is high, perhaps ten feet. He made an expansive gesture which seemed to indicate that we or I should go and get the ball.

No effort was being made by the two staff members to engage the residents, so I went to see what they were up to. Franco grabbed me by the arm and took me into his bedroom. He opened the wardrobe door. We stood and I made some comments about his clothing. He started banging gently, rhythmically, on the wardrobe door. Joseph was in the corridor. He made various gestures to me which seemed to indicate the various rooms. He rubbed his hair outside the bathroom. Later he went and had a look at a cupboard in the kitchen.

The evening meal

Tea is served close to six o'clock at 16 Temple Court. It takes quite a long time to support the men with eating. Then they are wheeled in front of the TV again for a little while, positioned in such a way to suggest that there is an expectation that they are watching. All the associated tasks of clearing away and washing-up have been completed by the time the night staff arrive at 19.45.

In contrast, at 96 High Street, the residents play some minor roles in serving the evening meal.

Kylie [staff member] starts the final preparations for tea at about six o'clock. She gets the cutlery out of a drawer and puts it on the worktop and asks Aphrodite to lay the table. Aphrodite does this, and fetches glasses from the cupboard. Alberto comes in and moves the knives and forks further apart. Brian's place is laid with a parfait spoon, which has a smaller surface area, to encourage him to put small amounts of food in his mouth.

Kylie carves the corned beef that she had cooked earlier in the day and puts it on the plates that she has put out on the work surface. She gets a large bowl of salad from the fridge and puts portions on each plate. On the table are a jug of water and a large bottle of orange juice. Julie [staff member] encourages people to choose between the two. Aphrodite gestures to Alberto to pass the orange juice. He does not. Kylie comes around and offers more salad. Julie fetches the tomato sauce and gives it to Brian. 'The meat may be a bit dry for you,' she says. Simon, another resident, puts some sauce on his remaining food.

The dessert was put into bowls on the kitchen counter by staff. Watermelon and another fruit for everyone except for Brian, who was given a banana in a bowl. Most of the residents took their plate to the kitchen and picked up their dessert. Brian gestured to a bowl that someone else was eating, but I was the only one who noticed.

We can see that once again that the residents are participating in tasks, but they are on the margins of the main event. Aphrodite laid the table. People took their dishes to the kitchen.

In thinking about the residents' participation here, one of the authors was reminded of his experiences as a child and later a teenager living in the family home. The kitchen was his mother's domain. She did the main tasks, remained in control of what was happening, but expected her children to 'chip in' or 'help out'. At 96 High Street the staff keep things going, and the residents chip in by laying the table, clearing their dishes, emptying the bin or hanging out the washing. Often this seems to be asked as a favour to the staff member, rather than an expectation or responsibility. This is very different to perceiving the resident as the person doing and owning the task, with the staff member there to give whatever support the person might need to complete it. Adults with intellectual disabilities often find themselves in the role of eternal children (Wolfensberger 1975). If someone is cast in the role of child, then it is no surprise to find that the staff sometimes take on the role of adult or parent.

The evening

At 96 High Street the staff take the lead in doing the housework after tea, loading the dishwasher, washing down the chairs and tables, sweeping the floor. The residents also make choices that should create uncertainty for the staff in how to respond.

Andrew [staff member] has started to sweep and mop the kitchen. All the chairs are moved away onto the carpeted area. He asks Alberto if he wants to mop the floor. Alberto shakes his head, so Andrew does the job.

There are a number of vegetables growing in pots in the garden. They are visible through the window. They are beginning to brown. I ask Rose, Sarah and Brian in turn if they want to water them. No one wants to.

How should the staff at the house respond when people choose not to be involved in such activities? If staff perceive that the ownership of these tasks rests with the residents, then one response may be to renegotiate when the task is done, so that the person chooses when they do it. But can residents choose absolutely? Can they opt out of activities that they don't like doing? In our own lives we may not like doing a whole heap of tasks, but still end up doing them anyway. Such situations are dilemmas and need to be discussed and resolved.

'An ordinary life' assumes that people either want to be supported to do household activities, such as cooking and cleaning, or should be responsible for them. In Chapter 5 we explore some of the assumptions behind these positions. For some residents and staff this may require a reframing of their respective roles.

Wherever people live, they have routines, which have varying degrees of flexibility. Many of the residents and staff in the group homes had behaviours that had been entrenched by the routines that they had experienced from living and working at Kew Residential Services for so long. For some residents, getting changed for bed after dinner was one such routine.

After dinner, just after seven o'clock, Dan appears in blue checked pyjamas and slippers. Richard [staff] turns on the TV to a news station. Earlier he had told me about the plane that landed at Tullamarine airport on a burst tyre. He thinks that I would be interested in seeing it.

Looking to change some of these 'fixed' behaviours has been a conscious strategy for one of the night staff.

John, the night staff, arrives at 19.45. John's strategy to keep people out of bed is to delay supper as long as is reasonable, because he says that some people will go to bed immediately afterwards. 'A couple of them, you give them a drink, and it's as if they think that's supper and they go to bed, especially Dan. What I've found, especially on the warmer days, is that I would give them a drink of cordial, but it won't be at supper, [which is] about nine thirty. I have to say to them, "I'll give you a drink, go and play basketball or whatever."'

I go to see what Franco is up to. As I approach he comes towards me and grabs both my arms by the wrist. He leads me into the shower. He leads me into his bedroom. We go back in the corridor. He holds me by one hand and circles around me. He leads me down the corridor by the other end of the house. Richard leaves at eight o'clock. He is coming back the following morning.

I look for Milan. He is in his bedroom. He is sitting naked on his bed. John says that if you leave him he will put on his pyjamas. Later he appears in pyjamas and a dressing gown. Milan is short, less than five foot. The sleeves on the dressing gown extend beyond his hands.

It was during an evening shift that the most concerted effort to get the residents to participate in a domestic activity was witnessed.

Joseph, Dan and Milan are going to day programmes tomorrow. John supports them to make their lunches. There is an array of things on the kitchen worktop. Brown bread, peanut butter, Vegemite, individual cheese slices, cream cheese, a processed meat, two boxes of different fruit bars, butter. John and the three men are crowded around the kitchen counter. Wally is in bed and Franco in another part of the house. John supports each person, one at a time, to make their lunch. Joseph actively chooses peanut butter and pushes away the processed meat that John holds out for him. Joseph puts a spatula in the peanut butter and puts it on the bread. John finishes spreading the peanut butter for him. He puts the cheese on the bread. John cuts the bread in half and wraps the sandwiches in cling film, and places it in the lunch bag, with a drink box, yoghurt and a fruit bar. John held up the two boxes and Joseph pointed to one box. The same process is repeated for Dan and Milan. Dan is directed to the fruit bar that would be easier to eat, as he has no teeth. When Milan is given the cheese slice to put on the bread he puts it in his mouth. 'I knew that was going to happen,' laughs John. Franco appears in the kitchen and watches what people are doing. The men put their lunch boxes in the fridge and then put the food away with support.

However, even participation in this task is not standard practice. John explains:

I think with me, at night I'll forget sometimes. I do try to get them to make lunches, but sometimes I'll sit down with them and we'll have a coffee or a Milo [chocolate malt drink] and then I'll forget about the lunches and it's really too late. I'll go ahead and make the drinks. I'll forget. It's getting out of those habits where you do more things for them. It's just getting out of that routine. These guys are capable of doing a lot of things. It's just getting into that mentality.

Supper

The final formal meal of the day is supper.

At about quarter to nine Neil made supper for everyone at 16 Temple Court. He put three biscuits on separate plates and made milky tea. Shane went over to the kitchen and watched the preparation with great interest. Meena asked me to put the electric kettle away in the cupboard under the sink in case he grabbed it. Christos, who was in his wheelchair, had jellied Milo which Meena supported him to eat. It took him a long time and Meena said he was very slow today. She sat patiently on the arm of the couch holding the Milo and a spoon while Christos looked around him then gradually let the drink slide down. He opened his mouth when he was ready for the next spoonful. David, Shane and Charles ate their supper at the dining table. Charles ate all the biscuits and Meena said he seemed very hungry. He drank all of the Sustagen [a food supplement] quietly by himself. Shane ate the biscuits and then gulped his tea. Charles's tea was left on the table for one minute, which Shane grabbed and drank. David refused to eat or drink anything, vocalising and holding his head in his hands.

As I sat with Shane the other men were taken to bed. It did not take Neil long to do this. The programme which had been on the TV was not finished as they were wheeled away and I wondered whether any of them had been watching it and what it meant to be taken away before it ended.

Supper at 96 High Street is a further example of the restricted nature of choice in this setting.

Julie [staff member] gets supper ready. She offers people a choice of tea, coffee or Milo. People seem to make a genuine choice from the three options. A packet of biscuits is put on the table. Brian's drink is thickened and put on the table in the measuring jug. He pours it into his mug. Alberto had tea, with the milk in the teapot. Aphrodite gestures to Alberto to pass the biscuits. Aphrodite takes two. Later she is told by Julie that she has had enough. When Julie is not watching she takes some more. People take their crockery to the kitchen when they have finished. Julie wipes down the chairs.

The residents are offered a choice of drinks, which was determined by the staff member. Obviously, there are other drinks that people might like, but there are other choices to be made, such as who makes the drink, what time people have it and where they drink it.

The night shift

Both 16 Temple Court and 64 Penny Lane have active night staff. At 96 High Street a member of staff sleeps in. After the men at 16 Temple Court are put to bed, Neil works on the communication book and checks the men every hour. He is anxious about doing this as each time he goes into Charles's room he wakes. He expressed his unease about this issue in a staff meeting earlier in the month.

Neil said he was concerned that he had to make an hourly check on the men who were subject to seizures and this was okay with Christos who was a heavy sleeper. However, Charles was a light sleeper and each time Neil checked him Charles jerked awake. He had tried leaving the door a little open but Charles still woke. Penny said she had been anxious the other day when she went into Charles's room and he was lying there very still with his eyes open. She was afraid he was dead.

The night shift brought out the anxieties about the men's health very clearly. This was an issue which emerged in many different contexts throughout our time at 16 Temple Court. Both night shift staff expressed anxiety about managing health crises when they were alone at night. Neil discussed the issues around health with one of the researchers after the men had gone to bed.

We talked about night shift. He said it was quite stressful and not many staff wanted to do it. If someone had a seizure he would wait for a minute or so and if it seemed to be getting worse, would call the ambulance and the on-call person within the Department. The on-call person could not offer assistance but reported to the cluster manager the next day that he had phoned in. He said that when the ambulance came to see Christos during a seizure they had wanted him to go in the ambulance with Christos to the hospital. He told them this was impossible as he couldn't leave the four other men. He was happy to answer any questions they had but couldn't leave the house. He told them that Christos had been admitted before and that his records were at the hospital. If Christos had a seizure during the day a member of staff went with him in the ambulance. I wondered what this meant to Christos if he came round with complete strangers in a new place.

Concluding remarks

The extent to which these 16 people with intellectual disabilities are leading 'an ordinary life' is a matter for conjecture. We think that the excerpts we have presented depict people's lives as extraordinary; a far cry from the lifestyle envisioned by Paul Williams in Chapter 1. In certain instances some residents were making choices, were engaged in tasks, but at levels that fall short of the aspirations envisioned in contemporary social policy documents. This is 'ordinary' as dull; lives characterised by prolonged periods of inactivity, disengagement and boredom. The outcomes for these 16 individuals measure poorly against the standard of 'an ordinary life'.

It would be disingenuous to claim that nothing has changed for people with intellectual disabilities in general, in the 20 years since *An Ordinary Day* (Dowson 1988) was published. Yet, as Steve Dowson subsequently wrote, 'Once we accept that people with learning difficulties are entitled to the same respect, dignity, basic rights and opportunities which we expect for ourselves, we have established an absolute standard. Against that standard...the industry still fails miserably' (1997, p.102). It is not unreasonable to claim that for many people with intellectual disabilities there is still a long way to go before their lives meet this standard.

We hope that, for these 16 individuals, we have merely recorded a step along the way to 'an ordinary life'. Chapters 4 to 6, in particular, present data from the action research projects that followed this initial period of participant observation. In these group homes, the goal of the action research projects was to change practice in line with the predetermined aims of 'an ordinary life'. The remainder of the book shares some of the lessons we learned from trying to move closer to that goal.

Notes

1   This average is broadly accurate. We were aware of two residents who had spent some time in other institutions, which were not included in working out the mean.

2   The Triple C has six stages of communicative/cognitive development. Stages one to three in particular rely on the communicative partner to assign communicative intent and meaning to the person's behaviour.

3   John Rose (1993) observed that moving to a group home from an institution requires direct support staff to take on an expanded role, which is underpinned by a 'different' service philosophy. The new position is subject to greater role ambiguity, requires higher levels of input and receives more pressure from management.

4   A vitamised diet includes food of a smooth and even consistency; the consistency of custard or yoghurt and not runny. Foods are often cooked for a longer period prior to vitamising. Oesophagitis is an inflammation of the lining of the oesophagus (gullet). In most people this

is caused by the digestive juices in the stomach moving upwards into the lower oesophagus (reflux). Reflux causes a burning sensation in the upper abdomen and lower chest, sometimes moving up into the throat. Dysphagia typically refers to difficulty in eating as a result of disruption in the swallowing process. Dysphagia can be a threat to one's health because of the risk of aspiration pneumonia, malnutrition, dehydration, weight loss and airway obstruction.

5   At the weekend one staff member will come in at 07.00 and a second at 08.00 as people do not need to be supported to get ready for day programmes.

Chapter 3

Homeliness

Introduction

In this chapter we discuss the concept of 'home' and examine ways in which a group home is unlike a 'typical' home. We present a model of 'home experience', which provokes questions about the nature of severe and profound intellectual disability, but also provides direction for those entrusted with the challenge of creating a homely environment in a group home setting.

Conceptualising a home

In Victoria, where we did our research, a 'group home' is more commonly called a 'Community Residential Unit'. In typical Australian style, this is often abbreviated to 'CRU'. We prefer the 'group home' term, because it supports the idea that people with intellectual disabilities should live in 'homes', whilst 'Community Residential Unit' and 'CRU' seem to reflect and evoke a 'service culture'. It is important not to overstate the role that language has in shaping people's perceptions, but we suggest that 'group home' is more congruent with the values and aspirations of 'an ordinary life', and that as a general 'rule of thumb' organisations should look to align their day-to-day language and written documents with their values.

John Annison (2000) points out that 'home' has been inappropriately applied to a range of accommodation for people with intellectual disabilities, many of which have been anything but 'homelike'. He argues that all residential service stakeholders need to have a clear understanding of what makes a 'home', because a 'home' has a key role in contributing to high-quality community living.

One problem related to the notion of a 'home' is that it has a strong subjective element. Therefore, what one person considers a home may be considered unhomelike by another. Parents on our research steering committee mentioned freshly cut flowers, bowls of fruit and the smell of a roast dinner as being qualities they associated with a home, and these perspectives influenced what they hoped to see and smell in the group homes where their sons and daughters lived.

Judith Sixsmith (1986) developed a helpful conceptualisation of 'home experience' that has physical, social and personal dimensions. The *physical home* encompasses the structural and architectural style of the building, together with the space and amenities that are available. The *social home* is a place for entertaining and enjoying the company of other people, especially friends and relatives, whilst the *personal home* is an emotional and physical reference point that is encapsulated by feelings of security, happiness and belonging.

One of the strengths of this conceptualisation of 'home' is that it moves beyond a restricted view of a house as 'bricks and mortar'. For the house supervisor below, 'home' is more than the physical building. It extends beyond the 'four walls', ultimately embracing the social relationships within the immediate neighbourhood.

I always say the house starts at the letterbox and finishes at the back fence. A lot of staff teams are very focused on the house, what's in the four walls. I think that's because they don't see the place as a whole. I think that's part of the philosophy good house supervisors have, that we improve everything. If the bushes in the garden need trimming back and you don't want to do it yourself, or you haven't got residents who are capable of helping you, get Jim's Mowing [an Australian gardening franchise], or get whoever. Don't sit there and have your neighbours getting cross at the junky-looking rental. This neighbourhood is very quiet, where people keep nice gardens, so if you want to be part of the neighbourhood, be quiet and keep a nice garden, otherwise they're not going to accept you.

It is all too easy to focus on the physical home, especially when buildings, décor and furniture are all brand new, as was the case in our research. However, a clear understanding of what makes a 'home' requires consideration of all three dimensions.

Issues for people with severe and profound intellectual disabilities

Some authors who write about homes for people with intellectual disabilities in broad terms fail to draw out the issues for people with severe and profound intellectual disabilities. As we argued in Chapter 1, this makes a fuzzy concept like 'home' harder to apply to people with profound intellectual disabilities, or easy to ignore. John O'Brien (1994, 2005a) has written about what 'home' might mean for people with intellectual disabilities, but some of it is rhetorical and fails to maintain a congruent position for people with severe or profound intellectual disabilities. Our aim in critiquing his work is to problematise certain aspects of the meaning of 'home' for people with these levels of intellectual disability, so that we can more clearly understand the challenge of providing a homely environment.

O'Brien (1994, p.2) identifies three dimensions of home. He writes that people with severe intellectual disabilities have their own homes when:

- they experience a sense of place

- they experience security of place by holding the valued role of home owner or tenant

- they, or their agent, control their home and the support necessary to live there.

A woman who had volunteered at Kew Residential Services for more than 25 years expressed her view that, 'It wouldn't make any difference to some of them where they were' (quoted in Doran 2004). She is expressing an opinion about the personal restrictions of severe and profound intellectual disability.

Sixsmith's (1986) tripartite division of 'home' arose from phenomenological research, where participants shared their own meanings of home. As we cannot directly access the thoughts, feelings and other inner mental states of people with severe and profound intellectual disabilities, O'Brien's emphasis on people 'experiencing' both a 'sense of place' and 'security' is problematic. As we discuss later, we can only make inferences about whether people with severe and profound intellectual disabilities 'experience a sense of place' from their behaviour.

According to O'Brien, 'individuals with a sense of place comfortably inhabit and *personalize* their homes' (1994, p.2, emphasis added), but he also suggests that 'individuals with profound cognitive disabilities live every minute with the decisions others make' (p.4).

The likelihood is that the settings people with profound intellectual disabilities live in are going to be decorated and furnished in ways that reflect the tastes of the staff who support them and their family members, as this house supervisor suggests:

> The house was a building, there was nothing; there was no character to it. A very sterile building that had rooms for the guys to go into, and that was about it. Everything that we've now got in this house, and the things that are starting to take place, like the veggie garden, the shade sail and the rug on the wall, everything that has contributed to the house, these are the staff's ideas. The house is becoming what it is, because everyone has put into it. This house has changed, and it is starting to become a more homely place, losing that sterile building feel.

For most people, a home may also be an important factor in shaping one's self-identity, a place where a person can express their individuality (Annison 2000; Sixsmith 1986). Christos, who we wrote about in Chapter 2, may not even have developed an understanding of physical and psychological self, i.e. that he inhabits his body and is a unique human being, distinct from other humans and non-humans. It seems more accurate to say that Christos's identity is constructed by the people around him. This is provocatively written about by Nick Hornby in his work of fiction, *A Long Way Down*. In the extract that follows, Maureen is talking about her son Matty, who has a profound intellectual disability.

They're Matty's, the posters, not mine. He doesn't know they're his, of course, but they are; I chose them for him. I knew that the girl was called Buffy, because that's what it said on the poster, but I really didn't know who Buffy was; I just thought it would be nice for Matty to have an attractive young woman around the place, because he's that age now. And I knew that the black fella played for Arsenal, but I only caught his first name, Paddy. I took advice from John at the church, who goes along to Highbury every week, and he said everyone loved Paddy, so I asked if he'd bring me back a picture for my lad next time he went to a game... I chose the posters the same as I chose all the other things...the tapes and the books and the football boots and the computer games and the videos. The diaries and the trendy address books... The jazzy pens, the cameras and the Walkman. Lots of watches. There's a whole unlived teenage life in there... Thinking about these things helped me to see Matty, in a strange sort of way. I suppose it must be what they want to do when they think of a new character for

EastEnders: they must say to themselves, well, what does this person like? What does he listen to, who are his friends, what football team does he support? That's what I did – I made up a son.[1] (2005, pp.117–19)

Accepting that we have a major role in creating a home and constructing the identity of people with profound intellectual disabilities is an important step in developing high-quality services. It highlights the importance of having time and space to reflect on our own practice and the behaviour of service-users. The former should help staff to become more conscious of their own behaviour, and allow them to have greater awareness of how they might develop a home. Focusing on the behaviour of service-users allows us to look for ways in which they might be indicating 'happiness' about where they are living. A sense of 'home' as an emotional and physical reference point is exemplified by this house supervisor's interpretation of a resident's behaviour.

> The one thing I find that gives me great hope that we're doing the right thing is Betty Joy likes to skip out of day placement to stay home because she enjoys being at home so much. I think in the past [when she lived at the institution], Betty Joy would've been probably keener to get out of home, to go to her day placement, to get away from it. And so that says to me, even though Betty Joy can't communicate in 100 words how much she likes living here, that says to me this is someone who likes this place, who wants to be here, who thinks this is her home and its something very important to her. (Quoted in Doran 2004)

In this instance, Sixsmith's (1986) conceptualisation of 'home experience' becomes an interpretative framework for understanding Betty Joy's behaviour.

It is probably the case that the concepts of 'home' or 'institution', and the roles of home-owner or tenant, will have no personal meaning to people with severe or profound intellectual disabilities. It is in this sense that we agree with the volunteer whom we quoted above. This is not the same as saying that it does not matter where people live. The research we have cited suggests that there are likely to be very different outcomes for a person who is a home-owner as opposed to a patient in an institution.

O'Brien suggests that, 'Individuals have control of their homes when they have a choice in selecting the place that they live and the individuals they live with' (1994, p.3). As we made clear in Chapter 1, these decisions are made by others for people with profound intellectual disabilities. He goes on, 'Individuals with severe disabilities need the option to control personal assistance funds and manage the individuals who provide them with help. This means that they should have the choice to hire, fire, schedule, train and supervise those who provide them with everyday assistance' (p.3).

People with severe intellectual disabilities are not going to control their own funds, or hire and fire staff. O'Brien also writes that, 'The cognitive disabilities of some individuals are so substantial [which surely must include people with severe intellectual disabilities], that they must rely on a guardian, usually a family member or friend, to exercise control on their behalf in order to ensure that they have a home and a support system that offers them a sense of place and respects their dignity and any expressed preferences' (1994, p.4). There is a big difference in whether a person with intellectual disabilities controls their home and support or whether this is in the hands of someone else, regardless of whether they are human service employees or a guardian.

This means it is important that processes exist for identifying ways in which people can exercise control over the physical environment, no matter how small. At 16 Temple Court, for example, one of the residents was being taught to operate the elevating back-rest on his bed which could be adjusted by an electric hand-control by one of the night staff.

Sixsmith's (1986) framework can just as easily be used to guide the development of the physical, social and personal home. This house supervisor explained how she had to work at shaping a staff group's perception of a social and personal home, which meant tackling the consequences of the 'meal break' policy, an issue we discuss later.

I find it really difficult to explain to some staff, 'When you're on duty you can walk in the house, when you're not on duty you have to ring the doorbell. When you're in the house, even if you're on shift, I don't really like you taking over the kitchen and making full gourmet meals for yourself, even if it's your meal break. It's your meal break but it's their home, you've got to respect that.' That's the difference between the personal and professional. Yes it is a home, and therefore you've got a good kitchen, and it is your meal break, but it's not your home.

A degree of conflict should be expected when people sit down to develop a clear understanding of what makes a home. 'Home', 'homely', 'homey', 'homeliness' and 'homelike' are all culturally defined concepts that we learn about from an early age (Thompson *et al.* 1996a).[2] They are complex multi-dimensional concepts, which are applied to detached houses in isolated rural locations and high-rise apartments in multicultural urban settings. Every member of staff will have their own understanding of 'home', and they will bring their lived experience to the group home setting. These understandings extend to the minutiae of day-to-day living, such as the frequency with which bed linen should be changed, windows cleaned, or whether milk should be served in a jug or remain in the carton. In an earlier longitudinal study, one of the authors observed a group home take on two distinctive interpretations of 'home', each reflecting the preferences of the house supervisor of the day. For the first two years it was a 'family home', bright and airy, tidy, well-decorated with pictures, place mats were used and the table laid carefully at every meal. For the next two years the house supervisor referred to it as a 'bachelor pad', and the house was untidy and unkempt, with a pool table dominating one of the lounge rooms. Given the time and inclination, a group of stakeholders with interests in a specific group home will be able to work out what constitutes 'homeliness' for residents in that setting.

A 'group home' is not an 'ordinary home'

Looking more closely at the characteristics of a group home reveals a number of ways in which it is not an 'ordinary home'. This produces additional challenges for creating a homely environment. In this section we point out some important ways in which a group home is different from a typical 'home', and show that some of the ways in which we commonly think about a group home can be both helpful and limiting.

In the absence of alternative ways of thinking, we are drawn to familiar concepts. Influential policy documents that shaped residential services in the UK advocated that people with intellectual disabilities 'should live in small family-type groups', that homes should create a 'substitute family group', and they should have a 'family atmosphere' (Atkinson 1998). Thus, the concept of 'home' and an idealised notion of 'family living' can be seen in the design and organisation of group homes.

Attending to the group dimension

Whilst the 'group home' term reflects the aspiration to create a 'home', the prefix suggests there is something unusual about it. Historically, people with intellectual disabilities have spent much of their time participating in activities in the immediate company of other service-users, all of whom were treated the same and required to do the same thing. In Chapter 2 we described how four residents were taken to a café in a shopping centre and bought the same orange drink and a doughnut. This pattern of activities led Goffman (1961/1978) to coin the term 'block treatment'. Contemporary social policy and organisational rhetoric that promotes an individualised approach to supporting people stands in stark contrast to this practice.

As a congregate setting, a group home, by definition, establishes tensions between individual members of the group. The rhetoric of individualisation and person-centredness means that the group dimension of shared residential services is often neglected (Mansell, McGill and Emerson 1994). The group dimension is an important facet of the social home, encompassing not only relationships between the residents, but the type and quality of relationships between staff and residents.

As we argued in Chapter 1, individualised services are not possible for all residents in group homes all of the time. It is important to acknowledge, therefore, that staff working in a group home have, at times, to organise for people collectively and significant periods of home-life and leisure-time will be conducted in groups. In Chapter 5 we discuss how a keyworking system can be used to negotiate the tension that exists between individual and group needs so that a balance between these extremes is maintained.

Organising the household: Mealtimes

In this subsection we discuss the organisation of mealtimes in order to show that paying attention to group or individual interests produces different outcomes. Practice should be aligned with the outcomes that we are interested in.

The smooth running of a household requires that staff and residents must turn a number of domestic activities, such as budgeting, cleaning, gardening, household shopping, laundry and organising meals, into more formally recognised arrangements. People with mild intellectual disabilities will have their own ideas about how to run their home, but in a group home for people with severe and profound intellectual disabilities the management of the house is going to be primarily shaped by staff perspectives and the organisation's policies.

In Chapter 2 we described how staff had the most active roles at mealtimes, determining the limits of resident participation, the choices that were available, and taking the lead in serving food and drink. There are other ways of organising mealtimes that we discuss below, which underscores a key idea that stakeholders need to think through every aspect of how to organise a group home.

Two group homes that one of the authors worked in had contrasting approaches to how the main meal of the day was organised. In one, each of the five residents was supported in turn to cook their own meal, and in the other, the residents were supported to cook a meal for everyone, including the support staff.

The first was a group home for people with moderate and mild intellectual disabilities and mental illness in the USA, where individual choice over food to be eaten and teaching independent skills were privileged. In the second, mealtimes were organised along 'traditional family lines', where the main meal of the day was an event that everyone participated in. The latter allowed staff to model table manners. It also provided a naturally occurring social occasion to talk more generally, or specifically about how people were feeling, or what they wanted to do that coming weekend. The organisation increased the food budget to ensure that additional resources were available for staff to eat whilst at work. This was seen as a positive 'condition of service', given that direct support staff were not highly paid.

These differing approaches reflected the services' differing philosophies, rather than the residents, and both had pros and cons. Some important disadvantages of the individualised approach was that it generally took longer to prepare five meals than one; the quality of those meals was usually lower, as they tended to be less elaborate than a 'family meal'; and the social possibilities of a shared mealtime were missed.

The idea that staff can partake of the meal being cooked in a house is now anathema to many organisations, including the one where we conducted our research. Some organisations have cut their overheads by reducing the 'staff allowance' from the food budget, and where this is the case it is generally considered unacceptable for the residents to finance staff meals from their limited funds. At a staff orientation:

Participants are told that they have to bring their own food in. Staff are expected to make a contribution for any of the residents' food that they eat. The trainer says, 'A Community Visitor[3] may come in and see you eating something and accuse you of eating the clients' food.' People were urged to eat food out of containers that they had bought from home, as this would signpost that this was food that the staff had brought to work rather than being the residents' food. People get a receipt for any money they contribute.

This is reinforced in a formal policy statement about 'staff meals':

Staff are responsible for bringing or purchasing their own meals when on duty, though when staff share a meal at the unit or house, a contribution to the housekeeping expenses must be made. (Health and Community Services 2005, unpaginated)

The typical staff behaviour that we observed was in line with the message that had been communicated at the staff orientation. People brought their own food in to work and ate it at a separate time from the residents, who typically ate together. Not partaking of a meal together also creates 'social distance' between staff and residents.[4]

When working with people with profound intellectual disabilities it is all too easy to frame mealtimes as simply 'feeding' people, which can mean little more than putting food in a person's mouth (Schwier and Stewart 2005). If we reframe 'feeding' as 'dining' it helps us to conceptualise mealtimes as an enjoyable, shared experience, rather than an act that is done to someone else. We like Michael Smith's idea that '[sharing] a meal with others presents a powerful opportunity to enhance the sense of belonging and community in a life that often craves such normalcy' (2005, p.xxv).

It is possible that the formal policy contributed to the pattern of interactions that we described in Chapter 2. The specific 'staff meals' policy was bolstered by the institutionalisation of formal 'meal-breaks' in people's 'conditions of service', which formalised the separation of mealtimes for staff and residents. A shift length of five hours and one minute, for example, entitled a staff member to have a 30-minute meal-break. The 'hotel model' may be a more likely outcome when mealtimes are not shared occasions between staff and residents. When participation, conversation and enjoyment are not seen as important attributes of the social home, then preparing and serving food, and cleaning-up afterwards, can become disproportionately emphasised within the staff role.

The concept of an official 'meal-break' was unknown in the aforementioned service where the staff and residents ate together. Informal times for tea or coffee were either part of the natural rhythm of the day, or were negotiated. When residents arrived home from work or a day programme, it was habitual behaviour to put the kettle on and sit down together to discuss how people's days had been and make plans for the coming evening. When the residents were being supported to undertake housework, a natural point was inevitably reached when someone turned to the other to say, 'Is it time for a cuppa?' 'Breaks' were spent together, which facilitated closeness rather than creating and reinforcing 'social distance'. This is not to say that there may be specific settings where time spent apart from each other may not be beneficial, such as services where there is intense and frequent challenging behaviour. Breaks probably become more necessary when shifts are over-long.

Given that much of our lives are organised around eating food and the planning, shopping, selecting, preparing and cleaning-up that accompany it, then staff groups need to consider how mealtimes can contribute to the home in its physical, social and personal dimensions. When the residents need a lot of physical support to eat, this will require some creative practices.

The end result is likely to be a balance between sitting down together and supporting residents to cook separate meals at times to suit. This will be necessary if services are to support more individualised lifestyles in group settings. For example, one resident may have to eat his evening meal earlier or later than everyone else if he wants to attend an evening Adult Education class. Or if a resident dislikes the meal that is on the 'menu', then it seems reasonable to support him or her to make an alternative.

The group home as a 'workplace'

The presence of paid staff in a group home is the most obvious reminder that the setting is also a workplace. As we mentioned at the beginning of the chapter, the labels Community Residential Unit and CRU promote a service rather than a home. Group homes may have a number of features that draw attention to them as places of work. Embedded in this comment from a house supervisor is the aforementioned idea that people bring their lived experience of 'home' to work, that 'Occupational Health and Safety' regulations shape the group home as a place of work, which is in tension with trying to create a home for the residents.

> I think because you're in somebody else's home it's very easy for us as staff to confuse that sometimes, and have a sense of ownership and impose the things that you would impose at home and that you want to bring into work. I think the main thing is to remind people that this is the residents' home, it's not our home. It's also our workplace and that's more an OH and S [Occupational Health and Safety] thing, but it is their home. We all have to do things differently in somebody else's home and try and start that from the very beginning.

In Chapter 1 we stated that the houses were purpose built and in our view they have been designed with a number of characteristics that accentuate a 'workplace' over a 'home'. In designing, building and equipping the houses we thought that there were a number of ways in which the decision-makers had misjudged, or failed to consider, the impact of their decisions on the home environment.

Amongst the various claims that have been made for the architectural features of a group home are that they can:

- tell us a good deal about the policies that guide the service and the social organisation of the house

- have an impact on the way the setting is perceived by the residents, although this is moderated by a person's level of intellectual disability

- influence the lifestyle of the people with intellectual disabilities living in it; a home that looks like typical single-family housing will produce more positive outcomes

- influence how service-users are viewed and treated by support staff

- affect assumptions made by members of the general public about the attributes and behaviour of people living in it. (Egli *et al.* 2002; Thompson *et al.* 1990, 1996a, 1996b)

All of these claims are addressed throughout this chapter, aside from the final point, which was addressed indirectly in Chapter 1. The rhetoric of 'ordinary houses in ordinary streets' marks out the terms of the debate, that people with intellectual disabilities have a right to live in the community, in a house furnished with typical domestic equipment. This provides the context in which to promote ordinary patterns of living. People living in homelike settings may be more expected to make their own choices, to mix with others in broader society, and to be entitled to privacy. Of course, the general public may not take on board these messages.

Purpose-built houses, uniform in design

As the group homes were designed, built and equipped specifically for people with intellectual disabilities, the end result does reveal something about how the 'imagined' residents were perceived and role of the staff was understood. At 16 Temple Court, neither the work surfaces nor the kitchen appliances had been installed for use by people who use wheelchairs. We were told that it was not envisioned that the residents would be involved in activities like cooking. This omission was rectified in group homes that were built at a later date.

To date, about a hundred of these purpose-built group homes have been built in Victoria, and as such they can be considered a 'service model', akin to the Locally Based Hospital Units in the UK and the Intermediate Care Facilities (ICFs) in the USA. Their physical similarities mean that intellectual disability service 'insiders' are able to identify them from the outside, even if they have no prior knowledge of a specific location.

Figure 3.1 The lounge at 64 Penny Lane

Figure 3.2 The lounge at 16 Temple Court

As well as having a similar internal layout, a relatively uniform solution to decorating and equipping the houses had made the interiors noticeably alike. They had been painted in a limited range of colours, equipped with comparable furnishings, and some rooms were laid out in a similar manner. Figures 3.1 and 3.2 show the lounges from two group homes. The garden furniture, which can be seen through the rear window, is identical.

Although streets often contain housing that looks similar, from the Royal Crescent in Bath to less glamorous contemporary housing estates, such a large number of group homes with a similar architectural style and décor had consequences. Given that there is a significant movement of staff between the houses, either to work in other settings or support residents to visit friends and acquaintances, we would suggest that the similarity is a strong cue to staff that purpose-built group homes are a service solution to the housing and support needs of people with intellectual disabilities. This cue would have been less stark if 'ordinary' housing, which has greater architectural variety, had been used. A 'service atmosphere' could have been further reduced if more freedom had been given in the selection of décor and furnishings. Organisations make constraints for themselves in this regard, by creating restricting regulations about purchasing arrangements. Mansell *et al.* (1987) recommended allowing service-users and direct support staff as much control over this decision-making as possible. If residents are unable to choose how their own homes are decorated and furnished, then this at least ensures that these decisions are made by people who 'know' them best, i.e. staff and family members. The inclusion of family members may be an important safeguard against the imposition of particular understandings of home, particularly when service-users come from an ethnic minority.

Figure 3.3 shows a bedroom in a group home visited by Alan Robertson and Patsie Frawley as part of their preparation for an investigation into 'homeliness' (Robertson, Frawley and Bigby 2008). Its horizontal stripes, painted in bold colours (green, lavender and purple), may not be to everyone's taste. Yet it is a good example that illustrates how people close to a person with profound intellectual disabilities experimented with décor on the basis of what they thought the person might like.

According to Thompson *et al.* (1996a), the 'Absence of personal individualizing decoration reflecting the interests and tastes of the residents reinforces the impression that the residents have little control of their own residential space' (p.310). We found that the residents' personal possessions tended to be confined to their bedrooms, and the lack of personal possessions in common areas made them look somewhat bare. Moving beyond the 'basic' physical home takes time, and over the course of the project there was evidence that greater personalisation was taking place. The most outstanding example was a number of large paintings hanging on walls of one house, which the residents had been supported to complete (Figure 3.4).

Figure 3.3 An attempt to personalise a resident's bedroom

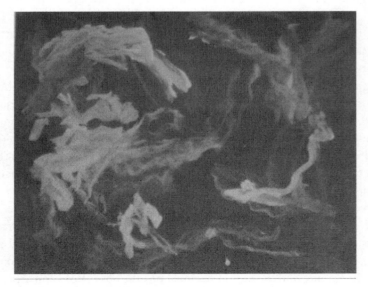

Figure 3.4 A painting completed by a resident with support at 64 Penny Lane

The houses had some additional features that detracted from perceptions of 'homeliness' and enhanced a 'service' feel. As in an earlier study, these were the result of guidelines that tended to create more institutional environments in settings that are meant to mirror domestic housing (Thompson *et al.* 1996a). For example, each house had a state-of-the-art fire prevention system, the legacy of a tragic fire at Kew Residential Services in 1996 (Freckelton 2005). Although this system raised the standard for fire safety, the high visibility of sprinklers, extinguishers, fire blankets and 'exit' signs created the impression of a public space rather than private home (see Peace 1998).

Staff facilities

The group homes had a sleepover room/office, staff toilet and shower. The latter was a requirement that had been agreed with the recognised trade union: 'Each house built...shall have exclusive toilet, shower and hand basin facilities for the exclusive use of the employees in each CRU' (DHS and Health Services Union of Australia 2002, p.10).

Our experience was that the office looked like the most 'lived-in' room in the houses and the staff bathrooms typically seemed more homelike, with hand-towels, air-fresheners and soap available, which was often not the case in the residents' facilities.

We thought that this exclusive use of a toilet and shower for staff reflected 'institutional thinking', which was formally endorsed through rules, and physically built into the structure of the building. Just as the institutions had separate amenities to divide 'staff' from 'patients' (O'Brien 2005b), so the distinct facilities influenced the social home, enhancing 'social distance' and impacting on the type of relationship that existed between 'staff' and 'resident'.

When asked about such matters, some informants stood reality on its head, arguing that separate staff facilities ensured exclusivity and privacy for the residents. Whilst the staff were free to use any of the facilities, the staff toilet and shower was 'off-limits' to residents; a 'rule' that had to be stated and enforced. As the residents' toilets often had no soap or hand-towel, and sometimes no toilet paper, the staff were always more likely to use the one room that had all three.

When separate amenities are formally endorsed by official policy, then it should be no surprise to find that informal practices also develop that make unnecessary distinctions between residents and staff. We observed, for example, the naming and use of staff mugs and plates, which were stored on the 'staff shelf' or in the 'staff cupboard'.

Offices in group homes are not so different from 'nursing stations' found in institutions; formal centres of power and control. In the Thompson *et al.* (1996a) study, the more administrative space a residence had (e.g. staff offices), the more institutional it was seen as being. Although sleep-in staff, by definition, require a bed, there are more imaginative solutions to the administrative requirements of a group home than 'a staff office'. One house supervisor who we interviewed had relocated the computer from the office to the lounge, so that it was more readily available to the residents, and the staff and residents could more readily use it together. A solution such as this may not be appropriate where challenging behaviour may result in a lot of property damage, but as Mansell *et al.* (1987) point out, some responses to issues such as challenging behaviour or incontinence can result in barren environments that are designed to be indestructible.

Mansell *et al.* also write that, 'Sometimes unusual solutions are proposed on the basis of trying to design away problems the people who live in the home may have' (1987, p.72). Nowhere was this more evident than in the design solutions that had been developed to restrict people's access to the kitchen. At 18 Finch Grove a wall and doors had been specifically built to achieve this, which was colloquially known as 'the Berlin Wall'.

The kitchen is very small. A screen at head height and two locking doors have just been built to make it secure, so that the residents cannot get in. It means the residents cannot easily see in and staff can't see out. I was told the alteration had been done at the request of the house staff to enable the residents to be kept out of the kitchen to prevent them from knocking things off the work space and touching hot things. An earlier attempt to solve the problem using child-proof gates had not worked. The house supervisor complained that this was not what had been intended, that staff could not see out if they were in the kitchen, and it also obscured the view out into the garden through the big window in the dining room.

Some six months later the screen and doors were cut down to waist height. Although the residents could now observe what was happening in the kitchen it remained inaccessible to them, unless they were admitted by a staff member. Mansell *et al.* argue that, in general, 'The appropriate response to these kinds of problems is largely made up of what staff do and how well they are organised and trained' (1987, p.72). Mansell *et al.* (2004) make the case for allocating staff to areas of a group home. At 18 Finch Grove, another group home where we were participant-observers, there were always two rostered staff, which meant that one staff member could be allocated to support the residents in the kitchen when it was being used to prepare food and drinks.

Occupational Health and Safety

Human services have become increasingly fixated with 'risk' (Sykes 2005). Although this parallels a preoccupation with 'safety' in the broader environment (see Furedi 1997, for example), this concern has been a driver that has changed the group home environment. Nowhere is this more apparent than the focus on Occupational Health and Safety.

In the research houses, front-loading washing machines and tumble-driers were positioned on purpose-built plinths so that *staff* did not have to bend down to load and unload these appliances. Each house was supplied with a raised laundry-basket on wheels, again so that *staff* did not have to bend down to pick up the basket, but also so that it could be pushed rather than carried. Although the residents could also benefit from these back-saving adaptations, we have emphasised the staff in the preceding sentences, because Occupational Health and Safety legislation exists to protect employees and make 'workplaces free from risk, injury and disease' (Victorian Workcover Authority 2005).

Services for people with intellectual disability have had an ambivalent relationship to risk. In an oft-quoted article, Perske (1972) made the case for making sure that people with intellectual disabilities were exposed to the benefits of ordinary risk-taking. An employee focus on Occupational Health and Safety, rather than Perske's client focus, reduced the extent to which some service-users could participate in specific tasks, and in the worst cases created dependence rather than independence.

Large areas of flooring were made out of materials that could be easily cleaned, just in case food, drink or bodily fluids should be spilled on them. Rather than carpets, much of the flooring was made of easily washable synthetic materials. These materials are more likely to be found in an institutional setting rather than a home (Egli *et al.* 2002).

The commercial-style mops and buckets that had been provided to each house had been purchased with an emphasis on Occupational Health and Safety. To be able to operate this equipment independently you have to have 'normal' motor skills, which may be impaired in some people with intellectual disabilities. You have to be able to use both feet at the same time. One foot goes on a stabilising plate on one side of the bucket and the other foot is used to press down a lever that operates a mangle-type arrangement over the bucket through which you pull the mop. Whereas some service-users might be able to mop the bathroom or their bedroom on their own with a different type of mop and bucket, the degree of coordination that is required to operate this equipment means that, for some, it will always be a job that requires the support of a staff member.

The institution as a point of reference

As well as drawing attention to the group home as a place of work, we have suggested that certain features had the characteristics of institutional settings, such as the flooring, staff toilet and office. There were other aspects of the physical structure and architectural style that also brought to mind 'the institution'.

A number of writers have evoked the institution when writing about community-based services. In her study, for example, Janice Sinson (1993) described group homes as 'micro-institutions' and Sharon Landesman (1988) defined 'institutionalisation' as the processes by which *any* residential setting actively or passively adopts depersonalised and regimented practices that were associated with the negative consequences of institutional living. Like a science fiction story, the institution 'shifts its shape and assumes the disguise of an ordinary looking house' (O'Brien 2005a, p.261).

For many people, institution is the antithesis of home. For people with direct experience of living or working in institutions, their first-hand knowledge is a comparative benchmark for both appearance and practice. As the years drift by, however, fewer staff will have this reference point and will have to be guided more by their own understandings of homeliness or make comparisons with buildings that do not typically function as homes, such as hospitals. Architectural features, such as the proportion of floor space devoted to corridors, the number of doorways, the wall, floor and ceiling materials, the style and size of furniture pieces and disability-specific adaptations, are all associated with whether a building is perceived as being homelike (Egli *et al.* 2002).

The houses were designed to be wheelchair accessible, and the emphasis on accessibility has resulted in wide passages and doorways (Figure 3.5), large empty bathrooms with specialist equipment such as grab-rails (Figure 3.6) and open-plan communal areas.

These features suggest that there is something slightly 'different' about the residents, but also give the houses a more institutional feel. According to Egli *et al.* (2002) long sound reverberation times can create the impression of a noisy public foyer. The group homes with their spacious, open-plan design, together with flooring and furnishings that did not provide adequate sound absorption, had this feel. Achieving the right balance, particularly when people require specialist equipment or additional room to manoeuvre, is a challenge.

Home versus workplace: A paradox

We have suggested that the houses we have described have a number of features that accentuate the group home as a place of work. We believe that although a group home is also a place of work, it is the home that needs the greater emphasis, i.e. it is a home where people work, rather than a place of work where people live. Yet the comments of some managers drew our attention to a paradox. In the opinion of three managers, conceiving of the group home as a 'home' undermines a strong work ethic.

Figure 3.5 A corridor that ran the length of the house, from the front door to the rear

Figure 3.6 A bathroom, where access and ease of cleaning were paramount design features

---

It's difficult in this environment 'cos we're in a home, and we're supposed to be modelling what it's like to be at home and I think some staff get confused. This is still ultimately a professional working environment, but as you get to know the clients a little bit more you become a little bit more lax in how you communicate. As you get to know people, that professional distance, the lines get a bit blurred.

I think we tend to see our workplace more as a home environment rather than a workplace. I think that's why [the professional and personal] boundaries tend to get a bit merged at times. I think people are very conscious that they're trying to provide a homely environment for the clients who are living within our service but at the same time they forget that it is a workplace and their role is that they are coming to work to provide a service.

I try to wrack my brain. Why is it that in houses, why is it so easy to let go, and lose perspective of why they're really there? I believe it is the environment. I come to work, you go to work, you go to an office, there's the computer there, everyone's there, it's work. A CRU [group home] is well decked-out with tea and coffee at your disposal, couches, some houses with cable TV, you actually lose perspective of work, it becomes a second home to some people. It's like coming from a home to another home, and you lose perspective of work. I'm not saying that that's the case, sometimes I wonder, could that be a reason? People lose perspective that it's work, because it's a home, someone's home, it's like you're going to another house, you've got television, you can watch your favourite programmes, you've got tea or coffee... I don't know.

Getting the balance right between a home and a workplace is a constant challenge. In a sense, it seems that it is possible to end up with the 'worst of both worlds'. A sense of 'home' is undermined for the residents by workplace rules and regulations, and some staff may perceive a group home as just another home, where the normal rules that guide workplace behaviour don't apply. These are ideas that are worthy of further investigation.

The staff group as a pseudo family

It is not surprising that since residential services have been conceptualised as an alternative to the family home, ideas about 'the family' should be apparent in the way we think about group homes.

In a discussion we were having with a staff team about how they organised external leisure activities, one of the support staff explained that, 'Usually everyone goes out. If we are going in the bus I take all the boys.' To which the house supervisor added, 'Bus trips are the whole family.'

The way in which staff draw on the concept of 'the family' to describe the atmosphere of residential services has also been commented on by Dorothy Atkinson (1998). As we have tried to suggest in our discussion of mealtimes, some helpful insights can be gained by thinking in this way. 'The family' as a simile or metaphor can be used to emphasise positive qualities, such as warmth, care and the expectation of doing things together. However, this may blind us to any negative outcomes that may result from extending the simile too far, or believing that a group home is exactly like a family.

The home is also the place where children are nurtured and family members are 'cared' for (Peace 1998). According to Jill Reynolds and Jan Walmsley (1998) the dominant ideology of 'care' in Western society is derived from parenting young children. It is all too easy for people with intellectual disabilities, especially those with severe or profound impairments, to be cast into the role of eternal children (Wolfensberger 1975).

It is this dynamic that makes us feel ambivalent about a group of middle-aged men with intellectual disabilities being referred to collectively as 'the boys', as in the fieldnote extract above. Although it is common practice for some non-disabled adult men and women to refer to themselves as 'boys' and 'girls', they are not seen as perpetual children or adolescents.

If residents are cast in the role of children, then it is no surprise to find that the staff sometimes take on the role of adult or parent. This dynamic is apparent in many of the fieldnote extracts in Chapter 2. For example, the many ways in which staff take responsibility for the running of the home. From this perspective, 'the family' as metaphor or simile may infantilise the residents, positioning them as people who need looking after, and create dependency and helplessness (Atkinson 1998). Some research shows that adults with intellectual disabilities, who remain living with their families well into adulthood, where parent–child relations are more entrenched, have restricted opportunities for taking on the roles and responsibilities of adult life (Reynolds and Walmsley 1998).

As Mansell, McGill and Emerson write, 'Managers simplistically conceptualize the environment as a family, which the (overwhelmingly female) workforce is expected to make work' (1994, p.71). A highly gendered workforce, without the benefit of professional training, is likely to draw on concepts of caring that they have learnt from family and kinship systems. This lived experience is imported into the workplace and can shape the type and quality of relationships in a group home.

Although the concept of 'care' has been strongly critiqued, by the feminist and disability movements in particular, John Swain and Sally French point out that 'care' is not intrinsically oppressive. They argue that, 'It is oppressive...when it incorporates a mould for the "cared for" as a person, for behaviour, for appearance, and for lifestyle' (1998, p.82). As we have argued in this chapter, the lifestyles of people with severe and profound intellectual disabilities are particularly susceptible to being shaped by the values and practice of staff. Although the resident in the fieldnote extract below could select his own clothes and dress himself, one member of staff has strong views about how he should look and behave, which another staff member goes along with.

Alberto was wearing shorts and a T-shirt. He was not wearing socks. Andrew said 'Look what I've found' and showed him some socks. Julie shouted, 'Don't make him wear socks. He pulls them right up and looks a dork.' Andrew took the socks away again.

Although Julie's practice was influenced by her understanding of 'normalisation', i.e. that Alberto's appearance should help him be valued by other people in the community, it is hard not to see this interaction as 'oppressive', where choice and control is taken away from the service-user.

Even though contemporary understandings of family have expanded way beyond the traditional nuclear family, the group of non-relatives who are paid to provide support in a group home do not fit any of these conceptualisations. Some authors (Gibson and Ludwig 1968; Kurst-Swanger and Petcosky 2003) have applied the term 'pseudo family' to refer to paid staff. This highlights its artificiality, but also emphasises the important role that support staff play in the lives of adults with intellectual disabilities living in out-of-home care settings.

Ruth Marquis and Robert Jackson usefully remind us that, 'Service lives are not "ordinary lives". Service lifestyles are "service specific" and, as such, have other dimensions to day-to-day living which need to be understood by people managing and evaluating services' (2000, p.412). So, group homes are neither 'ordinary homes', nor are they exactly like families. We need to be careful about the application of 'familiar' concepts.

Concluding remarks

In concluding this chapter we want to give a little more attention to the physical home, rather than the social or personal dimensions, which receive greater attention throughout the book. We want to be careful not to overstate the role that the physical setting can play in realising high-quality outcomes, but it is an important characteristic that must be taken into account by architects and designers, policymakers and direct support staff. In the twenty-first century, with more than 30 years of knowledge and experience of managing group homes behind us, there is little excuse for designing and furnishing group homes in ways that are more 'work-like' than 'homelike'.

It may be the case that group homes for people with severe and profound intellectual disabilities must always have a degree of ambiguity about their character. The aspiration to create an 'ordinary home' can be undermined by features that reflect the specific needs of its residents, such as wide corridors and bathroom hoists, and the fact that the setting is a place where people come to work. However, the overall impression created by a building depends on combinations of characteristics, and it should be possible for the features that emphasise 'home' to outweigh those that suggest 'service'.

We like Sixsmith's (1986) model because it is simultaneously a framework for thinking about homeliness, a practical guide for creating a home, and an interpretative framework for understanding a specific setting. As such, it goes a long way to meeting Annison's (2000) recommendation that all residential service stakeholders should have a clear understanding of what makes a 'home'.

Issues for consideration

- Are you clear about what a group home is?

- To what extent have the physical, social and personal dimensions of the home been considered?

- Do senior managers in every functional department have a clear understanding of what makes a home?

- Can the stakeholders in a specific group home be brought together to work out what constitutes 'homeliness' for the residents in that setting?

- Can greater levels of decision-making be pushed downwards to allow service-users, direct support staff and family members as much control as possible?

- Are processes in place so that stakeholders review every decision in relation to the goal of creating a 'home' environment and the impact on the residents' lifestyles? For example, architectural design and décor, policy and procedure, rules and regulations, practice.

- Has enough consideration been given to the group dimension of the group home?

Notes

1   Buffy is the main character in the television series *Buffy the Vampire Slayer*. Arsenal is an English football club who used to play their home games at Highbury, before they moved to the Emirates Stadium. *EastEnders* is the name of a British soap opera.

2   These terms have multiple meanings, and in certain cultures some of them do not have positive connotations. Homely, for instance, can mean 'plain' or 'unpolished', and when applied to a person can mean 'not beautiful' (Simpson and Weiner 1989). Our intention has been to use all of them in a positive way, as aspirational outcomes.

3   In Victoria, a Community Visitor is a trained volunteer who visits disability residential services to observe the quality of services, talk with residents and staff to identify problems, and follow up on complaints raised by residents.

4   The concept of social distance has been used relatively frequently in intellectual disability research. It describes the distance between different groups of society and is a measure of people's willingness to participate in social contacts of varying degrees of closeness.

Chapter 4

Planning and A(
for Individualised Outcomes

Introduction

We have pointed out that the group dimension is an important aspect of life in a group home. This is because individualised services are not possible for all the residents in a group home all of the time. Staff have to organise for people collectively, and without the assistance of 'natural supports' (see Chapter 6) significant periods of time in the home, and in the community, will be conducted in groups.

This does not mean that the staff in a group home have to adopt regimented practices where all the residents are treated the same and required to do the same thing. On the contrary, it is possible to live in a group home and not lead the same life as everyone else. Indeed, it is almost impossible not to organise certain practices along individual lines, e.g. providing support for health and personal care. Yet good practices in these areas are rarely sufficient to establish the highly individualised lifestyles aspired to in the social policy. In this chapter we highlight the planning and action that is necessary to realise individual lifestyles and outline a number of issues related to the implementation of a keyworking system designed to achieve this outcome.

The personalisation agenda

A number of staff who work in group homes for people with profound intellectual disabilities must wonder whether the senior managers and Government mandarins who write policy documents have ever visited such a setting. As one

...taff said, 'It's good to talk about issues, but you can only do so ...people who are more severely disabled. The people who write the ...need to have a look.' We use this quotation not as an attempt to set limits ...what can be achieved for people with intellectual disabilities in general, but ...to point out that direct support staff can feel frustrated by the benchmarks set for them. This is likely to be exacerbated if they have not been given the necessary resources or guidance to achieve them.

As far as the day-to-day running of group homes is concerned, nowhere does the gap between the aspirations of social policy and its actual delivery seem more acute than in recent discussions of 'personalisation' in England, where it has been promoted as the cornerstone of contemporary public services (Department of Health 2008b).

Iain Ferguson asserts that, 'Many social workers would be hard-pressed even to define the term, other than the common-sense meaning that services should be more tailored to individual need' (2008, p.79). As such, 'personalisation' is little more than a fashionable substitute for individualisation; a concept that has been central to human services for decades. It is therefore not a fundamental break with the past, but a new marketing term intended to give the impression of a fresh approach. The tendency to introduce different terminology is confusing and undermines the need to develop a common language. Nonetheless, the Department of Health (2008b) writes that 'personalisation' means that:

> Everyone who receives social care support, regardless of their level of need, in any setting, whether from statutory services, the third and community or private sector or by funding it themselves, will have choice and control over how that support is delivered. It will mean that people are able to live their own lives as they wish, confident that services are of high quality, are safe and promote their own individual requirements for independence, well-being and dignity. (p.4)

> Every person who receives support, whether provided by statutory services of funded by themselves, will be empowered to shape their own lives and the services they receive in all care settings. (Department of Health 2008a, unpaginated)

We tend to agree that 'People want support when they need it, and they expect it quickly, easily and in a way that fits into their lives' (Department of Health 2008a, unpaginated). However, congregate settings do not quite work like this. Anyone who has worked or lived in a group home will be acutely aware that it is a setting where individuals' interests compete with each other. Although not the whole story, the support available to residents is constrained by the available staff resources. This does not mean that the provision of additional staff will result in more time being given to supporting the residents. A number of studies have shown that as the number of staff in a setting increases each staff member spends a smaller proportion of their time interacting with service-users (see Mansell, Felce and de Kock 1982, for example). As we shall see, the organisation of staff through systems of support planning is an important factor in developing effective working practices (Felce 1998).

The residents' needs for staff support in a group home have a natural rhythm of peaks and troughs. Although the careful allocation of staff and the sensible organisation of the day can help to lessen problems associated with 'demand' at peak times, there are periods, such as 'first-thing in the morning', when giving people the support 'when they need it' could only be realised by having greater numbers of staff present.

Wally came out of his bedroom. His bed was wet. He said 'piss the bed' a number of times. There was a lot of activity going on at this time. Martin and Keith, the two staff, did not seem to communicate very much, but just seemed to know that there were a series of tasks that needed to be done. Milan appeared from his bedroom, grabbed hold of my arm and took me to the bathroom. My understanding was that Martin and Keith had agreed that the residents would have breakfast first and then have a shower, even though Dan had also recently indicated that he was ready for the shower. I tried to explain this order of things to Milan, but he took off his pyjama top, then his pyjama bottoms and went and sat on the wooden bench by the shower. I went and told Keith what had happened and he went to help Milan shower. Wally, whose pyjamas were damp with urine, had to wait because Milan had taken possession of the bathroom, an available staff member, and was naked and waiting. Martin was preparing breakfast for Franco and Joseph, who had been helped to shower and get dressed earlier by the night staff.

The two staff on duty have to share themselves between five residents. Although it could be argued that Milan exercised some 'control' in this instance, the residents of 64 Penny Lane are more subject to having their lives organised by the staff. Milan could just have easily been made to wait for a shower, whilst Wally, who had more pressing needs, was supported to wash and dress. Martin could have stopped preparing breakfast, and helped Wally to shower in the second bathroom, but then Franco and Joseph would have had to wait for their breakfast. Dan, who wanted a shower, but was going to be given breakfast, would have had to wait for both. At times, a group home is not an environment where people get the support when they need it, when they expect it, or in a way that fits into their lives!

Balancing the needs of the individual and the needs of the group

The house supervisor at 96 High Street made a comment that reflects the difficulties of providing a completely individualised service in a group home. He stated that, 'If each resident had their own routine, it would be chaos.' The unfavourable ratio of staff to residents creates two possibilities:

1. A resident must defer his or her needs and wants to those of another individual or group, and wait until a member of staff is available.

2. Staff members have to support a group of residents, which is why some activities are inevitably conducted in groups.

In the first instance, comparing a group home with a family seems helpful, because it highlights the 'give and take' that is necessary from all members if a sense of harmony is to prevail (Atkinson 1998). In her research Dorothy Atkinson described residential settings that were either orientated towards groups or individuals; a distinction which she used to differentiate between residential 'climates'.

> When [the needs of the individual and the needs of the group] were, more or less, in some sort of equilibrium then the climate seemed fair and settled. When the balance swung rather too much towards the needs of the group, then the atmosphere changed and disgruntled individuals spoke out, or 'acted out', against it. (1998, p.21)

Group homes typically provide a better context for an individualised service than larger residential services. They generally afford opportunities for private space, especially through single bedrooms, and single-use bathrooms and toilets. These structural features help to avoid the worst examples of 'block treatment' associated with the institutions, such as communal bathrooms and toilets.

In contemporary services, residents get significant amounts of individual support, such as when receiving personal care and addressing health-related issues (e.g. medical appointments and accommodating particular dietary needs).

Supporting people to participate in household tasks is often done on an individual basis, such as making a bed or loading the washing machine. The risk for many people with severe or profound intellectual disabilities is that deferring their needs, or more likely having their needs temporarily put to one side by staff, may result in periods of disengagement. Whereas people with mild and moderate intellectual disabilities have the skills and motivation to engage in many activities independently, this is less likely to be the case for people with severe and profound intellectual disabilities. Therefore, outside of 'basic' activities that require 1:1 support, people with severe and profound intellectual disabilities not only find themselves sharing the same space with their fellow residents, or other people with intellectual disabilities, but sharing the same lives (Smull 2002). Thus they sit down to eat lunch collectively; are given a drink in the afternoon at the same time; are sat in the lounge together facing a television that they may or may not be watching; or go on the same outing together, such as a picnic or a trip to the shopping mall.

The challenge for staff in a group home is to find the right balance between an individual and group-orientated approach, so that it becomes possible to support individualised lifestyles, keep everyone engaged, whilst at the same time avoiding 'block treatment'.

Individualised support as 1:1 support

Figure 4.1 shows nine community-based activities that Brian, a resident at 96 High Street, participated in during one month. They were recorded on Activity

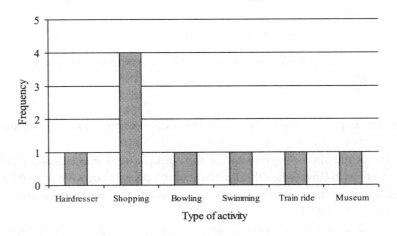

Figure 4.1 Brian's community activities for May 2006

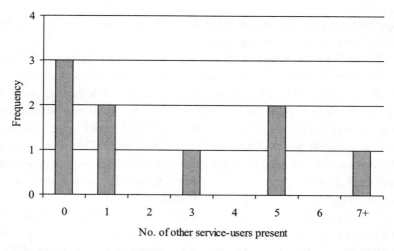

Figure 4.2 Number of service-users accompanying Brian when undertaking community activities – May 2006

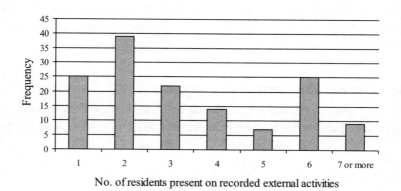

Figure 4.3 Number of service-users present on external activities from August 2006 to March 2007

Learning Logs, a written record of activities occurring within each resident's life, which are discussed more fully in Chapter 5.

Figure 4.2 shows the number of other people with intellectual disabilities who were with Brian when these activities took place. They were always fellow residents, apart from when he went bowling, which involved service-users from another group home.

One third of the activities (hairdresser, swimming and a shopping trip) were undertaken with only a member of staff present. Such an analysis shows that

Brian does undertake activities unrelated to 'basic' tasks on an individualised basis. Yet, since a group is defined as two or more people, 67 per cent of activities were undertaken with another service-user present. One third of the total number of activities had six or more service-users present.

Figure 4.3 shows that group outings accounted for 82 per cent of the 141 external activities recorded at 96 High Street over a seven-month period.

If we look more closely at the individual activities that comprise this data, much of it reflects Michael Smull's (2002) notion of people with intellectual disabilities sharing spaces and sharing lives. The two most common larger group activities at 96 High Street were classified as 'outings' and 'eating out', which usually happened at weekends and when the day programmes closed for enforced 'holidays'.[1] The Activity Learning Logs revealed that all or most of the residents went on these trips. Outings tended to be relatively self-contained activities, such as a drive to a local park for a walk or picnic. The residents went on about three of these trips in a month and ate out about once every three weeks. In Chapter 6 we argue that when community-based activities take this form, then there are few opportunities for people with intellectual disabilities to build more socially inclusive relationships.

Towards individual lifestyles

A focus on '1:1 activity' embraces a narrow understanding of individualisation. It is possible for a person with profound intellectual disabilities to receive a significant amount of 1:1 support, yet still primarily be seen as a person with intellectual disability. Developing an individual lifestyle is also about the formation of an identity that negates the externally imposed category of intellectual disability. Swimming, for example, had been identified as an interest favoured by Brian. If pursued regularly, it may allow him to be perceived as a 'swimmer' rather than a 'person with an intellectual disability'. The formation of an adult identity may be somewhat easier away from the group home environment, where it is possible to link into alternative social networks. For each resident it is helpful to ask:

- To what extent is this person seen as an individual in his or her own right; that is, distinct from the other people with intellectual disabilities that he or she lives with, knows and associates with?

- To what extent does this person have his or her own personal belongings, undertake activities that have particular personal significance and reflect him or her as an individual with his or her own self-identity?

It is, of course, feasible to pursue individualised interests when a staff member is supporting more than one resident. If we embrace the notion of 'give and take' that we referred to above, it is possible that one staff member can support two residents to pursue separate individual interests during the same outing. The first resident could receive help to go to the library and borrow a music CD, and then have to wait patiently whilst the second is supported to choose and purchase wool to knit a new scarf. Supporting people like this becomes harder, and the amount of 'individualised' time becomes diluted, as the size of the group increases.

We would suggest that the balance between individual lifestyles and group activities was out of kilter at 96 High Street, as it was in all the houses in our research, and that more emphasis needed to be put on individualised outcomes. This does not mean abandoning all activities that are organised along group lines. There are occasions when it is appropriate to do things as a household. For example, at 96 High Street a meal at a restaurant was organised for all the residents as a way of celebrating the anniversary of moving into the house.

Moving beyond physiological and safety needs

Figure 4.4 shows a depiction of Abraham Maslow's (1954/1987) well-known psychological framework, commonly known as the 'hierarchy of needs'. The 'physiological' and 'safety' needs, the bottom two levels in the pyramid, are, in many ways, 'easier' to meet. Making sure that people have food and drink, are

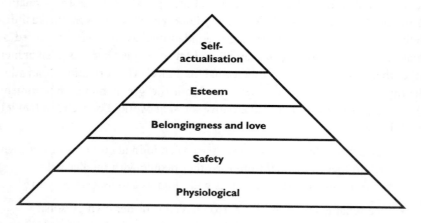

Figure 4.4 A diagrammatic representation of Maslow's hierarchy of needs

clean and well clothed, free from pain and discomfort and living in decent accommodation where they are warm and safe are standards about which there is little disagreement. These needs are often associated with 'caring for' people with intellectual disabilities, and it is in these areas that the five houses in our research performed relatively well. They represent an 'unofficial' minimum acceptable standard for supported accommodation services for people with severe and profound intellectual disabilities. Supporting people to 'get a life' will require support staff to address the broad range of 'quality of life' outcomes (de Waele *et al.* 2005).

A house supervisor made this most telling comment, which reflected the staff group's priorities and questioned their commitment to help service-users realise good outcomes in regard to the upper levels of the 'hierarchy of needs'. She said:

We do the best we can, one step at a time. First and foremost in the house the priority is client care. Recreation and other things come along. Client care is our priority. If there is spare time you can go for involvement. People should be fit, clean and comfortable. The other things come after that.

The upper levels of the hierarchy are harder to achieve for people with severe and profound intellectual disabilities. These are the areas that received the greater attention for the duration of *Making Life Good in the Community*, and are the focus of this book. It is in these domains that 'outcomes' are generally weaker for people with severe and profound intellectual disabilities. Meeting people's 'social needs', through friendships, intimacy and being accepted by 'the community', is possible, but requires hard work. Profound intellectual disability is not a positively valued characteristic, and so being respected as a person will not come easily. This will require a break from the externally imposed category of intellectual disability. Notions of self-esteem, confidence and 'becoming all that we are capable of becoming' are difficult concepts to apply to people with severe and profound intellectual disabilities, and consequently they may be seen by some people as having no relevance. Once basic needs are met, there is no certainty that staff activity designed to meet higher needs will simply 'come along'. Achieving good outcomes in regard to these higher needs requires a more formal approach to planning and organising support that is focused on long-term goals, but linked to day-to-day practice. The pattern of support that we observed in our research resulted from a combination of habitual practices and informal and short-term approaches to planning.

Unless we can attend to these issues, then for many people with severe and profound intellectual disabilities outcomes related to physiological and safety needs may be the best services can deliver. Outcomes associated with belongingness and love, esteem and self-actualisation will merely remain aspirational and the possibilities for a high 'quality of life' afforded by group homes will remain unfulfilled.

Routines and habitual practices

Most people's lives are organised around routines, by which we mean a more or less unvarying sequence of actions. In this regard, the residents' lives in the houses were highly routinised. Often we take routines for granted rather than spending time thinking about how they came about or what their function is. Chapter 2 describes a number of routines, which made up a 'typical' day for the residents and staff in the houses. During the weekdays people were woken up, helped to shower and dress, ate their breakfast, and then were driven to day programmes. The house was cleaned; dirty laundry was washed. Any residents who remained at home had 'morning coffee', then lunch, and may have gone on an outing before people were picked up from day programmes. On return, people had a snack, relaxed whilst tea was cooked, which they ate; then relaxed some more, before having supper and going to bed.

Shelagh, a staff member at 64 Penny Lane, described how she conceived the morning routine:

If I come in the morning I know to shower the guys, pack their bags, give them breakfast, get them ready and neat and tidy, get them off to the programmes and come back, clean the house. There is a routine in the morning that you need to get through before you do anything else. There's not really a cemented routine. We're pretty easy going. It depends what shift I'm on really. For example, one morning I might come in and I'll be working with Keith and we might give breakfast before we shower the guys. On another morning I might come in and I'll be working with Linda and we'll shower the guys before we give breakfast. It's pretty easy going. We just go with the flow. If the guys seem hungry and are all sitting at the table and they want their breakfast, you know what I mean? We work with each other.

By labelling such routines as habitual action, we are suggesting that there was little conscious understanding or discussion as to why routines were organised the way they were. This can be useful as it frees up our minds to do other things, but it can also become problematic.

At 96 High Street it was common practice for all the residents' toiletries to be purchased at the same time. Usually one resident would go and purchase the toiletries for all or a number of residents at the house. Yet, there was no valid reason why each resident could not be supported to buy their own toiletries. Purchasing the toiletries in the way that they did deprived each resident of an individually supported activity, of personally spending their own money, of interacting with members of the community and so on. 'Routine' can also be used in a pejorative sense when life becomes regular, mechanical and unvarying.

Much of the time it was left to the staff on duty to work out for themselves how they would organise support to the residents. They had the aforementioned routines to structure the day. Informal planning allowed the staff to achieve short-term goals and immediate priorities, such as doing the shopping or going to the beach for a picnic. In addition, staff groups had established 'norms' for external activities, i.e. patterns of behaviour that were accepted by the staff group (and by the residents). With a strong group-orientation, community-based activities were planned around a group of residents, either doing activities on the basis of what had happened before, such as trips to parks, beaches, etc., or more spontaneously where staff asked, 'What shall we do today?'

We noted a general antipathy towards longer-term planning. This may have been because long-term planning on behalf of the residents required staff to use systems that were alien to their own lives, but also because they did not have the knowledge or skills that are required to make long-term plans. Yet, as we stated previously, developing individual lifestyles requires more formal planning and a longer planning cycle.

Planning systems for organisations and individuals

Planning, the process for establishing goals and courses of action for achieving those goals, is one of the cornerstones of modern organisations. Organisations produce mission statements and strategic and operational plans (Stoner, Freeman and Gilbert 1995). As well as this 'organisational planning', human service organisations have utilised specific methods of planning for service-users for more than three decades.

'Lifestyle planning' is a term that encompasses a number of comprehensive planning systems, such as individual programme and educational plans, and an array of approaches under the Person-Centred Planning umbrella. Services also develop more narrowly focused plans for service-users, such as behaviour management plans and teaching programmes. Systems for planning, supporting and monitoring resident activity are associated with positive outcomes (Emerson and Hatton 1994). A recent study has shown that Person-Centred Planning was linked to statistically significant changes on a number of key lifestyle-related outcome variables (Robertson *et al.* 2006).

Although planning systems for people with intellectual disabilities have been a key feature of intellectual disability services, they have also attracted their fair share of criticism, usually where they have failed to improve people's 'quality of life' (Robertson and Emerson 2007). More often than not, it is not the planning system itself that deserves condemnation, but how the system is used. In evaluating the efficacy of such systems, Robertson and Emerson argue that we need to be concerned with issues of quality, content, process and outcomes. In their review of 'lifestyle planning' they summarised a number of weaknesses in regard to the quality and content of plans:

- restricted range of goals

- lack of long-term focus

- inadequately prepared plans

- lack of information on how and by whom goals are to be implemented

- vaguely expressed goals

- preferred activities not corresponding to the actual preferences of service users. (2007, p.286)

Many of the formal planning processes and products that we observed were weak. The 'lifestyle planning' system was in a transitional period, where the Individual Programme Planning system was being replaced by Person-Centred Planning. This had effectively put the older system in abeyance, with little attention being given to reviewing previously identified goals. We found scant use of formal systems for identifying what the residents could and could not do (e.g. adaptive behaviour assessments), and therefore there was no systematic way for establishing individual teaching programmes. There was no formal system for planning what the residents did at a home on a day-to-day basis, beyond the basic routines, such as getting up, showering, mealtimes, etc., or for how staff would allocate their time on a specific shift. Some staff took on tasks tacitly. For example, where a person was understood to be the better cook, he or she would be responsible for lunch or dinner. Formal hand-over time was underutilised. Planning for the day was more likely to be done on an improvised basis, perhaps during a coffee break. When pressed, staff were able to comment in greater detail about what residents had done, but not about what they were going to do in the future, i.e. little attention was given to planning for the longer term.

The need for action

It is not enough to have good planning meetings that produce good plans for people. Plans need to be translated into action. This is well captured by an aphorism attributed to the management guru Peter Drucker, 'Plans are only good intentions unless they immediately degenerate into hard work.' The planning process needs to have a long-term perspective, but it also requires a means of incorporating objectives into day-to-day activity (Robertson and Emerson 2007). This allows us to move from where we are now, to where we want to be.

In the remaining part of the chapter we outline a system that has been developed to promote better individualised outcomes for service-users in a group context, known in many residential settings as 'keyworking'. Keyworking was seen as a way to improve the service at one group home in a number of ways, such as increased opportunities for resident choice, greater participation in the house and focused effort to facilitate *community participation*. The next part of the chapter contains general information about keyworking, which arose from the first phase of an action research project at one group home. This information can be applied to any residential service, because although some keyworker responsibilities will vary from setting to setting, we would suggest that the role has core tasks, irrespective of service context.

Keyworking

Keyworking is based on the simple idea that individualised lifestyles can best be developed through a named individual, called a 'keyworker'. Mallinson (1995) suggests that the concept has been around for more than 30 years, although the term for the 'named individual' varies between contexts and the role has had different emphases over time and place. Equivalent terms named by Mallinson include: attached worker, care manager, linkworker, primary carer, primary nurse, primary worker, rehabilitation assistant, senior care assistant and special interest worker.[2] Where the role of the keyworker is part of the day-to-day workings of a group home then it should be formally listed on a person's job description and incumbents given guidance about how they are supposed to fulfil the role.

For discussion purposes, we begin by offering a definition of a keyworker from the Social Care Association (1991, quoted in Mallinson 1995, p.x), which may appear initially as being somewhat dated.

A keyworker is part of 'A system for providing individualized social care through named persons. A keyworker is the person who has responsibility and accountability for the care of the service user and for decisions relating to their situation.'

Contemporary services that put a greater emphasis on self-determination may suggest that this definition has a paternalistic flavour, and 'care' is now understood as a problematic term (Brechin *et al.* 1998). A more recent definition puts greater stress on service-users making their own decisions.

The keyworker is someone who has responsibility for ensuring that a named service user receives a high quality, personalised service according to his/her needs and wishes.

The keyworker is not solely responsible for delivering the service; this is the role of every member of the support staff when on duty. The keyworker, however, builds a closer relationship with the service user in order to become more acutely aware of the service user's needs and wishes. (Pearce and Smith 2000, unpaginated)

In line with the position we have argued, discovering a person's needs and wishes is harder in some contexts than others. This is especially the case when supporting people with severe and profound intellectual disabilities. We suggest, therefore, that both definitions have something to offer. A keyworker may aspire to provide a service in accordance with a person's needs and wishes but in some circumstances it is more likely that people in an individual's support network will be making decisions about the service he or she receives and day-to-day lifestyle choices.

Benefits of keyworking

In Mallinson's (1995) research, keyworkers stated that they undertook the following tasks, which are ranked in order of importance: physical care; supporting daily living; assessment; advocating; counselling; admitting; recording;

arranging activities; and arranging outings. They also listed the following, but not in order of importance: buying clothes; attending to medical needs; attending to spiritual needs; buying Christmas and birthday presents; liaising with relatives; supporting people with their diet; and sitting and listening to people's joys and worries.

Mallinson's research was not conducted in services for people with intellectual disabilities, but in the context of residential care for older people. However, his findings revealed positive outcomes that would be welcome in any residential service. He concluded that keyworking contributed towards improved individualised support and his research respondents thought that keyworking enabled:

- staff and service-users to get to know each other as people
- the fulfilment of service-users' personal needs
- individualised care on a one-to-one basis reflecting service-user choice and trust
- monitoring and reporting of any deterioration in the general well-being of service-users
- job satisfaction and accountability
- a greater knowledge of the needs of the individual
- decisions involving supporting, resolving and planning
- roles to be clarified
- a more relaxed atmosphere
- attention to small but important matters
- decision-making via advocacy or counselling
- healthy competition between staff to improve their service.

Keyworking: A system and a process

Mallinson argues that the effectiveness of keyworking is 'dependent upon the calibre of a broad tapestry of systems and structures' (1995, p.125). Figure 4.5 shows his ingredients for effective keyworking.

In this chapter we are not going to provide any real detail about the systems and structures that support keyworking, other than to refer to two important management systems, formal supervision and house meetings, and the 'lifestyle planning' approaches that help people with intellectual disabilities to map their

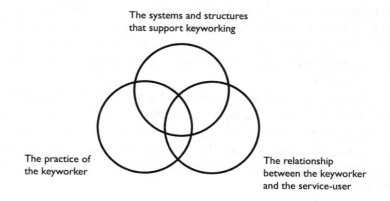

The systems and structures
that support keyworking

The practice of
the keyworker

The relationship
between the keyworker
and the service-user

Figure 4.5 The elements of effective keyworking

future and organise the supports they need. The management systems are discussed more specifically in Chapter 8 and there is a wealth of resources on Person-Centred Planning.

Keyworking in a group home: A good match

Implementing a keyworking system in a group home has certain advantages over larger residential settings. In Mallinson's (1995) study of 58 different establishments, the mean number of service-users that a keyworker supported was 4.5. A group home for people with severe or profound intellectual disabilities is likely to have a staff team that is, at the very least, equivalent to the number of residents. At 96 High Street, with six staff members and six residents, an obvious arrangement was to pair one employee with one service-user.

The keyworking system still needs to work when staff members exit or are absent from a group home, perhaps due to annual leave, for example. The staff team at 96 High Street considered two options for allocating keyworkers to residents, which took account of the specific issues they faced with its implementation.

In the first option a primary and secondary keyworker would be allocated to each service-user, so that the secondary keyworker could take on the responsibilities when necessary. This arrangement also offered the primary keyworker a named person to talk to about resident-related issues, although not to the exclusion of the rest of the staff group. As two members of the staff group at 96 High Street also had weak English literacy, careful selection meant that each staff pair could contain an individual with the prerequisite reading and writing skills to use the system effectively. In addition, as the part-time staff were not rostered to attend the house meeting, this arrangement would also mean that each resident was 'represented' by a staff member at the house meeting. The second option was for the house supervisor to take on the role of secondary keyworker for all the residents, which would mean that one direct support worker would have to be the keyworker for two residents. However, since the house supervisor should keep an overview of all the residents and meets with the direct support staff in formal supervision meetings, this option has some distinct advantages. A keyworking system will need to be tailored to the particular context in which it is being implemented.

The relationship between the keyworker and service-user

The relationship between the keyworker and a person with severe or profound intellectual disability is important because, amongst other things, the former must get to know the resident and make his or her likes and dislikes more widely known. Discovering a service-user's likes and dislikes has been a core task in human services over the last 30 years. Only the language has changed, fluctuating between needs and wants, hopes and fears, strengths and weaknesses, dreams and nightmares, gifts and capacities, interests and preferences, and so on.

The important issue here is that, in order to identify likes and dislikes successfully, keyworkers need to 'get to know' the people they are working with. Given this premise we would suggest avoiding routine changes to staff/service-user pairings that we have seen in some services. Even though staff in a group home are well placed to do this, in our research the way in which they talked about the residents suggested that discovering their interests and preferences was a task that they found difficult.

One reason for this can certainly be attributed to the residents' levels of intellectual disability in our research. Zijlstra, Vlaskamp and Buntinx (2001) argue that the needs and wants of people with more severe intellectual disabilities only become known after a great deal of effort has been spent becoming familiar with the individuals concerned. They put forward a useful categorisation of direct support staff, which draws our attention to the need to have a critical mass of 'well-known faces' in a staff team if people's preferences are to have a better chance of being correctly identified (see Table 4.1).

Even though the entire staff group at 96 High Street eventually came to meet the time criterion to be classified as 'well-known faces' they still struggled to identify people's interests and preferences.

Table 4.1 Categorising direct support staff (adapted from Zijlstra et al. 2001)

Well-known face	A staff member who has worked six months or more in a group home and is capable of building a relationship with an individual with profound intellectual disability in that group.	A minimum of six months is required to perceive, interpret and respond adequately to the signals of an individual with profound intellectual disability.
Known face	A staff member who has worked more than 25 days but less than six months.	Someone who can to some extent see, interpret and respond adequately to residents' signals.
New face	A staff member who has worked 25 days or less in a group home is a new face to a person with profound intellectual disability.	Someone who is wholly or mostly blind to the signals given by the resident.

At the house meeting, about seven months after the residents had moved into the group home, there was some discussion about the role of the keyworker in investigating and seeing what a particular resident liked. Brenda commented that the residents only want to go out and eat and Julie added that she made them exercise afterwards by walking. Frank, the house supervisor, said that, for him, it was not always obvious what a resident was interested in and that he 'didn't have a clue what Sarah would like to do'.

As well as illustrating weaknesses in the quality and content of a resident's Individual Programme Plan (IPP), the following extract also suggests that six months may not be long enough to build the kind of relationship required to be an effective keyworker. There may be specific barriers to overcome, such as lack of verbal communication, or a staff member may not have the skills or have made the effort to get to know the individual.

I asked Andrew what individual things were happening with Rose. He mentioned issues with her weight and getting exercise. He struggled to name anything else, so we looked at the IPP in the folder, which was dated 2003. As well as objectives about her weight there were also goals about vacuuming, a holiday and communication. 'We can't get her to vacuum, so we get her to dry the dishes,' he said. When I probed him, he admitted that these goals, apart from the holiday, would not excite her. A holiday had not been organised for her, unless a week at her mother's house was counted. Andrew said that he had tried to get her to draw – 'Not interested'; carpet bowls – 'Not interested'; walks – 'She moans and complains of mosquito bites.' (Rose's communication dictionary states that when she said 'I've got a Mozzie bite' it might mean 'I don't like doing this' or 'I don't want to do this'.) 'She does like make-up and music.' Andrew thought that he was not well matched with Rose and added that he thought that no one would be particularly well matched.[3]

According to Brost and Johnson (1982) getting to know a person requires a keyworker to engage in the processes of interviewing, observing, reading, and sharing time with a person.[4] In more than 25 years, this basic advice hasn't changed. The Disability Services Division (2007) in Victoria published essentially the same advice in *Planning for Individuals* (Table 4.2).

Table 4.2 Strategies for getting to know a person

Where to go for information (adapted from Brost and Johnson 1982, pp.29–30)	Finding out about the person (adapted from Disability Services Division 2007, p.29)
• The person being assessed is the first and most important source of information. The person must be consulted at every stage of the process; his/her preferences carry the most weight	• Listen to them
• Observing in many service settings and environments	• Spending time with them in different situations and different settings
• Talking to all significant others	• Talking with others who know them well
• Checking files and records	• Although this section does not specifically mention written records it is possibly implicit in the following: 'Depending on its relevance, a person's life history and personal information may be gathered from a number of life stages and areas of importance'

Difficulty in identifying people's interests and preferences was a recurring theme in the *Making Life Good in the Community* research. Sometimes it is hard to know what a person with intellectual disabilities prefers. On other occasions we may feel personally uncomfortable with what a person says he or she prefers. A keyworker is in a difficult position when people either do not, or are not able to, talk about their wishes, do not seem to have any preferences, cannot seem to express interest in any specific alternatives or seem to have peculiar preferences. Brost and Johnson (1982) could not provide 'off-the-peg' solutions to these issues, and this situation is unlikely to have changed in 25 years. This reveals something about the nature of profound and severe intellectual disability, where preferences typically have to be inferred from interpreting people's reactions to events (Ware 2004).

Unfortunately, Reid, Everson and Green (1999) have demonstrated that relying on the views of direct support staff does not represent a consistent way of accurately identifying the preferences of people with profound intellectual disabilities. In their research, 25 per cent of a sample of preferences identified through Person-Centred Planning (PCP) were found out to be non-preferred by using systematic preference assessments. At the very least, services need to ensure that residents and staff receive extensive and ongoing training and support in order to establish the communicative competence of all communication partners when augmentative and alternative communication systems are used (Perry *et al.* 2002).

Brost and Johnson (1982) listed a number of factors that may affect a person's preferences and people's interpretations of them (Table 4.3). Some of these factors were evident in the data that we collected, which contributed to the weak individualised lifestyle outcomes we found. All of the other residents were limited in the ways they could express their desires and the staff were constrained in understanding them. Simon, the only resident with a significant vocabulary, declined to speak to us. He had spent 40 years of his life living in an institutional setting, so it was not surprising that he declined our overtures to come and sit down and discuss his aspirations with us.

Our fieldnotes contained numerous examples where the values of the staff group impacted not only on how the preferences of individual residents were perceived, but on the day-to-day running of the houses. In one very candid interview, a member of the staff group gave a number of reasons why she was poor at facilitating community-based activities in the evenings.

Table 4.3 Determining individual preferences (adapted from Brost and Johnson 1982, p.44)

What an individual prefers might be influenced by:	How a keyworker interprets 'personal preferences' might be influenced by:
• The number and kind of experiences or opportunities the person has had • What, how and for how long the individual had received services • The opinions and preferences of family members, guardians, advocates and significant others • The number of ways available to express desires • The skills and resources the person possesses and can use in alternative situations	• For how long and how well the keyworker knows the person • The values of the keyworker • How willing and capable the keyworker is at interacting with the person • What limits the keyworker sets on a person's capacity for growth and learning

They've been out at the day programmes all day having fun so they don't want to do anything else... When I've been out at work all day I don't like to go out again... People like to have a bit of a breather... It's the weather. You don't feel like going out on the dark winter nights when it's cold. I like to settle in.

Another member of the staff group was equally adamant that she would only support community-based activities that she would enjoy, and stated very clearly to the staff team that she would not support the residents to go to church. The same staff member was, however, very thorough at completing all the keyworker tasks and arranging community-based activities, but we were less sure that she had taken on board that individualised planning required her to '[assist] people with a disability to identify *their* goals, aspirations and needs' (Disability Services Division 2007, p.10, emphasis added). Sanderson *et al.* claim that this 'requires a significant shift in power, from professionals having "power over" to have "power with" [people with intellectual disabilities]' (2002, p.20).

It should be noted that there is nothing intrinsically wrong with direct support staff taking a lead in planning and organising the lives of people with more severe and profound intellectual disabilities. This reflects the reality of supporting people with these labels. However, when a person is unable to clearly articulate their 'dreams and nightmares' or 'interests and preferences', then there should be safeguards to make sure that individual staff members' interests do not dominate, as this house supervisor articulates.

The biggest issue that we have I believe, as carers, is the fact that 'I want to turn somebody into another me' is very often the ideology. People aren't aware of it, they're not conscious of it, but its values that come in to it. So when we talk, am I effectively hearing what they want? Am I placing my judgement on that? How do we encourage and support and nurture them to be them, not miniature us, but them?... I am working towards satisfying their life's desires. Can I say that again, it's very often missed. I am working towards satisfying *their* life's desires.

Human service organisations need to promote reflective practice amongst direct support staff, so that assumptions, feelings, interpretations and values can all be subject to scrutiny (Ellis 2000). When a person is unable to articulate their preferences, then planning should be guided by the service's principles and values, and not those of an individual staff member.

Recording, monitoring and feedback

It is self-evident that being an effective keyworker requires specific knowledge, skills and abilities. Pearce and Smith (2000) list accessing resources, advocating, communicating, coordinating, enabling, liaising, planning, recording and team working as the prerequisite 'skills'.

Group homes routinely collect information about the day-to-day activities of service-users. Figures 4.1 and 4.2 were created from data collected at 96 High Street, and illustrate the types of summary information that a keyworker might be expected to complete and present to the staff team at a house meeting or discuss in a formal supervision meeting. This information could equally be presented in textual form, but we happen to like graphs and agree with Gary LaVigna and his colleagues (1994) that visual feedback in the form of a graph allows performance to be seen.

Amongst other things, direct support staff require analytic and reflective skills. At 96 High Street keyworkers were expected to produce a written 'monthly' report for presentation and discussion at the four-weekly house meeting. Having to write and deliver a report at each house meeting was one way in which a keyworker demonstrated responsibility and accountability to a particular resident and the rest of the staff team.

Good practice in relation to paperwork and recording is a core competence for direct support staff, so keyworkers should be able to make use of written information. In the *Community Support Skill Standards*, it states that a competent direct support staff 'learns and remains current with appropriate documentation systems, setting priorities and developing a system to manage documenta-tion…[and] maintains accurate records, collecting, compiling and evaluating data, and submitting records to appropriate sources in a timely fashion' (College of Direct Support nd, unpaginated).

It is common practice for house meetings to be structured in such a way that each resident is discussed in turn. This allows each staff member to put forward their ideas about the service each service-user is receiving, which reinforces the importance of the entire staff team having an interest in all the residents.

A keyworker report should take a 'look back' over the recent past and also look to the future. The 'look back' is intended to be 'brief' and requires the keyworker to identify important activities, events or issues that need to be noted, discussed and acted upon. Keyworkers have to do some preparation by having a look at the formal records kept by the staff group. At 96 High Street some of the sources that informed the monthly report were 'conversations' with the specific resident, the Communication Book, Activity Learning Logs, IPP/PCP goals, and other more specific documents (e.g. at one house there was a concern that a resident was underweight, so the person's weight was routinely recorded and reported on).

There is no need for a keyworker report to be completed on a standard document. However, the staff at 96 High Street wanted to have a standard form to complete, which also helped to set boundaries around the task. Figure 4.6 shows an example, completed by Alberto's keyworker.

The report contains items that may merely need to be noted, for example the community-based activities that Alberto undertook in the previous month. Other items need to be discussed and acted upon. For example, the statement '[Alberto is] learning to operate DVD player 1:1 so he can put on his DVDs inde-pendently' is recorded as a matter of fact, but it raises issues for discussion and action that need to be addressed by his keyworker. The rest of the staff group need to know how Alberto is being taught to use the DVD player, and they need to agree how to provide consistent support.

A keyworker might be interested in knowing about the types of activities that a resident has done in the past month and how often he or she did them. The keyworker should also want to know whether the activities had been a success or not and would want to 'draw out' what had been learnt from supporting the person to undertake these activities. It is useful for a keyworker to probe how well these activities reflect the person's interests and preferences.

The keyworker may use a house meeting to get the team's views about an issue. For example, Brian's keyworker used a monthly report to establish an objective of going out to purchase his own toiletries. Raising this as an issue at the house meeting allowed the staff group to discuss the existing 'norm' for buying toiletries, and replace it with practice that was more individualised for all the residents.

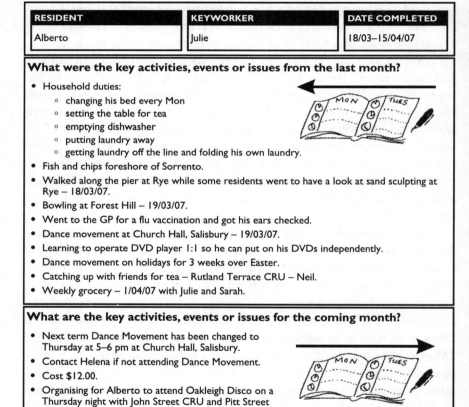

RESIDENT	KEYWORKER	DATE COMPLETED
Alberto	Julie	18/03–15/04/07

What were the key activities, events or issues from the last month?

- Household duties:
  - changing his bed every Mon
  - setting the table for tea
  - emptying dishwasher
  - putting laundry away
  - getting laundry off the line and folding his own laundry.
- Fish and chips foreshore of Sorrento.
- Walked along the pier at Rye while some residents went to have a look at sand sculpting at Rye – 18/03/07.
- Bowling at Forest Hill – 19/03/07.
- Went to the GP for a flu vaccination and got his ears checked.
- Dance movement at Church Hall, Salisbury – 19/03/07.
- Learning to operate DVD player 1:1 so he can put on his DVDs independently.
- Dance movement on holidays for 3 weeks over Easter.
- Catching up with friends for tea – Rutland Terrace CRU – Neil.
- Weekly grocery – 1/04/07 with Julie and Sarah.

What are the key activities, events or issues for the coming month?

- Next term Dance Movement has been changed to Thursday at 5–6 pm at Church Hall, Salisbury.
- Contact Helena if not attending Dance Movement.
- Cost $12.00.
- Organising for Alberto to attend Oakleigh Disco on a Thursday night with John Street CRU and Pitt Street CRU.
- Staff need to take Alberto to his bedroom before going out to programme and check if there are any dirty clothes and wet PJs.

Figure 4.6 Alberto's monthly report

From the individual to the group: Keeping an overview

There are times when it is useful to collate information in order to make comparisons between residents and look for broader trends about what is happening in a house. Figure 4.3 might be the type of analysis undertaken by the house supervisor who should keep an overview of practice in the house. In this instance, the graph could kick-start a move towards a more individualised focus. A further example is given in Figure 4.7, which shows the number of times that each resident went shopping over a three-month period.

The most glaring difference is between the occasions that Rose (2) and Simon (14) went shopping. Both the house supervisor and Rose's keyworker ought to be questioning this disparity. Why is there such a difference? Is Rose getting 'a fair go'? What should be done about it? We do not believe that Rose had less of an interest in shopping than any of the other residents. We would suggest that the differential picture is accounted for by the absence of a system for planning what the individual residents would do on a day-to-day or weekly basis. There was a selection bias when an individual staff member could ask any resident whether he or she wanted to go shopping.

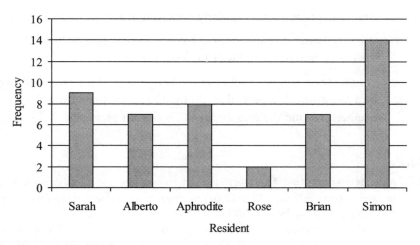

Figure 4.7 Total number of times each resident went shopping in a three-month period (May–July 2006)

Concluding remarks

Although some activities in group homes will inevitably have to be undertaken in groups, it is possible for residents to be supported to develop individualised lifestyles. However, achieving individualised lifestyles will not just happen. It will be enabled by a formal approach to planning that is focused on the long term, with mechanisms in place to incorporate goals into daily living. Helping people with severe and profound intellectual disabilities to 'get a life' requires more than 1:1 support; it is also about developing a lifestyle that challenges the category of intellectual disability. Keyworking is simply a means to an end, a process and system to enable an individual to get the support and services they need (Bigby 2007). In the following two chapters we focus on two related aspects of an individualised lifestyle, participation in meaningful activities and the quality of people's social relationships.

Issues for consideration

- Are there planning systems that support effective work practices?

- Are plans audited with respect to the quality and content of plans, process and outcomes?

- Is the balance between individualised lifestyles and group activities 'right'?

- Are there processes for regularly reviewing the routines in a house?

- What activities do each resident have that allow him or her to be seen as an individual in his or her own right?

- Do the direct support staff have the knowledge, skills and abilities to be a keyworker? In particular, do they have 'communicative competence' and the knowledge and skills for planning?

Notes

1   All of the residents attended day programmes, which were organised around group activities.

2   In a more recent article Marie Knox (2007) uses the concept of case management to discuss keyworking in a group home where her son lives.

3   Various issues arise when attempts are made to 'match residents to staff' or allow residents to choose their keyworker. The former may fail to make or find a suitable match and the latter may result in a particularly competent or likeable staff member being swamped with requests. It is probably more helpful to understand the keyworker role as a series of tasks that are underpinned by certain competences, which a direct support staff needs to be able to carry out with any resident.

4   In our research settings, not only were there copious historical records of varying use, but each resident also had a number of up-to-date assessments, which had been done at the time of their move from the institution to the group home. Very little use was made of this information. As a consequence, the current staff made little use of past 'knowledge' about the people they were supporting.

Chapter 5

Participating in Your Own Home

Introduction

This chapter focuses on a particularly important outcome for service-users, 'engagement in meaningful activity', an idea that we introduced in Chapter 1. Although 'meaningful activity' can take place in any setting, in this chapter we are specifically concerned with activities that take place in 'the home'. We link 'engagement' to a number of other previously discussed concepts and outline a technology known as 'Active Support' that has been shown to increase levels of engagement for people with severe and profound intellectual disabilities. We discuss the weak implementation of Active Support at one of the focal group homes, 16 Temple Court, and raise a number of issues related to its implementation and sustainability that have more general applicability.

Practices that lead to low levels of engagement

As we stated in the opening chapter, it was hoped that the use of 'ordinary' housing for people with intellectual disabilities would establish 'ordinary patterns of living' (Felce and Perry 1995). And what could be more 'ordinary' than being involved in the running of one's own home through such activities as making a cup of tea, paying the electricity bill or using the washing machine?

Yet the research that we cited in Chapter 1 and the descriptions of people's lives presented in Chapter 2 reveals that many people with intellectual disabilities experience low levels of engagement in their own homes. This is despite the fact that they live in settings that are equipped with all the amenities necessary for 'ordinary' living (the physical home). We suggested that certain staff practices we observed excluded the residents from participating in many household activities, and we used the concepts of ownership, parent–child interactions, staff as the principal actors and the 'hotel model' to describe these dominant patterns of behaviour. These concepts are loosely tied together by the fact that the major roles in the group homes were played by staff and the minor ones by residents.

In general, staff practices determine the parameters of resident participation in household activities and the choices that are made available for people with severe or profound intellectual disabilities. The fact that a number of staff complete certain activities with little or no resident participation impacts directly on their levels of engagement. In most cases, people with severe and profound intellectual disabilities are disengaged not through their own 'choice', but because the assistance they need to participate is unavailable (Stancliffe et al. 2008).[1] If staff do the cooking, cleaning and laundry, then these activities are removed from the available list of opportunities that residents can participate in. When a staff member undertakes an activity by herself, she has effectively made herself unavailable to support a resident in an activity. In our research, the houses were not so 'activity-rich' that they could afford to reduce the number of available activities without there being consequences for the overall levels of engagement. It follows from this that if people with severe and profound intellectual disabilities are to participate in activities there must be available activities, available staff support, and the right level of assistance given by support staff (Jones et al. 2001a).

Engagement: A particularly important goal

'Engagement in meaningful activity' is acknowledged as a particularly important concept because the extent to which any person spends time engaged in household, leisure, personal and social activities is understood to be a significant feature of his or her 'quality of life' (Felce and Perry 1995). More recently, Jonathan Gershuny (2005) has argued that a 'busy lifestyle' has come to be seen in an increasingly positive light and signifies high social status.

'Engagement in meaningful activity' can be linked to some of the guiding concepts that we have discussed in previous chapters. Imagine, for example, a 'supported living' arrangement, where James, a man with mild intellectual disabilities, lives by himself in his own apartment. When the door-bell rings, James opens the door and invites his neighbour in for a cup of tea. Table 5.1 relates this scenario and the activities of answering the door and making a cup of tea to some of the aforementioned concepts.

Table 5.1 Linking an activity
to core concepts: An example

Framework	Sub-categories	Possible outcome
Five Accomplish-ments	• Community presence • Choice • Competence • Respect • Community participation	This example embraces all five accomplishments. One's own home is an ordinary place. James makes a positive choice to invite the person into his home, and has the skills to be able to open the front door and make his neighbour, part of his network of social relationships, a hot drink. Being a homeowner and neighbour are valued roles.
Home experience	• Physical • Social • Personal	The home has the amenities necessary for engagement, such as a kettle, fridge and so on. It is a place for James to enjoy the company of his neighbour. Being able to invite his neighbour into his home may make James happy and give him a real sense of having his own home.
Ordinary life		Opening one's front door, making tea and entertaining a neighbour are opportunities that most people have.
Hierarchy of needs	• Self-actualisation • Esteem • Belongingness and love • Safety • Physiological	This example moves beyond meeting physiological and safety needs. Inviting a neighbour into his home underscores that this is James's home. Being a homeowner and offering hospitality may result in James feeling good about himself and enhance how the neighbour perceives him.

It seems obvious to us that these are good activities for James to participate in, and we believe that this remains the case if we substitute a person with profound intellectual disabilities in James's place. However, our experience tells us that such a view may not be shared by everyone, and so we think it important to 'unpack' what the aims of 'engagement' are for people with profound and severe intellectual impairments.

Some of the sub-categories incorporated by these overarching concepts are harder to relate when we use an example that involves a person with severe or profound intellectual disability. This can have the effect of making the concepts seem less relevant. In the following illustration, the author contrasts disengagement with being engaged:

> Imagine watching a man with severe disabilities sitting in a wheelchair in the living room of his residential home. He is just sitting there, not doing very much – perhaps dribbling a bit, perhaps making some humming noise. A member of staff comes in, walks to the other side of the room to pick up the paper and walks out. He is not spoken to. A visitor comes into the home and is shown into the living room by the member of staff, but the man is basically ignored while the member of staff tells the visitor about all the activities the people have on their weekly planner sheet.
>
> Now imagine the same person, holding the shopping basket on his knee, with the member of staff talking to him (using signs or pictures) as they hand him the carrots one by one to put in the basket. Someone comes up to say hello to the member of staff, who introduces the man and says 'I'm just helping John to do his shopping.' See the smile on his face as he is pushed to the checkout, holding a big sack of potatoes on his knees. Hear him laugh as the checkout staff reaches over to scan the potatoes and says 'Are you all right there?' You hear the member of staff say 'You are OK, aren't you John. When you laugh like that you are happy.' (Beadle-Brown 2006, p.10)

The author puts her 'spin' on these scenarios, which are implicitly related to some of the concepts in Table 5.1.

> What you are probably experiencing is a completely different impression of this person. Suddenly this is someone who can do things, who is competent in doing the shopping. Suddenly you see someone involved in, and enjoying, the everyday activities of daily living. You see someone who can communicate, because they have been given the means to do so, and a member of staff who helps to facilitate not just communication but also interaction with other people. You see someone with whom others are bothering to interact and you probably feel more comfortable because you can get some sort of idea of this person's skills and characteristics, just from this short experience. It is very likely that you would experience an increase in the respect you have for this individual. (Beadle-Brown 2006, p.10)

We wish that changing people's orientation to a person with severe or profound intellectual disabilities were so simple. Although we fully support the practice of involving the person, we are not entirely convinced that every direct support staff will share this interpretation. They may not see someone who is competent in shopping, but someone who can participate in shopping with significant help. Likewise, they may see a staff member who understands that he has a key role in mediating interactions with other people and explaining the person's behaviour, rather than someone who can 'communicate'. When interactions are brief, it is unlikely that either the checkout staff or the staff members' unnamed acquaintance are likely to have their view of the person transformed by their encounter.

In the revised version of the earlier scenario that we posited, where we substituted James with a person with profound intellectual disability, it is likely that the staff member will have invited the neighbour in for a drink. It is much harder to say for sure that this individual, who is supported to open the front door and share a cup of tea with a neighbour, experiences any change in regard to the abstract sub-categories of belongingness, esteem, personal home, respect and self-actualisation. We have to rely on interpreting the individual's behaviour, as we have no access to his thoughts, feelings and other inner mental states.

We are sympathetic to people's efforts to extol the virtues of people with profound intellectual disabilities. However, our experience suggests that 'cheerleading' is rarely a successful strategy for convincing direct support staff to change their practices when they hold beliefs that are incompatible with involving residents in the running of their own home.

Promoting 'engagement' may be taking place in a context where the staff group contains a range of attitudes towards people with intellectual disabilities, and differences in how individuals understand organisational policies and their role. For example, in a group home there is not always a consensus about the extent to which residents should be involved in the purchasing and preparation of their food; an understanding that resident involvement is consistent with the organisation's goals; and the direct support role is to enable this to happen.

A range of views is illustrated in the following fieldnote extract, where we raised the idea of involving the residents in household activities with the staff group at 16 Temple Court. One of our colleagues (Kelley) had visited the residents' day programmes and was involved in a free-flowing discussion about what she had seen. As researchers, we were 'outsiders', and our primary method of influencing staff practice was to try and persuade people that involving people in the running of their own home was a goal worth pursuing. Managers from the same organisation can also be perceived as 'outsiders' if a staff team is 'close-knit'. Maria asks Kelley if she will tell them about what happened when she went to the day programme.

Kelley: I watched Shane in a cooking programme. He was at the stove stirring things. He was in the kitchen for two hours.

Maria: By himself? Maybe he can cook for you, Penny?

Ray tells the group how Shane will grab a hot pan. 'When you're cooking at the house you've got a lot going on. You've got a frying pan going, a pot boiling.'

Meena, the house supervisor, explains, 'It may only be [supporting him to cook] for five minutes. The kettle may be going, but you are standing next to him. He only grabs it when he walks in to the kitchen.'

Neil: If we got Shane in the kitchen and something happened, then who's to blame?

Ray: You get distracted at the house. The telephone may go and you have to answer it. You can get 18 phone calls in two hours. If we had a gate on the kitchen...

Kelley: Your issue here is duty of care?

Meena: It's about giving them the chance. You're not asking them to cook the whole meal. There's no way he can learn the whole skill.

Neil: It's about involvement.

Maria: You should give him the recipe, Penny.

Meena: This is about the dignity of life, this is living, you wouldn't be blamed...

Kelley reminds people that it is expected that people will involve people in activities like cooking.

Ray: That's what we're doing. You have to be realistic; Shane will pick up a jug that has hot water in it.

Penny: When I was on the phone he grabbed my coffee.

Meena: He's so clever. He does it when your back is to him. But if you're stirring with him...

Ray: He'll get bored with that eventually.

Kelley: In the day programme Shane was in the cooking programme for two hours.

Meena: Before [at the institution] they didn't even know what an apple looked like. We're giving them a chance...

Kelley: You've got different chances here.

Meena: In [the institution] the food came from the central kitchen...

Ray: There's a limit to what you can do.

In this short fieldnote there is some support for the idea of involving the residents in household tasks, particularly from the researcher and the house supervisor, but also a number of statements that reflect barriers. The residents' behaviours and lack of interest in cooking are seen as problematic; ironic statements serve to undermine the idea of participation; there is a focus on risk and worries about resident safety; concern to protect the staff's own position; and comments that suggest that involving people in this way pushes the realistic limits of what staff can achieve.

During the meeting one staff member expressed a particularly strong view which suggested that involving the residents in household and community activities was neither realistic because of the men's level of impairment, nor practical due to limited resources.

It's pretty hard with our ones, they can't talk. The more able bodied can participate... We have to be realistic, realistic about people's levels of abilities and disabilities... We must be realistic about the amount of time. Perhaps when you've got a long shift?... We have to do things like this on top of the workload that is already there.

Jingree and Finlay (2008) call this 'practicalities talk'. In this instance, participation is not possible because the staff member identifies both 'internal' and 'external' obstacles, i.e. the personal limitations of profound intellectual disability and environmental barriers due to a full workload. Practicality-based judgements made by direct support staff, particularly those based on levels of intellectual disability, are likely to impact on the realisation of 'an ordinary life'. Although people may express positive attitudes towards people with intellectual disabilities in general, when the distinction is made between people with mild or severe intellectual disability, then attitudes change (Antonak et al. 1995; Bigby et al. 2009; Jones 1975). During the interview process a potential recruit may fully support the goal of 'running one's own home' for all people with intellectual disabilities and also believe that it is not practical for the individuals with severe intellectual disabilities he ends up supporting. Although the Allen et al. (1990) study is relatively old now, they reported that more than half of the community staff group in their research seemed to have some reservations about the practicality of the goals of community-based services for people with intellectual disabilities. A key issue was 'practicality', based on the potential and ability of people with intellectual disabilities.

Questioning the assumptions behind 'engagement in meaningful activities'

Active Support, a way of assisting people with intellectual disabilities to engage in meaningful activity that we outline below, assumes that people prefer to participate in activities rather than 'do nothing', and that individuals with intellectual disabilities wish to be involved in the same range of activities as other members of the community.[2] We are going to accept the first point as axiomatic, but our research findings suggest that some direct support staff find the second more contentious.

Felce and Perry argue that the driving force for engagement in 'ordinary' activities is 'the desire to take responsibility for the conduct of one's own daily life and to learn and be supported to do domestic chores such as cooking and cleaning' (1995, p.800). Although this argument is also put forward by articulate self-advocates (see Attrill, nd, for some views from residents living in group homes in Victoria), we have little or no idea about how people with severe and profound intellectual disabilities view this goal. The claim has to be *accepted* by the staff supporting them and applied in their everyday practice. As direct support staff make minute-by-minute decisions about how residents are supported, some of which are contrary to the assumptions underpinning 'meaningful engagement', we can assume that the goal is not universally shared, or not held to be relevant all of the time. This may be for a number of reasons:

- As we argued above, a concept like 'ordinary living' is seen as less practical for people with profound intellectual disabilities. If direct support staff believe that it is not practical to involve people in household activities they are likely to focus on meeting people's basic needs and provide a cooking and cleaning service for the residents.

- Staff hold other beliefs that they think of as being more important. Some staff may therefore consider peeling potatoes or cleaning the toilet the kind of 'ordinary' activities that they would like to avoid, and therefore perceive themselves as doing the residents a favour by providing a catering and housekeeping service along the lines of a hotel. Or perhaps they believe that people should not be pushed to adopt a particular lifestyle, but to lead a different lifestyle more suited to their level of disability or needs. And so on.

There is a significant 'industry' that promotes activities that are likely to be seen as outside of an 'ordinary' lifestyle, many of them 'therapeutic', such as the use of multi-sensory rooms, sensory boards, physiotherapy, play, therapeutic massage, walking programmes and so on. There is value in some of these activities, but we would suggest that they should supplement 'the domestic curriculum', not be an alternative to it.

An advantage of using the domestic activities available in an 'ordinary house' is that there are hundreds of naturally occurring activities, so staff do not have to generate activities for 'engaging' people (Jenkins *et al.* 1987). An activity like wiping down the dining table could stimulate a person's senses as well as any sensory box, as it may involve hot and cold water, sponges, cloths, smells of cleaning materials and so on. If domestic tasks are removed from the list of available activities, other endeavours do not simply 'come along' without significant planning and action.

A group home equipped with all the necessary amenities only provides opportunities for engagement, which can be used or ignored. The fact that many residents who live in group homes have low levels of engagement suggests that involving people in the running of their own home is not always a shared goal and staff do not have the skills and knowledge to do this intuitively. As we showed in Chapter 2, the intuitive practice of some staff results in low levels of engagement, exactly the opposite outcome that services aspire to.

It is all too easy to focus on the incongruent attitudes of 'resistant' staff and get caught up with thinking that we need to change attitudes as a means of changing behaviour. In such cases we often resort to emphasising guiding philosophies, 'cheerleading' or telling positive stories. A better tactic might be to impose congruent roles and responsibilities on the group home staff (see Beer, Eisenstat and Spector 1990). For many direct support staff, 'seeing', with the service-users they support, 'is believing'. As Mansell *et al.* write, 'It is the task of the project organisers to *show* staff how these opportunities can be used to the full' (1987, p.123, emphasis added). Once this has been done, staff need to be taught the working practices that will result in high levels of engagement (Mansell, McGill and Emerson 1994).

Active Support

Active Support, which was originally developed and tested more than 25 years ago, is a technology to assist people with intellectual disability to engage in meaningful activity. As such, it has the potential to improve the 'quality of life' of people who live in group homes and ensure that the opportunities afforded by these settings can be used to the full.

It has a number of 'organisational systems' that address planning, monitoring and management. It combines a number of training techniques that have been shown to change staff practice, which increases the amount and type of support residents receive from staff, and sustain it over time (Jones and Lowe 2005). There exists a body of consistent research evidence which shows that group homes that adopt Active Support procedures produce increased levels of resident engagement in 'meaningful activities' (Bradshaw *et al.* 2004; Felce *et al.* 2000; Jones *et al.* 1999, 2001a, 2001b; Mansell *et al.* 2002; Stancliffe *et al.* 2007). The recent reviews by Stancliffe *et al.* (2008) and Totsika *et al.* (2008a) are a good introduction to the relevant literature. Figure 5.1 illustrates the main features we have described, as well as Active Support's influences and hoped-for outcomes.

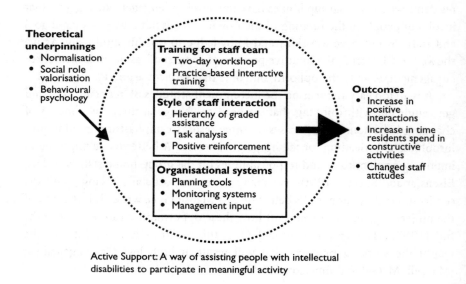

Active Support: A way of assisting people with intellectual disabilities to participate in meaningful activity

Figure 5.1 Conceptualising Active Support (adapted from Jones and Lowe 2005)

Although Stancliffe *et al.* (2008) suggest that there is agreement about what Active Support is, there is significant variation in the way in which it is implemented and monitored. Our aim here is not to provide readers with a 'definitive' version of Active Support, but to use our research context as a real-life example, so that we can highlight some issues for its implementation and sustainability that readers can consider in their own organisations.[3]

The 'version' of Active Support that we describe below was implemented at 16 Temple Court, and used elements from the 'official' sets of training materials (Jones *et al.* 1996b; Mansell *et al.* 2004), some faithfully and others adjusted, in combination with existing 'in-house' procedures. This probably reflects the reality of implementing a system like Active Support, in that it will be subject to changes, some for better, others for worse, that reflect the local conditions in which it is put into practice. At 16 Temple Court there were a number of organisational systems:

Activity and Support Plans

A basic weekly timetable that covers all the regular domestic, self-care and leisure activities in a particular group home. A working draft is created by the staff group at an Active Support training event, which is then subject to ongoing revision. The timetable contains both regular activities and a 'menu' of household and optional activities to choose from. It provides a means of planning activities over a short period and allocating staff to support specific residents. Figure 5.2 shows an Activity and Support Plan for Monday morning, which would be used by the rostered staff to plan the residents' support.

Opportunity Plans

A number of small goals, colloquially known as 'opportunities', that residents are supported to undertake by staff on a regular basis (see Figure 5.3). Opportunity Plans and Activity and Support Plans are related. A goal that is initially identified on an Opportunity Plan may end up as the next revision of the Activity and Support Plan. Emptying the mail box, a goal on Charles' Opportunity Plan, could become an optional activity on the Activity and Support Plan, which in the future could be done by any resident. Likewise, an optional activity from the Activity and Support Plan, such as polishing furniture, could become a regular short-term goal on a resident's Opportunity Plan. Jones *et al.* (1996a) list a number of reasons for putting goals on Opportunity Plans:

Support worker shift times
1. Trevor from Night to 07.20 2. Meena from 07.00 to 16.30
3. Maria from 07.00 to 18.00   4. _____ from _____ to _____

Monday

Time	David	Staff	Charles	Staff	Matthew	Staff	Michael	Staff	Shane	Staff	Household	Staff	Options
07.00	Get up, shower, dress / Prepare breakfast		Get up, shower, dress / Prepare breakfast		Get up, shower, dress / Prepare breakfast		Get up, shower, dress / Prepare breakfast		Get up, shower, dress / Prepare breakfast		Put bins out / Set table / Clear breakfast / Wash up/load dishwasher		Good walk / Water plants / Gardening / Cut the grass / Polish furniture / Clean windows / Lunch out
08.00	Breakfast		Breakfast		Breakfast		Breakfast		Breakfast		Start washing clothes		
08.30									Bus to day programme		Unload dishwasher and stack coffee cups		
09.00	Bus to day programme		Clean bedroom and bathroom		Shopping for lunch items		Bus to day programme						
10.00			Drink		Drink in café						Clear lunch		
11.00			Physiotherapy		Hang clothes on line						Wash up/load dishwasher		
12.00			Unpack groceries / Prepare lunch		Prepare lunch								
12.30			Lunch		Lunch								

Figure 5.2 Activity and Support Plan

Resident's Name   Charles

Date Opportunity Plan Started   5/11/07

No.	Opportunity Who, will do what, when, and with what help...
1.	Charles will load the dishwasher after breakfast with direct physical assistance on the days he is not at the day programme (Monday and Tuesday).
2.	Charles will open the front door every time the bell rings when he is at home with direct physical assistance.
3.	Charles will water the tomato plant every evening after tea with direct physical assistance.
4.	Charles will check the mail box when he arrives back from the day programme (Wednesday to Friday) with direct physical assistance.
5.	Charles will purchase a litre of milk and loaf of bread from the corner shop with direct physical assistance once a week.
6.	Charles will write and mail a postcard to his sister once a month with direct physical assistance.

Figure 5.3 Monthly Opportunity Plan

- A person can almost, but not quite, do the activity now, so it looks feasible to help them learn the activity through regular practice.

- A person can do the activity already but at present has no chance to practise it.

- The goal has been set, or included in the larger goal at [a planning] meeting.

- The person enjoys the activity or has indicated that he or she would like to learn the skill.

- The person gains more control over their day-to-day living.

These reasons seemed less applicable at 16 Temple Court, where the residents had profound intellectual disabilities.[4] At 16 Temple Court the fundamental reason for putting activities on Opportunity Plans was, as argued earlier, that people prefer to participate in activities rather than 'do nothing'.

Activity Learning Logs

A record of how each resident's 'opportunities' were supported by staff, completed by the relevant staff member, with details of the person's interest in the activity (see Figures 5.4 and 5.5). The form was not limited to recording the goals on Opportunity Plans, but could be used to record more spontaneous attempts to engage a resident in activities that were worthy of note. This form was a local variation, specific to the organisation involved in the research, and is not part of the 'official' training materials.

As well as documenting the types of activities occurring within a person's life, it was hoped that the Activity Learning Log would help the staff team to gain a better understanding of a person's interests and the choices provided, and enable any lessons to be shared. This information could be incorporated into Person-Centred Plans (Warren 2004/2006).

Household and Personal Protocols

Standard ways that a particular activity is carried out, either for everyone in a group home or with a specific individual. They are written as a task analysis, containing as many steps, and as much detail, as is deemed necessary (see Figure 5.6).

At 16 Temple Court, the use of these forms was linked to the keyworker system. Figure 5.7 illustrates how this was meant to work at the house.

Resident's Name: Charles

The Learning Log at 16 Temple Court primarily records opportunities written on the Monthly Opportunity Plan. It can also be used to record new or significant activities. An aim of the Learning Log is to share information about how we support the residents so that we can provide the best-quality support.			
Date and time	**Opportunity**	**Others involved?**	**What was significant about how I supported this opportunity?**
	Fill in the number from the Opportunity Plan or write in full if a new opportunity.	Supporting staff and any other relevant people	Look at the Prompt Sheet to help you think about what to write here.
05/11 08.55	1 (See Figure 5.3)	Meena	Charles completed as much of this activity as his reach allowed. His wheelchair has to be placed on the right of the dishwasher, or at right-angles at the front, so that he can reach in with his left hand. He needed physical assistance to guide the items into the correct places, and released them when I removed my hand from his.
05/11 09.30	Cleaning his bedroom and bathroom	Meena	This activity provided a great natural opportunity for using the cleaning materials (e.g. polish) and toiletries (e.g. soap) as smells. Charles seemed to like the smell of the lavender soap, as he smiled when I held it close to his nose. Perhaps I could put it in his hand next time?
05/11 11.05	2 (See Figure 5.3)	Meena and Maria	I'd arranged with Maria for her to ring the bell when she arrived back from doing the shopping with Mathew. Charles needed physical assistance to press the handle all the way to the bottom, and then it was a bit difficult manoeuvring his wheelchair away from the door, as it opens inwards. He smiled when he saw Maria and Mathew and was able to carry some of the shopping back to the kitchen on his lap.

Figure 5.4 Activity Learning Log

Completing the Activity Learning Log at 16 Temple Court

Here are some questions that might help you to think about what to record in the final column of the Activity Learning Log, 'What was significant about how I supported this opportunity?'

You do not have to provide answers to all of the questions. The aim of the questions is to help you to think about how you support the residents.

Questions about the person I was supporting

- What did the person do to make me think they liked the activity?
- What did the person do to make me think they did not like the activity?

Questions about how I provided the support

- Did I prepare the situation so that the flow of the opportunity was maintained?
- Did I present the opportunity well to the resident?
- Did I provide graded assistance?
- Did I enable the resident to experience success?
- Did I provide support in a positive helpful style?

General questions

- Did anything work especially well?
- Did anything not work that well?
- Is there anything I would do differently next time I support this opportunity?
- Is there anything that I must definitely do the same next time I support this opportunity?

Figure 5.5 Activity Learning Log Prompt Sheet

INSTRUCTIONS:

- All staff are to implement the agreed protocols in a consistent way
- Any proposed adaptations need to be discussed with other team members prior to changing

BACKGROUND:

Protocols are designed to make particular activities as predictable for both residents and staff (including new staff and relief/agency staff).

Importantly, *Protocols* are designed to ensure that activities occur in a consistent way that assists residents to develop skills and maximise their independence in the specified task.

Protocols are prepared by staff during their staff meetings. Thereafter, they should be implemented by everyone and reviewed at staff meetings. Individual staff should avoid making changes or varying protocols between meetings, except when it is essential to do so (e.g. for safety reasons or a significant change in a resident's needs).

ACTIVITY: Buying a drink from the corner shop

DATE PROTOCOLS DEVISED: 12 November 2007

FOR WHOM: Shane

WHEN: Saturday or Sunday. Time is flexible.

WHERE: Corner shop (Banksia and Grevillia Streets)

PROTOCOLS/STEPS:

1. Preparation. Make sure that Shane has a $5.00 note in his purse. The purse should be in his right-hand coat pocket. Take a plastic beaker with you.

2. Shane needs physical guidance to stop and cross the road.

3. Once across the road he can walk by himself. The staff member should walk on his left-hand side down Banksia Street, i.e. closest to the road.

4. Guide him to the refrigerator, which is around to the left of the door. Shane needs physical assistance to open the door. He will pick a bottle or can without being prompted.

5. Guide him to the checkout and physically guide his right hand to the pocket with his purse in.

6. If he does not get it out himself, reach in and put the purse in his hand, and gesture towards the shop assistant.

7. If necessary prompt him to wait for the shop assistant to return his change and purse, and return it to his jacket.

8. There is a bench outside the shop, where you can stop and consume the drink. Open the can or bottle yourself but give physical assistance to pour the drink into the beaker.

Figure 5.6 Active Support Protocol

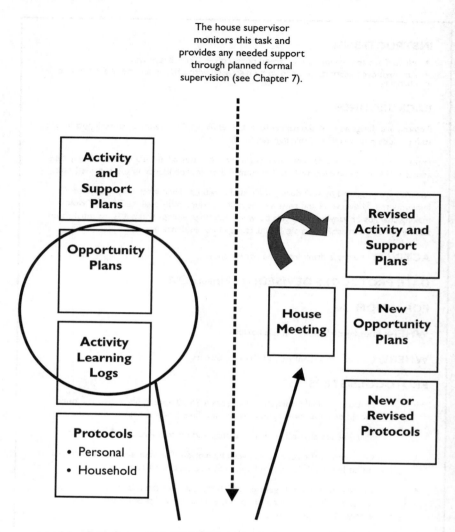

A keyworker is a named staff member who has the responsibility for making sure that a particular resident receives a high-quality individualised service.

Keyworkers are responsible for reviewing the *Activity Learning Logs* and drafting a new *Opportunity Plan* for the next four-week period.

A summary of the lessons learnt about supporting the residents to engage in these activities is prepared for the house meeting.

The new *Opportunity Plan* is presented and ratified at the house meeting, with any amendments made if necessary.

Figure 5.7 Keyworker responsibilities at 16 Temple Court in relation to Active Support

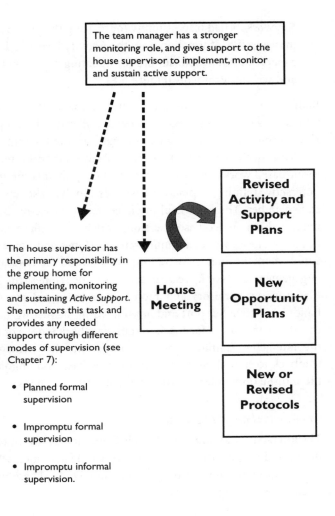

The team manager has a stronger monitoring role, and gives support to the house supervisor to implement, monitor and sustain active support.

Activity and Support Plans

Opportunity Plans

Activity Learning Logs

Protocols
- Personal
- Household

The house supervisor has the primary responsibility in the group home for implementing, monitoring and sustaining *Active Support*. She monitors this task and provides any needed support through different modes of supervision (see Chapter 7):

- Planned formal supervision

- Impromptu formal supervision

- Impromptu informal supervision.

House Meeting

Revised Activity and Support Plans

New Opportunity Plans

New or Revised Protocols

The house supervisor has specific responsibility for updating the *Activity and Support Plans* and revising or writing new *Personal or Household Protocols*.

Figure 5.8 House supervisor responsibilities at 16 Temple Court in relation to Active Support

Keyworkers had responsibility for revising the Opportunity Plans and summarising the information from the Activity Learning Logs, whilst the house supervisor had responsibility for updating the Activity and Support Plans and writing Protocols (Figure 5.8).

Staff are instructed in the use of these forms at the Active Support training, which consists of both classroom-based and onsite training. It is generally considered preferable to train an entire staff team at the same time.

Most of the research literature on Active Support refers to a two-day classroom-based workshop that covers the theory and planning. This is followed by 'interactive training'; a practice-based session that takes up to two hours for each staff member. The successful implementation of Active Support is thought to require this practice-based session, which takes place in the relevant group home, or close by in community settings (Jones and Lowe 2005). In a research study where the interactive training was omitted there was no change in resident engagement levels or increase in staff assistance (Jones *et al.* 2001a). It is essential that house supervisors and more senior managers are skilled in providing hands-on Active Support and are trained in facilitating interactive sessions so that they can provide feedback to staff. Feedback is not a one-off event related to the interactive training, and it is important that managers provide regular feedback to staff about their performance, based on ongoing observations and the information collected from the monitoring systems.

Immediate changes in practice

The interactive training at 16 Temple Court demonstrated to the staff group that they could support the residents in household activities, which they had previously considered impossible and/or impractical. These extracts are from the interactive training.

Maria [staff] asked Charles to help her get the washing in. She wheeled him to the laundry, put the plastic basket on his lap and wheeled him out to the back yard. Maria unpegged the laundry from the line, gave Charles the item in his left hand and Charles moved it slowly and dropped it into the laundry basket. He did this until the left-hand side of the basket was full. Because of reduced mobility in his arm he could not fill the right-hand side of the basket. Maria spoke to him throughout and wondered whether the basket might be too heavy. When the basket was full Maria piled the rest of the clothes onto Charles and took him back inside. Maria gave Charles an item of clothing and supported him to fold it on his lap. Paul [the trainer] suggested that Charles might find it easier sitting at the dining table. Charles was wheeled to the table and he was given another item. He was involved in folding towels in half and then in half again. He held the item in two hands and folded it away from him. The table surface was a bit slippery and Paul reminded Maria about the non-slip mats that they had seen at the training day. Maria used a hand to steady the items. Paul made the point that Charles did not have to fold all the laundry. Maria made piles of towels and clothes on the table. At the end, the items were put on Charles' lap and he was wheeled away by Maria to put the items in cupboards and wardrobes.

Neil [staff] was asked to support Charles to make a drink. Neil wheeled him in the kitchen, opened the cupboard and took out cans of Nesquik [milkshake] and coffee. As in one of the DVD training extracts he asked 'Do you want Nesquik or Milo?' and shook each item in turn. I could not see a clear indication and Neil suggested that Charles was looking at the oven. Neil opted to give Charles the Nesquik. Charles was given the mug to hold. Neil spooned in the powder and some water and milk and then asked Charles to stir, which he did. 'I never knew he could do that,' he said. 'Usually the drinks are made by staff and brought to the table.' Charles was taken to the sink and prompted to put the spoon in the sink which he did and then wheeled to the dining table to drink the Nesquik.

Neil was asked to support Charles to peel some carrots. He took Charles to the fridge and got out two carrots. Charles was wheeled back to the dining table with the carrots and peeler. Maria prompted Neil to get a chopping board. With hand-over-hand guidance, Charles was able to peel the carrots. Neil went to get a sharp knife from the kitchen and with physical guidance was able to get him to cut the carrots. Maria said 'I cannot look' and walked away. 'It's alright,' said Paul, 'Neil's got full control.'

Although the interactive training demonstrated that the staff could offer the right kind of assistance to involve the residents in domestic tasks, the task of embedding this way of working into staff practice remained. Our later data suggested that Active Support was not incorporated into staff practice at 16 Temple Court in a way that high levels of engagement were consistently achieved. We suggest that this was linked to the following factors, which we discuss in the second half of the chapter:

- The paperwork was not implemented with any great fidelity. The use of the paperwork was limited by staff characteristics, particularly their knowledge, skills, abilities and orientations (KSAOs).

- There were low levels of direct observation and hence little feedback from managers. Both the house supervisor and the team manager experienced constraints in observing staff practice.

Implementation and sustainability

As we suggested earlier, there is significant variation in the way that Active Support is implemented and monitored. One key debate centres on the relative emphasis that should be given to the use of written plans and records of resident participation, as opposed to managers watching staff supporting residents and giving them feedback about their performance (Jones *et al.* 1996b; Mansell *et al.* 2004).

Recent reviews of the research evidence concluded that there are no studies that compare 'paperwork' with 'management observation' (Stancliffe *et al.* 2008; Totsika *et al.* 2008a). At 16 Temple Court, both a paper-based system and direct observation were employed over a 12-month period. Our research was not a comparative study, so the comments that follow must be treated with some degree of caution, but our findings contain lessons for managers in other settings charged with successfully implementing and sustaining Active Support. They also help to inform the 'paperwork' versus 'observation' debate.

Table 5.2 lists the rationales for paper-based recording and direct observation given by Stancliffe *et al.* (2008). Of note here is the qualitatively different way that the 'bullet points' are written, which hints at the discussion to come. Whereas the reasons for paper-based recording are stated positively, those for direct observation address problems that have arisen with 'paperwork', in addition to listing some benefits of observation.

Table 5.2 The rationales for paper-based recording and direct observation (Stancliffe et al. 2008, pp.208–209)

Paper-based recording	Direct observation
• It signals the importance of participation to staff and managers in situations where paper records are important to the organisation • It allows quantitative analysis for use in feedback	• Focusing directly on user engagement avoids the possibility of staff completing the paperwork irrespective of whether they are supporting user participation • Direct observation focuses managers' attention on the quality of support and interaction, rather than on the number of opportunities presented

PAPER-BASED PLANS AND RECORDS

We want to begin by looking at the logic of the paper-based system that we have outlined, which can be linked to a basic learning cycle. We plan, take some action, review that experience and then draw some conclusions before repeating the cycle (Honey and Mumford 1992). In the previous chapter we highlighted planning as a fundamental management process. At 16 Temple Court, many of the activities that staff were expected to support residents to participate in were predetermined and written on Activity and Support Plans and Opportunity Plans. Many interactions with residents were also pre-planned, through protocols and the use of 'performance' statements, which detail the level of support that will be given (see Figure 5.3).

A distinct advantage of the system is that anyone with the relevant knowledge and skills ought to be able to come to a group home and read Activity and Support Plans, implement Opportunity Plans and follow protocols. This offers direction to casual staff in particular, who move between settings. The chief beneficiaries are the residents, because activities are supported in a consistent manner. These 'planning' documents are not ends in themselves. Certainly, they act as a cue to the staff working in a group home that these goals are important, but they are expected to 'degenerate into hard work'. The primary purpose of completing the Activity Learning Log is not to record that a resident has been supported in that activity, but to encourage a staff member to reflect on the activity and share any lessons with the rest of the staff team, so that better outcomes for the residents are delivered. In settings where opportunities for face-to-face communication are often minimal, these written lessons may be really helpful to the person who is working the next shift or day, or the following week.

Individual staff should read the Activity Learning Logs on a daily basis to see what they can learn from them. Keyworkers should look at the Activity Learning Logs in order to provide some distilled feedback to the rest of the staff group at the house meeting. The feedback can be both qualitative and quantitative. Figure 5.9 shows the number of times that five goals from the residents' Opportunity Plans at 16 Temple Court were recorded as having happened in a three-month period following the interactive training. The five goals were: 'Darren to water the indoor pot plants three times a week';[5] 'Charles to collect the mail from the mailbox every day'; 'David to put his lunchbox in his workbag Monday to Friday morning'; 'Mathew to walk around the lounge rooms, kitchen and his bedroom to close the curtains every evening'; and 'Shane will select and carry a towel and flannel to the shower every day.'

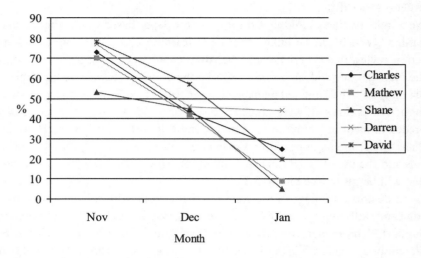

Figure 5.9 Number of times (%) an opportunity was recorded as being offered to the five residents at 16 Temple Court

The house supervisor or her team manager (the house supervisor's line manager) at 16 Temple Court might have produced this graph. A keyworker might have produced a single data series for one resident. However, it was produced by one of the authors, and was used to make the following points to the staff group:

- The graph reveals some flaws in the way that the staff team had implemented the Opportunity Plans. New Opportunity Plans should have been written every month. Goals should not have been rolled-over from one month to the next.[6]

- If appropriate, goals should be incorporated into the Activity and Support Plans. A goal like 'watering the pot plants' could be added to the menu of optional activities (see Figure 5.2).

- Other goals ought to be incorporated into the day-to-day practice of staff relatively quickly. Staff who have taken on board the principles of Active Support would support David to put his lunchbox in his workbag and Shane to collect a towel and flannel prior to showering as a matter of routine.

- The graph clearly illustrates a process of decay, which is a serious issue for sustaining Active Support in the long term. All we were able to say for sure is that over time there is a decrease in staff recording information about each goal. We did not know whether there was a corresponding decline in actually supporting the residents to undertake these activities. This same pattern was evident in the recording of the Activity Learning Logs for most of the residents' goals over this period.

- The graph is unable to show that there were comments written on the Activity Learning Logs that illustrated the kind of helpful information that might be gleaned from taking the time to read and analyse these documents. Mathew's goal of 'closing the curtains' is a good example. Recording of this activity plummeted, which we inferred as being due to the fact that the staff had recorded that they were struggling to support Mathew to do this activity. Mathew was enjoying the 'walk and talk' but not doing the activity. This was evident from reading the first few entries and is a good example of how successful engagement in some activities needs timely follow-up, problem-solving, coaching and supervision from the house supervisor and/or the team manager.

Some broader points about collecting data were also made. Most importantly, at the group home level, data needs to be analysed regularly if there is to be any point in collecting it. Without regular analysis, there are a number of consequences:

- The task of analysing data becomes too time-consuming, as there is too much of it. As a consequence, it is less likely to be analysed and subsequently any lessons that can be learnt from the data will be lost.

- People will stop recording data if they do not get any feedback. Without feedback, collecting data has become an end in itself. Direct support staff need to see that their recording efforts are worthwhile and that there are benefits for the residents and themselves.

- Team morale could suffer. This is more likely when one or two staff keep recording data when others have given up.

This feedback to the staff team captures the unavoidable tension between the planning and coordinating function that written records are meant to serve for direct support staff, and the monitoring function that documentation has for the house supervisor and team manager. Although it was one of the authors making these points, it could just as easily have been an external manager. One of the problems with paper-based recording is that it is all too easy to accentuate the managerial function of written records so that staff believe that they are being used to monitor their performance, rather than understanding that their primary function is to have an impact on the residents' 'quality of life'.

Unfortunately, data presented in a statistical way, such as that shown in Figure 5.9, can contribute to the practice of staff manufacturing records in order to inflate the recorded numbers of goals offered to the residents, which then has little relation to what staff are actually achieving. This is one of the arguments put forward for using direct observation rather than paper-based records. We observed characteristics of the written records that readers may be familiar with, which suggested that the paperwork was perceived as being of little use to the staff team: brief entries, which were little more than a 'written tick' to comply with the request to complete the paperwork; multiple entries in the same handwriting that looked as if they had all been written at the same time; and 'joke entries' that suggested that the Activity Learning Logs were not to be taken seriously. For example, Darren had a written goal of 'Going for a 15-minute walk in the local neighbourhood every day with staff support'. An entry on the Activity Learning Log about what was significant about the support offered simply reads, 'One foot after the other'.

STAFF KNOWLEDGE, SKILLS, ABILITIES AND ORIENTATIONS

Some people believe that direct support staff do not like completing written records, which may be based on a kernel of 'truth'. A pilot project to implement Active Support in Victoria identified the 'paperwork' as a problem (McCubbery and Fyffe 2006). The authors reported that one of the most frequently ticked items on their questionnaire items was 'Staff don't try and fill in forms accurately and get frustrated, confused or annoyed'. They added that, 'The problems with the paperwork requirements have been identified throughout the project' (p.9). At the end of the research at 16 Temple Court a staff member articulated his ongoing scepticism about the usefulness of the paperwork and highlighted practice as being more important. There is little acknowledgement that there might be any relationship between paperwork and practice.

Unfortunately that's the way now with staff thinking, if the staff think that [the paperwork] is more important than the activity, no one can benefit, especially the client, it's just 'Tick, tick, tick' and it's done. In our role it's more important to involve the clients, not focus on the way we record or write. It confused me, at the beginning, when they were talking about the way you're writing, the way you are repeating words, it really confused me. I said: 'Well, it's not important the way we write, just express your opinion, the activity is more important, not the way you are writing.' In the past we already involved the clients in an activity but for some reason the staff didn't write it down, didn't record it or forgot, it doesn't mean that they were not involved. Records are important but we should focus more on practice than on writing.

It should be clear from reading this chapter that the Active Support 'organisational systems' require a certain standard of English literacy. The same point could be made about many of the organisational systems in a group home, such as administering medication; keyworking; Person-Centred Planning; recording behavioural data about people with challenging behaviour; even reading the 'communication book'. If the Active Support paper-based processes in a group home reveal themselves to be weak, we should not be surprised if many of the above processes also turn out to be similarly poorly implemented.

Effective use of these 'systems' requires more than the prerequisite standard of English literacy. Numeracy, basic computer skills and speaking and understanding English, even as a second language, are seen as foundation skills for working in health and social care in Victoria. The need for direct support staff to have these abilities has increased over the last 20 years, rather than decreased, and this trend appears set to continue. Basic computer skills, in particular, have become more important as many organisations are putting their paper-based systems 'online'. There is often a significant gap between what direct support staff are expected to do and the actual knowledge, skills and abilities that many of them possess to effectively undertake their role. In the UK, for example, more than 400,000 staff in the health and social care workforce have literacy levels at or below those of a competent 11-year-old and 550,000 health service staff have numeracy skills comparable to those children leaving primary school (Fryer 2006).

Staff members without the necessary 'foundation skills' are therefore going to struggle to undertake those aspects of the system that depend on them. Bob Fryer writes:

> *This situation constitutes a potentially very serious problem indeed, in limiting staff's ability to handle some aspects of their jobs effectively, including fully understanding written instructions...* This is especially crucial in social care, where half of all staff are estimated to be employed directly in the provision of services. (2006, p.19)

English was not the first language for three of the day-time staff at 16 Temple Court, a group which included the house supervisor. These three employees were also the only full-time staff, which gave them a significant role in the socialisation of new employees and casual staff into the day-to-day running of the house. The two direct support staff also had the weakest levels of English literacy within the staff group.

As well as being tools for self-reflection and monitoring by management, the paperwork can also be used for peer-monitoring, such as when a staff member reads his colleagues' entries, or sees a peer completing paperwork. More importantly direct support staff monitor each other when they see a colleague interacting (or not) with the residents.

Unfortunately, these processes, peer-monitoring and socialisation, can result in an outcome different from the one that is wanted. Powerful work groups can exert social pressure on individual employees to adhere to the group's standard (Roethlisberger, Dickson and Wright 1939/1964). We would suggest that these social processes were implicated in the weak implementation of Active Support at 16 Temple Court. Three of the part-time staff who attended the Active Support training, who demonstrated greater competence and greater enthusiasm for Active Support, left the house within eight months. The remaining full-time staff were not well equipped to promote and role model best practice in relation to the paperwork with new employees or casual staff, as they struggled with the associated tasks and placed little value on them. Serious weaknesses in English literacy are not susceptible to a 'quick fix', so the house supervisor was unable to coach these staff to competence. The house supervisor advised the team manager on a number of occasions that the staff group 'find the paperwork a chore and complain that they are writing the same things over and over again'.

The full-time staff were less likely to come into work and make the time to read previous Activity Learning Log entries, i.e. they were poor role models for the people they were working with. Reviewing and summarising multiple entries was beyond their level of likely competence, and so they never gave feedback grounded in the written records at house meetings. Their minimal entries were probably more of a response to their managers' contingencies rather than a result of seeing any intrinsic worth for themselves or the rest of the staff team (see Mansell and Elliott 2001).

DIRECT OBSERVATION

So, although the rationale for paper-based recording is strong, circumstances may prevail in which it does not deliver the expected benefits. Rational systems do not always operate rationally, which has led to direct observation being promoted as a better alternative. In the introduction to their training resource,

Mansell *et al.* write, 'Our experience was that, too often, staff understood active support to be about the production of paper plans rather than the quality of support they provide in practice' (2004, p.1). They claim, 'The most powerful evidence of good practice comes from senior managers looking and seeing for themselves how staff use person-centred active support' (p.125).

It is important to distinguish between the first-line manager in a group home, the house supervisor and more senior 'external' managers. In our research setting, once the training had been completed, the primary responsibility for ensuring that Active Support was correctly implemented fell to the house supervisor and her line manager, the team manager. Of the two, the house supervisor has the greater day-to-day responsibility for ensuring that the staff she manages perform in line with organisational expectations. As Chapter 7 is devoted to this role, and the concept of 'practice leadership' in particular, we are going to discuss the role of external managers in this section, in order to illustrate that the impact of direct observation can also be weakened.

'Looking and seeing' or 'direct observation' can be done more or less formally. A relatively informal way of getting any manager to observe staff performance in a group home and give feedback is related to the practice of 'Management by Walking About' (see Peters and Waterman 1982). For 'external' managers, this might be through making some unannounced visits to the house to 'catch' people doing Active Support (or otherwise), observe their practice, model their own good practice, give some impromptu feedback and provide staff with the opportunity to ask for help or advice. If direct support staff know that managers may 'pop-in' at any time to look for evidence about the implementation of Active Support, this may help staff to focus on carrying it out.

An organisation could also establish that staff practice will be observed more formally on a regular basis. This is more likely to be carried out by managers that have direct contact with a group home, such as the house supervisor and team manager. This could be done in exactly the same way that the staff experience interactive training. A house supervisor, for example, could watch a staff member support a resident to prepare his breakfast or make his bed, which is then the basis of a discussion between the manager and the staff member.[7] Mansell *et al.* (2004) provide some questions that would be useful for anyone observing another's practice to consider:

- Did the staff member prepare the situation so that the flow of activity was maintained?
- Did he or she present the opportunity well?
- Did he or she provide graded assistance?

- Did he or she enable the person to experience success?
- Did he or she provide support with a positive helpful style?

A key question is whether these types of direct observation can be incorporated into managers' work schedules. To date, we do not know how much 'observation' is necessary to ensure high levels of meaningful engagement. Stancliffe *et al.* (2008) claim that direct observation focuses people's attention on the quality of support at a point in time. As useful as this is, there also needs to be a focus on levels of engagement. One high-quality interaction observed by a house supervisor is little better than no engagement, if it is the only time in a week that a resident is supported to participate in a meaningful activity. As Fournies (1988) points out, managers cannot and should not have to watch employees all of the time. The reasons for doing Active Support must be important enough to direct support staff to influence their performance when managers are not watching.

As the team manager's role is more removed from day-to-day practice, he or she has a greater focus on monitoring the implementation of Active Support. Most obviously this is through attending house meetings and looking at the formal documentation. The team manager is also expected to coach a house supervisor and develop his or her practice through formal supervision meetings. At 16 Temple Court, the team manager committed himself to having a monthly supervision meeting with the house supervisor, reviewing the Active Support documentation, and attending the monthly house meeting. In order to include some direct observation he also committed himself to calling in at 16 Temple Court for at least 60 minutes once a fortnight.

It is important to note that the 'paperwork' and 'observation' are linked to other 'organisational systems', particularly formal supervision and house meetings. At 16 Temple Court, individual staff members were expected to provide a summary of lessons learnt from the paperwork at house meetings and the house supervisor should monitor this task and provide help at formal supervision (see Figures 5.7 and 5.8). An immediate discussion should follow the house supervisor's observations of a staff member supporting a resident, but this could also become a topic for a more formal supervision meeting. Staff performance is always under the gaze of the house supervisor at a staff meeting, even though this may simply be listening to staff present information.

In brief, our findings revealed that none of the team manager's goals were fully achieved. Supervision meetings were cancelled, and were unable to be rearranged before the next scheduled meeting. Active Support slipped off the team manager's agenda as crises or new organisation initiatives became his immediate concern. Workload priorities impacted on his ability to look at the paperwork and attend some house meetings. Sometimes he arrived after a meeting had started, on other occasions he left before the end. Sometimes he was not able to come at all. The informal visits to the house were disrupted by the team manager having to act-up for three months and they were not carried out by his short-term replacement.

As with paper-based recording, circumstances may similarly prevail in which direct observation and other supportive processes are weakly implemented and therefore fail to deliver the expected benefits.

Concluding remarks

It is important that we should neither conflate the issues related to the implementation and maintenance of Active Support, nor oversimplify the debate so that it is couched as either 'paperwork' or 'observation'. Even the least paperwork-intensive Active Support system (Mansell *et al.* 2004) has some paperwork. The issues related to initial implementation are likely to be different from long-term maintenance, and both paperwork and observation are likely to have a role to play, although their emphasis may change over time.

In the language of 'necessary and sufficient causes', a cause is defined as necessary if it must be present for a certain outcome to occur, or sufficient if by itself it can produce a certain outcome (Ragin 1987). It may be the case that neither paper-based systems nor direct observation are sufficient, i.e. neither can produce high levels of engagement by themselves. Both may be necessary, i.e. they are capable of producing high levels of engagement in combination with one another or in combination with *other* causes.

The documentation would appear to have a key role in laying the foundations for successfully implementing Active Support, especially as part of the classroom-based training and in the months that follow. However, in circumstances when staff have become successful at planning and coordinating their work, and support high levels of resident engagement as part of their day-to-day practice, they are *less* likely to notice Opportunity Plans and Activity and Support Plans and *more* likely to see them as unnecessary (Mansell *et al.* 1987). Mansell *et al.* suggest that in these circumstances it is hard to argue that the existing processes and procedures should stay the same. For a period, the expertise and experience that a staff group have gained in implementing Active Support will probably maintain good practice. However, over time, as decisions are made to remove or alter the elements of the system that contributed to the staff becoming skilled in the first place, the possibility of reverting to the previous low levels of resident engagement is increased. For example, skilled staff may leave a house or the system may suddenly become stressed and there is no guarantee that the previously helpful systems will be reinstated. This suggests that the purpose and function of the paperwork changes over time, and that a staff team need to actively review it as the dynamics in a group home change.

It is also unlikely that there is one best way to either implement or sustain Active Support, because context might determine the emphasis given to paperwork or observation. Paperwork may be helpful in settings where staff are competent in its use. But it may be less important where organisational structures enable frequent observation. Where there are either organisational barriers to direct observation or such practice is weak, paper-based systems may allow Active Support to maintain a minimal presence until the 'organisational systems' can be strengthened.

Although the staff at 16 Temple Court were unanimous in their criticism of paper-based recording they agreed that direct contact with the team manager had an important role to play. A member of the direct support staff commented:

I know team managers are very busy, I know that they're engaged in about six or seven houses, but it's crucial that they should be involved with the staff directly. You're always able to contact them through the email or through the telephone…but we're not able to see or ask each other what's going on. It is really good to engage or be involved with the staff directly, it's good to attend the house and whether casually or formally discuss things with the staff. Maybe one of the reasons [that performance drops off over time] is there's not feedback from management. Really encourage the staff, otherwise it becomes very boring, you just keep doing the same things. We're all human beings; we need more encouragement and less criticism, which encourages you to do better. I know the team manager is not directly involved in this house, as a carer, but he has a crucial role to ask, 'What are our problems, how are we achieving, what are we doing?' It's encouragement for the staff and it's very important. If a manager is attending [the house meeting] the staff take it more seriously.

The house supervisor reinforced this view but added how the team manager's presence impacted on her own motivation and performance.

His presence will be good for the morale of the staff, and will help to continue the active support, to keep him up to date with what we are doing. He will see for himself what the staff have been doing or have achieved and will give some encouragement and feedback. If the staff don't see it as important, then slowly it will slip away. Even for me [as a house supervisor], if the management just say 'Oh do it, do it' and then they never even bother to ask how you're doing, or visit the house...even as a house supervisor, I'll think, 'Well, they never come, they never bother to ask how the house is going, how the staff are going...so why worry, why bother?' But for them to be directly involved; [the team manager] will be representing the area manager or the manager of DAS [Disability Accommodation Services] and he will play an important role in keeping in touch with the house-staff and give them some feedback. He'll actually see for himself, and give me a lot of support. When he is present, I play my role a bit better, as a leader of this team. He's my team leader, so he has to set an example as well.

Mansell *et al.* write that, 'Senior managers have a special responsibility to create a climate in which staff know that the most important part of their job is providing person-centred active support' (2004, p.123). The concept of a senior manager extends to the top of the organisational hierarchy. One of the direct support staff was impressed by a visit from such a person:

I remember two or three months ago, Gabriel [the team manager] was here, and he told us that one of the big bosses of DHS wanted to visit to look at Active Support. He mentioned, 'Do you see how important Active Support is, because this high-level manager, who is in charge, is interested in this task?' It's really made me think, 'Yes, that's very important.'

To reiterate the point we made earlier, as important as the contributions of these external managers are, the house supervisor has the greater day-to-day responsibility for ensuring that Active Support is implemented correctly and sustained over time.

Future possibilities for Active Support

Recent iterations of Active Support have moved beyond engagement in the home to include engagement in community-based activities. At present it is not clear what impact Active Support can have outside of the home, but it may be the case that articulated hopes, often expressed in confused language, are outrunning both the way Active Support is taught and researched. Some people are hoping that Active Support will increase the frequency and variety of community-based activities; and the quality and extent of social relationships (Stancliffe *et al.* 2008).

To date a small number of research studies have used the *Index of Community Involvement – Revised* (Raynes *et al.* 1994) to see whether Active Support training produced increases in the frequency and/or variety of reported community participation. This tool is a relatively blunt instrument that provides frequency measures, i.e. how many times a person went to a café, bank, concert and so on. It cannot be used to answer some of the questions that are currently being asked by researchers. It does not measure engagement or who is doing the supporting. Neither is it a good measure of the variety of activities that a person participates in, as activities are squeezed into 16 broad *a priori* categories.

Where community-based activities are supported by direct support staff who have had Active Support training, we would hope for a change in how people were supported to undertake these activities, i.e. that engagement increases during community-based activities. At 16 Temple Court, for example, the staff took Charles to a café where tea was served as separate items, i.e. as a teabag, hot water and jug of milk, so that he could be involved in making himself a cup of tea.

If the frequency of staff-supported community-based activities is to increase, staff must have the capacity to do this. Organisations are often quite good at supporting *community presence*, and so Active Support may not impact on the frequency of community-based activities. Planning processes may help staff to think about the variety of places that people go, although this may not always be desirable. Building social relationships, the focus of the next chapter, is likely to be facilitated by going to certain types of places over and over again. Direct support staff may have a role in passing on their Active Support skills to members of the public, so that they too can interact more effectively with people with profound intellectual disabilities.

Issues for consideration

- Are managers clear about why 'engagement' is important to people's 'quality of life'? Can they put forward coherent arguments for 'engagement' that are likely to persuade sceptics?

- How can you bring to the surface people's issues about the involvement of residents in the running of their own household?

- As engaging people with severe and profound intellectual disabilities is not intuitive practice, how are you teaching staff the working practices that will result in high levels of engagement?

- Do direct support staff have the KSAOs to use all of the organisation's systems?

- Is the best use being made of the 'natural' curriculum of activities available in a group home?

- Are managers skilled in providing hands-on Active Support, running interactive sessions and giving feedback to staff? Do they have enough time to observe staff practice?

- What are the specific issues for implementing and sustaining Active Support in your organisational context?

- Do you have unnecessary paperwork procedures? Are the paperwork processes linked to good resident outcomes?

- Is the data you collect analysed and discussed regularly, or has it become an 'end in itself'?

- How are new employees being socialised into the direct support role?

Notes

1   In the absence of speech, some people with intellectual disabilities may exhibit behaviour that is interpreted to mean that they do not want to participate in activities, particularly those who have autism or challenging behaviour. Gary LaVigna (2005) suggests that the right to choose is not absolute, particularly when choices are made primarily to avoid participating in activities. He argues that in such circumstances people may end up having a poor 'quality of life'. These are discussions that need to be held with a person's support network and, if possible, with the particular service-user.

2   In this context, 'doing nothing' means endless hours of inactivity, not 'having a rest' in an otherwise busy life (see Mansell *et al.* 2004).

3   Although a technology like Active Support is always being refined, and there have been some changes since its early conceptualisation, it is probably worth reviewing local practice against that recommended in the existing training materials (Jones *et al.* 1996b; Mansell *et al.* 2004) or any subsequent revisions.

4   Clement and Bigby (2008) provide further discussion on this point.

5   Darren moved into 16 Temple Court, following the death of Christos. This accounts for why his name appears in Figure 5.9 but his demographic information does not appear in Table 2.2. Five of the residents died during the research period. This probably reflects the differential mortality rate for people with more severe disabilities.

6   In contrast to Opportunity Plans described by Jones *et al.* (1996a), which have space for up to eight goals each week and are reviewed at a weekly house meeting, the expected practice at 16 Temple Court was to set three goals that would be reviewed monthly.

A key characteristic of feedback is that it needs to be timely. A distinct advantage of weekly Opportunity Plans is that relatively little time passes before the goals are reviewed. At 16 Temple Court four weeks might pass before there was any formal discussion about implementing a goal. Our analysis of the Activity Learning Logs revealed that if there was an issue with either supporting a goal or recording it, then this would reveal itself in the first week. The house supervisor needs to intervene early in order to demonstrate that the records are being read and ensure that they have a positive function.

Our view is that, in general, household 'opportunities' should not roll-over. A different set of criteria come into play for community-based goals, where the frequencies are lower, and the aims may be additionally related to the goal of *building inclusive communities*. Rolling goals over has the tendency to make Opportunity Plans stale and encourages 'lazy' practice on the part of staff reviewing and writing goals.

7   Finlay, Antaki and Walton (2008) make the case for using video recordings of staff practices as a means of improving services, although they are wary of it being used by managers.

Chapter 6

Building Inclusive Communities

Introduction

This chapter illustrates the difficulties of implementing a broad social policy goal that is unable to reflect the entire range of issues faced by people with disabilities. We use the concept of 'social space' to discuss the 'social inclusion' of people with intellectual disabilities and make links with a number of other concepts that are commonly used to discuss social inclusion. In doing so, we suggest that processes that foster *community presence* are stronger than those leading to *community participation*, which helps, in part, to explain why the social exclusion of people with intellectual disabilities remains an enduring social problem.

From segregation to community presence

When people with intellectual disabilities lived in institutional settings it was easier to demonstrate their segregation from mainstream society. Indeed, for part of their history, segregation and confinement were their *raison d'être* (Potts and Fido 1991). In contrast, it was hoped that the use of 'ordinary houses in ordinary streets' would place people with intellectual disabilities at the heart of local communities, and thus they would become part of the wider community.

A large number of people have promoted ideas about what 'inclusion' means and how to 'include' people with intellectual disabilities in mainstream society, most of which have been embraced by human service organisations (Perske 1993). Variations of 'inclusion', and its forerunner 'integration', have been a feature of the rhetoric that has shaped service-provision for people with intellectual disabilities over the past 30 years (Robertson *et al.* 2001). Yet despite this, there is a consensus that many people with intellectual disabilities still live on the margins of society.

In those countries where deinstitutionalisation has been completed, or is almost complete, it is often said that people with intellectual disabilities are *present* in the community but not *part* of it (Flynn and Aubry 1999; Myers *et al.* 1998; Rapley 2000). What this comment means can be clarified by reference to O'Brien's (1987) distinction between *community presence* and *community participation*. It suggests that although people with intellectual disabilities make use of the ordinary places that define community life, such as shopping malls and leisure centres, there is something about the quality of their social relationships which means that their lives can still be described as socially excluded.

What form does contemporary social exclusion take?

It has always been the case that the majority of people with intellectual disabilities have lived in community-based settings. This was true even when the institutional population was at its peak (Bartlett and Wright 1999). If we accept the premise that people with intellectual disabilities are living in 'the community' in countries without a significant institutionalised population, then our attention is more fully focused on their 'social', rather than their 'physical', exclusion.

In general, most people with intellectual disabilities are said to have small and highly restricted social networks, which are organised around human services. Their social networks are characterised by interactions with other people with intellectual disabilities, human service employees and immediate family members. Any contact that they have with non-disabled members of the public is likely to be mundane, impersonal and fleeting, although they may have some casual acquaintances. Sustained meaningful relationships with non-disabled people, characterised by intimacy[1] and friendship, are typically lacking. The lives of people with intellectual disabilities are often reported as being lonely (Luckasson *et al.* 2002; Marquis and Jackson 2000; McConkey 2005; Myers *et al.* 1998; O'Brien 1987; O'Brien and O'Brien 1993; Ramcharan, McGrath and Grant 1997; Ramcharan and Richardson 2005; Robertson *et al.* 2001). Evidence of this pattern of social relationships can be seen in Chapter 2. It should also be noted that, because this is a generalised account, it will not be true for all people with intellectual disabilities all of the time.

'Inclusion' as a social policy goal

As we stated in Chapter 1, group homes are meant to realise broad social policy goals. A buzzword that encompasses a number of related goals is 'inclusion'. In England, 'inclusion' is one of the four principles underlying the English learning disability strategy *Valuing People* (Department of Health 2001). It is explicated thus:

> Being part of the mainstream is something most of us take for granted. We go to work, look after our families, visit our GP, use transport, go to the swimming pool or cinema. Inclusion means enabling people with learning disabilities to do those ordinary things, make use of mainstream services and be fully included in the local community. (p.24)

'Full and effective participation and inclusion in society' is one of the general principles of the *United Nations Convention on the Rights of Persons with Disabilities* (United Nations 2006). The Convention contains a more specific Article, *Living independently and being included in the community*, which states that:

> States Parties to the present Convention recognize the equal right of all persons with disabilities to live in the community, with choices equal to others, and shall take effective and appropriate measures to facilitate full enjoyment by persons with disabilities of this right and their full inclusion and participation in the community. (p.13)

In Victoria, the goal of *building inclusive communities* appears in the *Victorian State Disability Plan* (DHS 2002b). It is explained as 'strengthening communities so that people with a disability have the same opportunities as all other citizens of Victoria to participate in the life of the community – socially, economically, culturally, politically and spiritually' (p.9).

This is part of the Government's vision for the future, whereby:

> Victoria will be a stronger and more inclusive community – a place where diversity is embraced and celebrated, and where everyone has the same opportunities to participate in the life of the community, and the same responsibilities towards society as all other citizens of Victoria. (DHS 2002b, p.4)

The goal of 'inclusion' embodies the notion of the 'big hairy audacious goal' that we introduced in Chapter 1; being 'fuzzy' and conceptually weak. There are a number of other terms that can substitute for 'inclusion', such as participation and citizenship; there are not accepted definitions for any of them; and they tend to be hard to apply to people with severe and profound intellectual disabilities.

In addition to drawing attention to 'inclusion' in this way, we also want to problematise a number of other terms that appear in related policy statements that we found to be equally slippery: 'participation', 'community' and 'communities'.

Our experience suggests that many staff working with people with profound intellectual disabilities are likely to reject certain notions of inclusion as being irrelevant to the people they support. This is because a broad social policy goal established for a heterogeneous population does not detail the nuanced ways in which meaningful outcomes vary for subgroups. People with profound intellectual disabilities are unlikely to be in paid employment, or start a family, let alone look after them. It is also hard to envision any responsibilities people with profound intellectual disabilities have towards society. On the contrary, in Western countries, people with profound intellectual disabilities are typically identified as a 'vulnerable' population in need of protection.

In relation to the goal of *building inclusive communities*, a staff member at 64 Penny Lane commented, 'We cannot expect much from these men because of the time they have spent in institutions. It will be easier to have inclusion with the next generation.' The relatives of the residents at 64 Penny Lane also expressed views that the relationships that their sons and brothers had with non-disabled people were unlikely to change:

I don't really know. I can't really see it... I think there is a positive push and people are more active in society. How much you can do? I don't know, it depends. Someone with no communication skills, no verbal communication skills and things like that, that's more...maybe voluntary people assisting? I think that's just the way society is. But it may change I don't know. We can have too high hopes.

No, I can't see that, I can't see that no. Not with any of the boys really... I think it would be pretty hard, unless people's ideas change, which they will in the future, but it'll be probably too late for people like Dan and Wally, maybe other people with disabilities younger... It would be nice, it would be really good wouldn't it... I've got two other brothers don't visit. They've got their grandchildren and what have you. They don't see him as a person. He's just one of these people with a mental illness, he's away somewhere.

One of the core initiatives in *Making Life Good in the Community* focused on staff-led interventions to alter the residents' pattern of social relationships with non-disabled people (Clement, Bigby and Warren 2008). In particular we were interested in the possibility of facilitating sustained meaningful relationships with non-disabled people, in order to overcome the pattern of social exclusion experienced by people with intellectual disabilities that we described earlier. This chapter contains many of the lessons we learned from trying to realise this goal.

Lay understandings of 'inclusion' and 'participation' are not good enough

The meanings of many social policy terms are not intuitive, and commonsense understandings are not good enough. This is well illustrated by the meanings that staff attached to the words 'include' and 'participate'. The latter caused difficulties in particular, because people's lay understandings did not quite match with O'Brien's (1987) definition of *community participation*, which we advocated as a guiding principle.

Despite spending considerable time explaining and promoting O'Brien's (1987) differentiation between *community presence* and *community participation*, we were not always successful in developing a common vocabulary. When asked to explain the difference between *community presence* and *community participation*, a staff member said, 'I see community presence as the guys just following us around at the supermarket. Participation is pushing the trolley.'

Lay understandings are likely to be found in dictionaries. 'To include' means 'to contain as a member of a whole' and 'to participate' means 'to share with another or others' (Simpson and Weiner 1989). Neither of these definitions requires us to consider how people are included or participate. This 'ancient' quotation from Fred Davis (1961) highlights the fact that people can be included and participate in very different ways. Its age also suggests that, in some areas, life has not changed that much for people with disabilities: 'As with the poor relation at the wedding party, so the reception given the handicapped person in many social situations: sufficient that he is here, he should not expect to dance with the bride' (p.127). Lay definitions of inclusion and participation allow people to argue that a staff member supporting a resident to attend a wedding, go swimming at the local leisure centre or watch a film at a multiplex is both 'participation' and 'inclusion'.

However, comparing these activities to O'Brien's (1987) definitions of *community presence* and *community participation* can lead to a different conclusion. They meet the criteria for *community presence*, the sharing of ordinary rather than segregated places. Yet, they may not meet O'Brien's criteria for *community participation*. If the staff member is the primary person the resident interacts with during each of these activities, then the resident has remained in a relatively 'socially isolated state' in relation to the wider community. This is what we believe some people mean when they state that people with intellectual disabilities are *present* in the community but not *part* of it.

If we are going to support people with intellectual disabilities to have relationships with non-disabled people, we need to move beyond these lay definitions of 'inclusion' and 'participation' and examine the activities that people are doing; where they are doing them; who they are doing them with; and how they are doing them.

Towards an understanding of 'community'

According to the policy goals cited earlier, people with intellectual disabilities are expected to participate and be included in 'the community' and various 'communities'. This suggests that a larger community is comprised of smaller ones. For example, the Australian community contains numerous cities and towns. Melbourne, the capital of Victoria, is subdivided into a number of suburbs. And so on.

Thinking about community in terms of geographical area is only one way of conceptualising it. Table 6.1 gives five different types of 'natural communities'

Table 6.1 A typology of communities (McArdle 1998, p.106)

Type	Example
Centre-based communities	Students, teachers, parents and local residents involved with a school; or staff and users of a recreation centre; or people attending a day service
Geographic communities	Residents of an identifiable rural district, friends living in a particular street or neighbourhood
Issue-based communities	An environment group and people who share their concern about a specific environmental issue; people with a common disability and their carers
Interest-based communities	A sporting club, or craft group
Kinship communities	Including family, extended family and their friends

(McArdle 1998). This typology was given to a staff group at a training event we participated in, entitled 'Developing community connections at a local level' (Scope (Vic) Ltd 2005). The participants were asked to use this typology to identify types of communities that the residents they supported were involved with.

More than 50 years ago, George Hillery (1955) pointed out that 'community' is a complex and contested term. He analysed 94 definitions of community and beyond the fact that all the definitions involved 'people', there was no other common basis. Most of the 94 definitions included area (similar to geography), common ties and social interaction, as important elements of community. Common ties, or commonalities, are features that people share with others.

Since Hillery's article was published the concept of 'community' has been attached to 'virtual communities', such as an *e-community* or *online community*. Members of these communities do not really meet in a geographical area, but 'in the ether', making use of newer forms of communication, such as email, the internet and the mobile phone. These newer understandings of community alert us to the fluid nature of 'society' (Hughes *et al.* 2007). It would be interesting to see what possibilities they hold for people with intellectual disabilities. At present they are another type of community that people with severe and profound intellectual disabilities are little engaged with.

A 'distinct social space'

In considering a geographical area we draw boundaries around people and places, and in doing so we create an inside and an outside. An alternative term for 'area' is 'space', which is 'the physical expanse which surrounds something' (Simpson and Weiner 1989). Todd, Evans and Beyer named the generalised pattern of social relationships experienced by people with intellectual disabilities as a 'distinct social space' (1990, p.215).

At a particular moment in time, anyone can be said to be occupying a 'space'. You may, for example, be reading this book in an office or sitting on a train. A space is made 'social' by the presence, or the potential presence, of other people. This creates possibilities for interacting with them. If you are in an office by yourself, you can read uninterrupted, until there is a knock on the door or the telephone rings. Reading a book whilst commuting to work in a crowded carriage may be an attempt to assert a similar 'private space'. Yet someone may attempt to engage you in conversation about what you are reading, the state of public transport and so on. An office or a train carriage can be described in a number of ways. In a sense, both of them could be described as a 'distinct social space'. Being 'distinctive' simply means that one space has certain characteristics that make it capable of being told apart from another.

In contrast to non-disabled adults, what makes the social spaces occupied by adults with intellectual disabilities distinctive is that they are locations where they primarily engage with other people with intellectual disabilities, service workers who are paid to support them and immediate family members. Drawing the boundaries in this way, highlighting its particular characteristics and naming it a 'distinct social space' is a deliberate attempt by Todd *et al.* (1990) to represent the way in which people with intellectual disabilities are socially excluded. The description we provided at the start of the chapter also suggests particular kinds of actions that can be taken to make the social spaces occupied by people with intellectual disabilities less 'distinctive' (Eden and Huxham 1996). The following actions may help to make people with intellectual disabilities more socially included:

- Enlarge their social networks, particularly by engaging new people who are not known to everyone in the existing network.

- Change the composition of people's social networks, specifically by bringing non-disabled people into them.

- Change the quality of their relationships with non-disabled people, so that some are characterised by familiarity and friendship.

With its focus on area and people, the notion of 'distinct social space' shares qualities with the other major concepts we are using in this chapter. It encompasses the 'places' in *community presence* and the 'personal relationships' in *community participation*, and two of the three elements from a core definition of community: area and social interaction. The third element of community, common ties, is evident in the way that individuals have been grouped, either as people with intellectual disabilities, paid staff or immediate family members. The process of social categorisation is discussed below.

This 'distinct social space' is well illustrated in Figure 6.1, an outcome of a social network assessment instrument developed by Elizabeth Tracy and her colleagues (Tracy and Abell 1994; Tracy and Whittaker 1990). This assessment tool has been used extensively in research involving people with intellectual disabilities (see Robertson *et al.* 2005, for example), as well as in social work practice.

The figure is a visual representation of Simon's social network map. He lives at 96 High Street. All the people in the network are other people with disabilities (10), service workers who support Simon at his home and the day programme (9) and immediate family members (4).

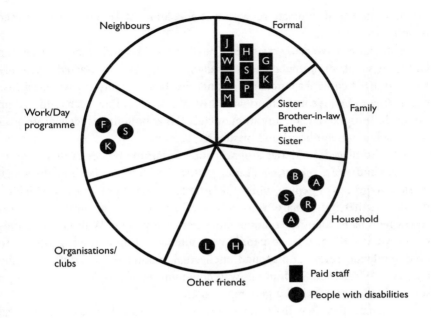

Figure 6.1 Simon's social network map

This assessment focused on important people in Simon's life who had had *active contact* with him in the month prior to its completion. The map does not therefore imply that Simon had no contact with non-disabled people, but as they were not included as part of his active social network, then it is likely that any interactions will have been fleeting, such as customer-based exchanges in shops and leisure settings.

Developing 'social space' as a useful concept

We have found the concept of a 'distinct social space' useful for describing the generalised pattern of social relationships experienced by people with intellectual disabilities. In addition, we think 'social space' is a helpful concept for analysing current social relationships and for imagining alternative future ones. It can therefore be used to explain how the social exclusion of people with intellectual disabilities arises, and provides ideas for human service employees who are looking to build more inclusive communities.

At any given time, we can draw a boundary around a person with intellectual disabilities, study the composition of people within this arbitrary space, examine the social interactions within it and look for common ties between people.

Boundaries have many qualities. They have insides and outsides. They can be big or small, strengthened or weakened, enlarged or contracted. Table 6.1 and Figure 6.1 contain a number of boundaries. It is probably easiest to visualise boundaries as being coterminous with the walls of a building, such as the group home, day programme, organisation or club. Other boundaries seem more arbitrary, such as a neighbourhood or suburb.

We also place boundaries around people using the processes of *social categorisation* and *social comparison* (Tajfel 1978). The former classifies the social world into groups of people, whilst the latter refers to the processes by which we decide whether individuals are members of a particular category. These processes help us to identify commonalities between people. Without these processes, we could not refer to people with intellectual disabilities; people with mild, moderate, severe or profound intellectual disabilities; paid staff; or family members. When thought of in this way, communities of people are defined by a social identity, rather than a geographical area.

Of course, people with common ties may come together in a geographical area. Families, for example, often come together at Christmas or Thanksgiving. Supporters of Arsenal Football Club go to the Emirates Stadium in North London on match days. This shows why it is important not to conceptualise a community as being confined to a geographical area. When the extended family return to their separate homes, they will still perceive themselves to be part of the same kinship community, even though they are no longer in the same physical location.

We want to suggest that boundaries are socially constructed, and because they are, they can change.[2] We propose that the boundaries of the 'social spaces' occupied by people with intellectual disabilities are typically in a state of flux and that people's actions influence their boundaries. People need to be able to deal with the paradoxical nature of boundaries. A danger of describing the boundaries of the 'distinct social space' in the way that we have is that it appears to make it clearly defined and fixed, when in fact this space is ambiguous, fluctuating and porous. This means that the lives of people with intellectual disabilities are a complex web of 'inclusionary' and 'exclusionary' situations and experiences (Hall 2005). People can be helped or hindered to cross the boundaries of the 'distinct social space' in either direction, which can alter the composition of people inhabiting it. In this way, the social spaces occupied by people with intellectual disabilities can lose their distinctiveness.

Applying 'social space' in practice

At this point, it may be worth re-reading the group trip we described to the shopping mall by foot and tram in Chapter 2 (p.60), which we want to refer to in order to ground our discussion of 'social space'.

If we think about that trip to the shopping mall we can see how, as the social spaces change, they retain a distinctive character. This 'distinct social space' is most obvious when the four residents are surrounded by the four walls of their group home, being supported by two staff members. Once the residents stepped over the garden boundary they entered public spaces, where interactions with other people are to be expected, and often actively sought, i.e. streets, a tram, a café, the shopping mall and a supermarket.[3]

In suggesting that people with intellectual disabilities predominantly have *community presence*, we can draw a boundary around the residents after they have left their home, imagining them as being in a 'bubble'. The four residents are isolated in public spaces, even as they move through them. Membership of any community is not automatically conferred by physical presence.

The residents and staff engage with no one else as they walk to the tram stop. Within the confines of a crowded Melbourne tram, one member of the public momentarily breaches the bubble by saying 'hello', whilst another creates as much physical distance as he can by moving to the far end of the carriage. As the residents push the trolley around K-Mart they engage only with the staff members.

In this instance, the actions of the supporting staff help to keep the residents relatively cocooned in the 'distinct social space'. At the shopping centre, the four men are seated at a table in a café whilst the staff go to the counter. In K-Mart, the staff member pays for the clothing. The staff miss opportunities to facilitate interactions between the residents and the shop assistants, whether this be ordering food, handing over money or acting as an interpreter for gestures and sounds. In contrast, the staff members move in and out of the 'distinct social space', holding conversations with fellow passengers on the tram and interacting with the café and K-Mart employees. The conversation with Linda, the off-duty staff member who happened to be shopping in the mall, does not change the general composition of the 'distinct social space', because she is part of it.

Facilitating community presence

A number of authors have written that wider cultural and social trends have resulted in a progressive withdrawal of people from public institutions and social involvement in recent decades (see Putnam 2000). It is important to acknowledge that this makes the contemporary task of facilitating meaningful relationships with non-disabled people harder. However, supporting people with intellectual disabilities to increase the number and variety of ordinary places they know and use is an important aspect of *building inclusive communities*. The fact that people with intellectual disabilities are said to be 'present' in the community reflects, in part, that the actions of human service employees enable *community presence* rather well. The trip to the shopping mall contains numerous examples of this, such as walking the street, riding on a tram and having a drink at a café.

Figure 6.2 shows some data collected at 64 Penny Lane about staff-supported community-based activities. The data is summarised at two points in time, which are separated by nine months. Each activity was categorised as *community presence, community participation* or a *segregated activity*. Of the 76 activities, 66 (87%) were categorised as *community presence*, three (4%) as *community participation* and seven (9%) as *segregated activities*.

In a discussion with the staff group (a 'member check'), we suggested that the broad pattern of activities they supported resulted in *community presence* but not *community participation*. This interpretation has *trustworthiness* (Creswell 1998), as the staff group could not provide any disconfirming evidence ('negative case analysis'). They agreed that they supported this broad pattern and could not identify an activity that they had initiated which would be likely to result in *community participation*.

Table 6.2 shows a more detailed description of the activities at Time 1.[4]

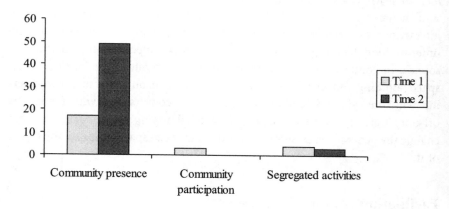

Figure 6.2 Chart showing the type of activities supported at 64 Penny Lane at two separate times

Table 6.2 Community-based activities categorised as community presence, community participation or segregated activities

	Community presence	Community participation	Segregated activities
Bus trips	• The beach at Ocean Grove • Tullamarine airport • Phillip Island • Healesville Animal Sanctuary • Federation Square • Trips to parks to go walking • Cinema • Dining out • Christmas lights		• Barbeque at another group home • Community Residential Services' Christmas party • Department of Human Services' regional office • Visit to other group home to see residents and friends
Community services	• Journey on the tram	• Dentist • GP • Hairdresser	
Shopping	• Safeway • K-Mart • Shoe shopping • Christmas shopping • Clothes shopping		
Walking from the house	• Walks around the block • Walks along Arthur's Creek		

There is nothing 'wrong' with any of these activities, but a closer look at the specific activities suggests that the possibility of breaking out of the 'distinct social space' is unlikely as a result of participating in them.

This is most obvious for the segregated activities that took place within the 'service system'. Segregated activities in segregated facilities need to be understood in relation to *community presence*. Highlighting the importance of using ordinary places was particularly necessary when people with intellectual disabilities spent much of their time in places that had been established for their sole use. For example, in addition to providing accommodation for people with intellectual disabilities, Kew Residential Services had its own school, swimming pool, shop, health centre and so on (Manning 2008). Nowadays physical segregation has a less overt form. A group home may be 'an ordinary house in an ordinary street', but it is still a specialist facility for people with intellectual disabilities, so going to a barbeque at another group home keeps people within the service system.

Changing the composition of the people in a group home can create a socially inclusive environment. The concept of the social home that we discussed in Chapter 3 and defined as a place for entertaining and enjoying the company of other people (Sixsmith 1986) has some utility here. This will include other people with intellectual disabilities and relatives, but it could also include non-disabled acquaintances and friends. This would help to transform a group home into 'a (more) ordinary house in an ordinary street'.

In contrast to the staff and relatives we quoted at the start of the chapter, this relative has a more positive vision of how things might be.

What I would like to see is the neighbours in the street just pop-in for a visit. Don't just close your eyes and walk past that place, pop-in and say 'hello', find out some more information about the staff and the residents... Even if you only do it the once and it freaks you out and you don't want to do it, but at least take that first initial step to see that these people live in this house, everyday normality, there is no difference in living in your home. I'd like to see a lot of people trying to understand and see these people are like us.

The development of acquaintances

We classified the use of the three community services, the dentist, GP and hairdresser, as *community participation*, because this was consistent with the definition we had given the staff team (see Table 1.1 earlier), where acquaintances can be seen as being part of 'a growing network of personal relationships'.

Going to the same place regularly can lead to the development of acquaintances. Acquaintances gain knowledge of each other through experience, but have little familiarity with one another (King's Fund Centre 1988). The residents at 64 Penny Lane routinely went to the same hairdresser, which led the house supervisor to state, 'There is a good rapport with the hairdresser, he knows people's names, and who likes the hair-dryers and who doesn't.'

Acquaintances are an important part of anyone's social network, and are a precursor to closer relationships. However, it is unlikely that repeated use of the same dentist or hairdresser will develop into close friendships. We suggest that many of the places that people with intellectual disabilities go, and the activities that they participate in when they are there, make it unlikely that close personal relationships, leading to friendships, will have any possibility of forming. This is because they are activities where interactions are too brief to develop familiarity, common ties and a positive decision to want to spend more time with one another.

Community presence as the end goal

All of the activities that we categorised as *community presence* were supported by staff, and most of them were undertaken with more than one resident. The 'bus trips' tended to involve the entire household. In Chapter 3 we quoted a house supervisor who conceived these trips as family outings, where everyone went out together.

None of these activities have *community participation* as a central goal. The activities are ends in themselves, to see a film, to go for a walk or to buy some shoes, which are supported by a paid member of staff. The way in which the staff member supports the residents plays a large part in determining whether they will have any interactions with other people, and what those interactions will be like. In contrast to the practice we described on the trip to the shopping mall, this staff member reported a number of interactions with shop assistants during this outing to see a film.

We saw *Shrek 3* at the movies. Joseph loves popcorn. He ordered it himself by pointing, then paid the money and collected the change. Joseph also picked his lunch by pointing out a dish from a shop in the food court. When we went to pick up Franco's birthday present, he chose a back-scratcher for himself, then went to pay for it. He collected the change and hasn't put it down since.

If many of the activities supported by staff will not lead to meaningful relationships with non-disabled people, then what type of activities will?

Enabling community participation

A number of authors have claimed that *community presence* is a precondition to 'being part of the community' (Flynn and Aubry 1999; Myers *et al.* 1998; Rapley 2000), i.e. it is necessary for *community participation* to occur. This statement needs qualifying, because, as we have tried to show, many activities that are supported by staff result in *community presence*, but are highly unlikely to lead to *community participation*.

None of the activities that we categorised as *community presence* in Table 6.2 are likely to result in friendships with non-disabled people. This is because they are activities that you tend to *do with friends*, rather than activities that you do in order *to make friends*. For the residents at 64 Penny Lane, the support to undertake these activities is provided by paid staff.

Perske (1993) argues that human service workers cannot create friendships for people with intellectual disabilities. What service-workers can do is to help people with intellectual disabilities go to places where friendships are more likely to happen. This will be in places where the same people can meet routinely so that they can make a judgement about whether they want to spend time with one another (Lakin *et al.* 2005; O'Brien, Thesing and Capie 2005). If we want people with intellectual disabilities to have the possibility of close friendships with non-disabled people, then it is important to pay particular attention to the type of activities people are being supported to do.

In the two years that we were involved with the staff group at 64 Penny Lane, there was really only one activity that had any chance of resulting in *community participation*. More than anything else, this arose from imagining ways in which a resident's preferred activity might be used to break out of the 'distinct social space'.

A number of clinical labels had been used to describe Franco, who was 51, and had lived in Kew Residential Services for 41 years. In addition to having 'profound mental retardation due to unknown cause', he had also been diagnosed as having autism, epilepsy, pica, a premorbid personality and a psychotic disorder. At the start of the research his behaviour was talked about problematically, especially in social contexts. The house supervisor stated:

I don't want to sound negative towards Franco but it's difficult to take him into a group setting, particularly in a closed community area because he gets very anxious. So we've got to take every opportunity that we can so the other fellas can experience that type of community access, where we go down a different line for Franco.

This 'different line' reflected the house supervisor's vision of what was important, and might be achieved for Franco: eating at a restaurant or café with staff support.

We've got a long process that's in place for Franco. I've got a goal of 6 to 12 months [where] we'll be able to take him into a restaurant or café without him getting anxious and wanting to get up and go. That's why it's very important that we [teach him to sit at the dining table in the house].

In addition to this goal, there was also a consensus amongst the staff team who supported Franco that 'walking' was an activity that he liked to do. He was often supported to go for walks, either 'around the block', along the local creek or driven to a place where he could walk. The most likely outcome of these supported walks was *community presence*. This was mainly because the staff group supported this activity in a service-centred way. A member of the staff 'took' Franco on a walk and 'brought' him back to his home, with little concern for whether there were any interactions with other people, although as one member of the staff team pointed out, 'A member of the public might say "hello" whilst walking along Arthur's Creek.'

During the research, one of the authors joined a bush-walking group in the area where he lived, which had a relatively large membership and arranged walks of varying lengths on a weekday and at the weekend. A bush-walking group is a *community of interest* (see Table 6.1). We suggested that if a similar group could be found close to 64 Penny Lane, then such a group offered a reasonable chance for facilitating *community participation*. A walking group provides the context where the same people participate in a recurring activity where social interaction is high. People walk and talk, and stop for rests, where they sit and take refreshment. Although a staff member would have to support Franco initially, we could envision the possibility that, in time, it might be possible for a member or members of the walking group to support him to walk once a week. This would require the staff member to find a way of shifting the support given to Franco from being *service-based* to being *naturally* available. This distinction between service-based (or formal) supports and natural (or informal) supports is made by Luckasson *et al.* (2002). *Building inclusive communities* requires support beyond that provided by human service employees (e.g. health and social care employees), to include resources and strategies provided by people or equipment in a person's 'natural environment' (e.g. friends and family members).

Rather than a bush-walking group, Franco's keyworker gathered information about urban orienteering. Orienteering is a family of sports that require navigation using a map and compass. Urban orienteering involves navigating through parks and streets, with the aim being to locate checkpoints on various natural and man-made features along the way, such as a bench seat or street lamp.

Urban orienteering seemed to offer the possibility for the same people to meet routinely. It had a rolling programme of events, which were likely to be attended by regular participants, and the nature of the activity allowed for interactions between people. Participants gathered together at the start of the evening, could stay for a drink at the end, and the less competitive participants could walk and talk between control sites. Presentation evenings provided a different context for social interactions.

The staff supported Franco to purchase some walking shoes. They served as an 'object of reference', which proved successful in communicating to Franco that orienteering would be happening in the near future.

He'll go and get those trainers in order to go orienteering. He'll show you, and put them on, and give you his foot to do up the shoelaces. He even grabs my handbag and my keys, like, 'We're going orienteering tonight.' He'll have dinner and then come in the office and get my handbag. He knows.

An entry in the Activity Learning Log, following Franco's first try, hints at the possibilities for engaging with other participants.

Orienteering at night-time. Franco was eager to go in the bus and on arrival paced until we picked up the map and card, and off we went, with the help of a kind woman. We walked for nearly one hour, Franco started to tire but went really well. We walked to different points and punched our card. He did not seem to mind at all about walking in the dark. I definitely think this activity should be repeated.

For a period of time Franco was not in the 'distinct social space' commonly occupied by people with intellectual disabilities, but was in the company of the staff member and 'a kind woman' who shared his interest in walking. Franco's involvement in this ordinary activity was especially encouraging, given the staff group's initial concerns about his behaviour.

Perceptions about people's long-standing behaviours of concern should not be dismissed, but neither should 'challenging behaviour' be a reason to exclude people with intellectual disabilities. As we have stated before, the appropriate response to these kinds of problems is largely made up of what people do and how well they are organised and trained. Members of the public can learn appropriate responses. Entries in the Activity Learning Logs reflected staff concerns about Franco's anxiety.

Franco was very excited before leaving the house as he was told prior that he was going on the bus. Once there I got Franco to hold the map and torch. Franco didn't really enjoy being near everyone else when it was starting as there were a lot of people but once everyone started to walk it was better for him and he relaxed a little. Very good night.

Supporting Franco to participate in this activity also helped to change the way in which the staff group talked about future possibilities for him. Nearly two years after the house supervisor's previous remark, another member of staff, initially a *community participation* sceptic, said:

You'd be surprised who we can [form] friendships with, people from different races, different beliefs, different everything. I know we're just taking a baby-step and I think we've got a long way to go. I'm not sure if Franco's going to form a friend with someone, we really can't say. I can't say to you that you're going to form a friend with someone tomorrow from a group you've never attended before but I think if we continue with these one-on-one activities I can see someone spending time with Wally and I can even see someone spending time with Franco, believe it or not, and saying, 'Come on mate, we'll go for a walk and then go for a Coca-Cola or a milkshake at McDonald's.' It's not farfetched, it can come real, but I don't know if it's going to happen or not because I'm not psychic. I think anything's possible.

Importantly, Franco's keyworker had also begun to think and act differently, understanding that she had a facilitative role in developing natural supports.

The people that run [orienteering] know Franco now. At the presentation night there was a trestle table set up and it had quite a lot of food and drinks. So, obviously not the ideal situation for Franco to sit in a room full of people with a trestle table full of food and drinks. I did speak to the guy that runs it and he said, 'You know, not a problem.' If by chance Franco did win [an award] he would do a presentation of who Franco was, where he'd come from and how he'd come to winning this thing, and that in turn makes everybody else more aware of Franco. He's there and he may have an intellectual disability but he'll still be there every week and he'll still do exactly what they're doing.

Figure 6.3 shows the three associations between *community presence* and *community participation* that we have discussed. The first keeps people in the 'distinct social space', the second alters its composition for short periods, whilst the third offers the possibility for breaking out of it.

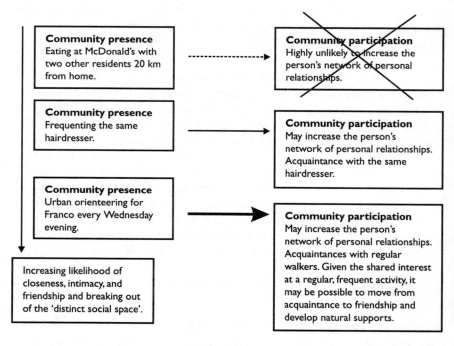

Figure 6.3 Staff-supported activities: Possibilities for transforming the 'distinct social space'

Ideas to help staff to facilitate *community participation* can be expressed relatively simply:

- Find places where the same people can meet routinely, and social interaction is high, so that non-disabled people can have direct experience of people with intellectual disabilities.

- Help people gain familiarity with one another so that they can make a decision about whether they want to spend time with each other.

- Ensure that staff understand that part of their role is to expand the social networks of people with intellectual disabilities to include relationships with non-disabled people.

- Give staff the knowledge and skills they need to provide support to people with intellectual disabilities in a way that looks beyond service-based supports towards informal or natural supports. (Luckasson *et al.* 2002)

Like many simple ideas, they are easy to write or say, but a lot harder to achieve. In the final part of this chapter we want to name some of the issues that surfaced in our research, which worked against the research goal of altering the residents' pattern of relationships with non-disabled people.

Intellectual disability: A label that sticks

Despite all the 'people first' rhetoric, it does seem that being categorised as a person with intellectual disability limits an individual from being seen in other ways (Finlay and Lyons 2005). There are numerous other bases of identity, such as being a fan of *Buffy the Vampire Slayer* or Arsenal Football Club, but they are often ignored in favour of 'intellectual disability'.

Although Howard Becker's (1963) sociology of deviance, or more specifically 'labelling theory', has less cachet than it once did, it still has some explanatory power. 'Labelling theory' suggests that a label, such as 'intellectual disability', defines an individual as a particular type of person. The term contains an evaluation of the person so labelled, and has a 'master status' that clouds all other characteristics. Other people view the person, and respond to that person, in terms of the label (Haralambos and Holborn 1991). This process seems to be extremely marked in regard to people with profound intellectual disabilities.

It is the case that any individual or group identity based on the term 'intellectual disability' is unlikely to have any personal meaning for people with severe and profound intellectual disabilities, i.e. their level of intellectual disability means that these abstract concepts will not be understood, recognised or applied to themselves. What is important about this fact is that the diagnostic label and the social category are more salient to the people that support them and the people they come into contact with.

Being labelled as 'intellectually disabled' has consequences for people with severe and profound intellectual disabilities. Most people in their lives see the disability as being an important fact about them, if not the most important fact, and most of their lives are organised around the social category. Societies invest a lot of energy in creating environments for people with intellectual disabilities and direct support staff can put a lot of additional effort into making sure that they spend time in each other's company.

The making of this 'distinct social space'

O'Brien and O'Brien write that, 'Modern patterns of practice and belief segregate and isolate people with developmental disabilities as a matter of course' (1993, p.10). Although human service employees have a significant role in combating social exclusion, their actions also ensure that segregation is an important opposing process.

Service-settings, such as a group home or a day programme, represent the 'distinct social space' in its most elemental form. Hundreds of thousands of people with intellectual disabilities live in group homes, supported by paid staff, where the major visitors are other people with intellectual disabilities and relatives. Day programmes tend to provide services to large numbers of people with intellectual disabilities. As people with severe and profound intellectual disabilities often use specialist transport services to get to and from day programmes, a significant part of their day is spent in this 'distinct social space'. Interacting with non-disabled people is impossible in many circumstances, because we create situations where the boundaries of the 'distinct social space' are relatively impervious, or non-disabled people are nowhere in the vicinity. Contrast the possibilities for interacting with non-disabled people when travelling to a day programme in a group home's minibus, as opposed to using public transport.

Governments also provide money to organisations to run specialist leisure services. Others are run by volunteers. The Wyreena Community Arts Centre in Victoria offers programmes specifically for people with disabilities called Art Action, Let's Create and Creative Capers (ERLS Inc. 2006). Rec-Line is a recreation, leisure and holiday service for adults who have an intellectual disability in Victoria (Oakleigh Centre 2006). There are hundreds of Gateway Clubs in the United Kingdom, offering sports and leisure opportunities for people with an intellectual disability. These clubs are the 'leisure arm' of Mencap, the largest disability charity in the UK. All of these settings bring people together on the basis of 'intellectual disability'. A person who lives in a group home, attends a day programme and then goes to the Gateway Club in the evening may spend the entire day in the 'distinct social space'.

Given that human service employees choose to use these settings on behalf of people with profound intellectual disabilities, it is hard not to argue that the residents are perceived as a type of people who should mix with one another in certain places.

Bonding and bridging relationships

We can make a link between the concept of common ties and the distinction between *bonding* and *bridging relationships* (Putnam, Feldstein and Cohen 2004). The former are relationships between people who have things in common, whilst the latter are links between people who do not *seemingly* have things in common.

Within the 'distinct social space', we have flagged 'intellectual disability' as a characteristic that one group of people have in common. In the context of our research we would include some additional common ties: the Department of Human Services' (DHS) service-users who are supported by DHS employees; people with a shared history of living in Kew Residential Services (KRS); and relative proximity within a geographical area. These characteristics meant that staff looked to make links, not only with other people with intellectual disabilities in general, but other DHS service-users and employees, and other people who used to live at KRS who live nearby. All of these links tend to keep people within the 'distinct social space'.

As part of the aforementioned training, *Developing community connections at a local level*, a group of staff identified ten-pin bowling as an activity to get a resident more 'connected' with the community. Two actions they suggested to 'achieve' this arose from seeing intellectual disability as the primary organising category. One participant suggested contacting the bowling centre to find out if they had a time for people with intellectual disabilities. Another suggested creating a bowling group, by contacting other group homes to see if other residents wanted to go bowling. If these options were pursued, rather than create meaningful connections with non-disabled people, they would merely create other spaces where people with intellectual disabilities would congregate together.

We observed some energy being put into developing links with residents in other DHS group homes. The men at 64 Penny Lane were supported to visit three other group homes during December, the season for Christmas parties. 'Intellectual disability', 'DHS service-users' and 'proximity' were important characteristics that bound people from different group homes together. By virtue of these qualities, people who might otherwise be strangers to one another ended up having afternoon tea together. A staff member recorded this entry in the Activity Learning Log:

Dan, Joseph, Milan and Wally went to another CRU [group home] for afternoon tea. The guys met the five residents and their families. They shook hands and then sat down to the birthday cake. The residents at [the group home] were very interactive with the guys, trying to engage them in chats. The guys were very eager to eat the party food and cake. One of the [group home] staff arrived with her dog, causing anxiety to Dan, Joseph and Milan. The dog was moved into the staff's car, but Dan was still anxious. Dan started pointing to the bus and the rest of the guys followed. We left shortly after.

Pragmatic concerns also resulted in links between staff members and residents in different group homes, such as sharing a bus ride to a day programme. We observed managers actively encouraging bonds to form with other group homes, in order to engender feelings of 'community' and of being more supported. This was referred to as a 'buddy system'. Another group home was termed a 'sister house'. 'Emergency Management Plans' were developed using this network. In one region, the fire evacuation policy was to put the residents in the minibus and drive them to the nearest group home. If your frame of reference is such that the nearest source of support is a group home five to ten minutes away, you may miss the possibilities for developing supportive relationships that are much closer.

One of the authors was preparing lunch for friends when his oven packed up. He went to his next-door neighbours and asked whether he could finish cooking the meal in their oven. Later the same week, another neighbour on the opposite side of the road, who has two small children, called to ask whether she could use the washing machine as hers had broken. People who work in group homes should not lose sight of the fact that the people who live in the same street and the immediate neighbourhood are potential sources of help and friendliness.

The development of bridging relationships may require a simple reframing of how we perceive commonality. Rather than thinking that the people who live next door to a group home have nothing in common with the five men at 64 Penny Lane, they could be perceived as neighbours, with common ties to the neighbourhood. Franco could be perceived as a person who likes walking, who is a fellow member of an urban orienteering club.

We found raising issues such as these with direct support staff to be contentious, as they often perceived our comments as a blanket condemnation of their current practice, rather than a recommendation for supplementary practices. There is nothing inherently 'wrong' with any of the human service actions that we have described in this chapter, as natural supports are unlikely to replace service-based supports entirely. Yet it is important that human service employees understand the consequences of their actions, i.e. they tend to keep people within the 'distinct social space'. If we are serious about 'inclusion' then there needs to be a better balance between the use of service-based and natural supports.

Building inclusive communities in confused and incoherent times

In suggesting that there is nothing 'wrong' with the human service actions we have described, we are 'tipping our hat' to that confused term 'post-modernism' (Osbourne 2002). In a post-modern world it seems much harder to equivocally state that something is 'wrong' or 'right'. Ideology should not deny a person the right to attend a Gateway Club if he or she chooses to do so. Many activities currently supported by direct support staff, such as going shopping at the supermarket, are not going to be entirely replaced by natural supports. Post-modernism encourages us to accept different perspectives, either as a pluralistic gesture of tolerance or as representing many truths.

Two other ideas that are linked to post-modernism are 'fragmentation' and the 'celebration of difference'. Since the 1980s intense community-building has been done in the name of 'difference', 'identity politics', 'multiculturalism' and 'the politics of recognition' (Anspach 1979; Gilson, Tusler and Gill 1997; Zola 1987). This has created a more fragmented environment; one in which working towards the goal of *building inclusive communities* seems more confused. As Jonathan Friedman writes: 'One of the things that is not happening is that boundaries are disappearing. Rather, they seem to be erected on every street corner of every declining neighbourhood of our world' (1999, p.241).

Some actions of the disability movement seem to have resulted in the strengthening of boundaries between people with and without disabilities (Fraser 1996). 'Disabled people' can now be seen as a particular community, group or population that have different experiences to non-disabled people. They have a particular identity and can promote their own interests. This description of Club Wild, for example, appears in an 'accessible and inclusive sport and recreation' guide: 'An organisation run by and for people with disabilities…[that] creates opportunities for people with disabilities to express their unique cultural identities, to celebrate and affirm these within their own communities' (ERLS Inc. 2006, p.20). Rather than these boundaries being drawn from the outside, they have been drawn from the inside, which Bauman (2001) described as a form of 'self-enclosure'. Club Wild could be seen as part of the 'distinct social space'. However, rather than enforced segregation, inhabiting this social space arises from the principle of self-segregation. So, one day a direct support staff may be asked to build bridging relationships with non-disabled people at an urban orienteering event; the next, support someone to attend an activity that appears to reify boundaries between people with and without disabilities, such as Club Wild or a self-advocacy organisation.

Some issues related to the 'marginalisation' of people with profound intellectual disabilities appear to be more clear-cut in comparison to people with moderate and mild intellectual disabilities. Whereas people with mild intellectual disabilities might choose to spend an evening at the Gateway Club, a self-advocacy meeting, visiting a friend in another group home or going late-night shopping with a friend with intellectual disabilities, this is not the case for many people with severe or profound intellectual disabilities. Spending a significant amount of their lives in the 'distinct social space' has very little to do with the 'choices' made by people with profound intellectual disabilities, but much more to do with the beliefs and choices made on their behalf by other people, predominantly staff and relatives. Yet taking a person with a profound intellectual disability to a Gateway Club is made more legitimate if a person with mild intellectual disabilities is electing to go to one too.

There is no blueprint for a society where there is 'full and effective inclusion and participation' (United Nations 2006). To borrow Zygmunt Bauman's phrase, it is a 'community of our dreams' (2001, p.4). Transforming society from how it is now to how we imagine it could be does not follow a linear path. Some contemporary spaces may merely be transitional ones. Bauman distinguishes between 'real' and 'voluntary' ghettos. Whereas the former are places from which insiders cannot get out, the chief purpose of the latter, where insiders are free to come and go as they please, is to bar outsiders from entry. Bauman writes,

'The real ghettos mean denial of freedom. Voluntary ghettos are meant to serve the cause of freedom' (p.117). A self-advocacy organisation, with a focus on speaking up for the rights of people with intellectual disabilities, epitomises such an organisation. The transitory nature of such spaces is suggested by Bridget Whittell and her colleagues:

> Ultimately...self-advocacy is only a means to an end. In the future, members [of self-advocacy organisations]...hoped they would be able to move on from belonging to a self-advocacy group as it would no longer be necessary when they had achieved equal rights and paid jobs. (1998, p.56)

Other contemporary spaces may turn out to be cul-de-sacs on the way to this imagined society. In the meantime we have to face the fact that there are social spaces that appear to be incongruent with the goal of *building inclusive communities*, such as institutions; others that are more clearly aligned to it, such as the supermarket and the urban orienteering club; and some that have a more ambiguous relationship, such as a self-advocacy organisation. What seems important is that the functions and purpose of all social spaces are scrutinised in relation to the larger goal.

Organisational capacity

Organisations only have so much capacity to achieve their goals. For human service organisations in Victoria, *building inclusive communities* is only one goal, and facilitating relationships with non-disabled people is but one facet of that goal. Making the distinction between what needs to be done and situations where there is greater choice is useful in explaining why people with intellectual disabilities are still socially excluded.[5]

In a group home, a significant proportion of staff time is taken up with tasks that need to be done. Food must be bought, cooked, eaten and the dishes washed. People must be helped to wash, dress and complete their laundry. There are a number of organisational tasks that are given importance, especially administrative tasks. People go to day programmes and may need to be driven there and picked up. People have to get their hair cut, buy new shoes and visit their GP. This reduces the amount of time available where people are truly free to decide how to spend it. When all these necessary tasks are completed, direct support staff have only a limited amount of unconstrained time to organise the lives of people with profound intellectual disabilities. Some might be spent relaxing at home, or going to the beach with a support worker or visiting another group home. These are legitimate choices, but they reduce the time available to work at *community participation*. Days may be filled with so many other tasks to do that there is no time, or negligible time left, for facilitating meaningful relationships with non-disabled people.

The more time people with intellectual disabilities spend in group homes, at day programmes, using segregated leisure facilities, in a minibus, participating in group trips, or engaging in activities that lead to *community presence*, then the less chance there is to change their pattern of social relationships.

O'Brien (1987) makes the point that 'inclusion' requires focused effort. Given that organisational capacity is limited, and that *community participation* may not be an everyday priority for many staff, ways need to be found of bringing it into focus and making sure that direct support staff allocate some of their time to work at it. Person-Centred Planning (PCP) may help in this regard, because a foundational principle is to strengthen the connections between people with intellectual disabilities and non-disabled people (Sanderson *et al.* 2002). However, even though the largest formal outcome evaluation of PCP to date found benefits in certain 'quality of life' domains, it showed no impact on 'inclusive social networks' (Robertson *et al.* 2005, 2006). A keyworking system, discussed in Chapter 4, is another planning mechanism that could help staff to focus on *community participation* as an outcome.

In the organisation we studied, and in many others that manage group homes, direct support staff have been given a key role in changing the pattern of social relationships for residents in a group home. This is on top of all the other tasks they have to undertake, many of which have a greater day-to-day priority. Other approaches to facilitating relationships with non-disabled people remove the onus from direct support staff. This includes specific schemes to link people with intellectual disabilities with volunteers (Gaskell 1985; Hardman and Clark 2006; Walsh 1984); the creation of specific positions to work with a small number of residents, called a 'Ties and Connections Worker' in one organisation (Whittington 1993); and the creation of 'circles of support' (Wertheimer 1995). If residential service providers are to have greater success in *building inclusive communities*, an effective strategy is likely to be multipronged, rather than one that leaves achieving this goal solely to group homes' direct support staff.

Community attitudes

In discussing the journey on the tram to the shopping mall, we described how one passenger had created as much distance as he could between himself and the residents, by moving to the other end of the carriage. The house supervisor spoke about this in an interview:

On the tram, as we were getting in, Joseph balanced and put his arm on another fella. I was quite surprised. The fella would have been in his mid-fifties. He got up for Joseph and I said, 'Thanks.' There was enough room to sit down. 'No, no, no, I'll go down the other end,' he said. So he got as far away from them as possible. He was right down the other end of the tram. Those sorts of things you experience.

Most direct support staff have stories about 'negative' responses to the people that they support. The worst stories reflect experiences of isolation, rejection, hostility and avoidance. Direct support staff have been charged with facilitating relationships with non-disabled people in what some writers have called a 'handicapist' or 'disabling' society (Abbott and McConkey 2006; Blatt *et al.* 1977/1981; Ramcharan *et al.* 1997). Identifying indifferent or negative attitudes within 'the community' was a theme that staff returned to throughout the research. Negative experiences may make human service employees less, rather than more, likely to act as facilitators of bridging relationships (see Clegg and Lansdall-Welfare 2003).

I think there needs to be more public recognition. There needs to be more acceptance of somebody with a disability. I believe the development of a person with a disability, whether physical, intellectual or even mental illness, is in the hands of the ignorant. Until we are able to establish a better education for the general community, those with disabilities will always struggle with acceptance.

It is no surprise to find that non-disabled members of any society hold disparate attitudes towards intellectual disability (see Yazbeck, McVilly and Parmenter 2004, for example). It is all too easy to dismiss people with less accepting views as ignorant, ill-mannered or bigoted. Jennifer Clegg (2006) suggests that it may be fruitful to focus on the difficulties non-disabled people experience when they first encounter somebody with significant disabilities. The fact that people with intellectual disabilities spend a lot of time in the 'distinct social space' means that many non-disabled people have little or limited direct experiences of them. Clegg writes:

When first meeting an adult with intellectual disability you do not know whether they will speak to you and, if not, whether their silence indicates shyness or inability. Some speak with such poor articulation that you cannot understand; or the omission of a crucial piece of information means you understand the words but not their meaning. You may find it hard to look at the person because of unusual features. The person may be warm if somewhat over-friendly as they hug you; equally, they may be suspicious, distressed or rejecting. Small wonder that many find this interactional space disconcerting. (pp.128–9)

As well as an intellectual disability, people may have a secondary disability such as blindness, deafness, physical impairment or epilepsy. 'Other difficulties or behaviours include incontinence, movement disorders, self-harm or assaults on others. The person may also have socially disconcerting features: dysmorphic faces, baldness, drooling, stereotyped behaviours, or they may make strange noises' (Clegg 2006, p.127).

Dan, who is in his fifties and a resident at 64 Penny Lane, was supported to go swimming. A member of staff wrote these entries in the Activity Learning Log, from separate visits to the leisure centre:

Once Dan was in the pool he made lots of movement in the water with his hands. He was happy for me to lead him through the small kiddie pool, sliding along on his bottom. He waved his arms and smiled a lot when we were sitting near the water jets. The small pool had a gradual decline to the water so Dan was able to sit down and scoot forward on his bum. He picked up a flotation device and held it up to a jet to deflect the water. With a small amount of encouragement, Dan put his head under water and lay on his stomach. Dan scoffed down chips as a treat on the way home, smiling a lot and pulling my hand and pointing out the window.

We arrived half an hour before the session to give Dan time to get used to the surroundings. An hour would be better. Dan was very reluctant to get into the small pool by going down the step. After a while in the small pool, we headed to the larger pool. Dan was very unsure on his feet getting down the eight or so steps. Once at the bottom Dan was clearly uncomfortable, grinding his teeth and had a very anxious look on his face. We moved out of the larger pool. He was happy however to spend another half an hour in the small pool.

Other swimmers at the leisure centre may have heard Dan grind his teeth or seen a middle-aged man scooting along on his bottom in the children's pool, in both instances accompanied by people who are there to 'care' or 'support' him. Given that people with limited direct experiences of intellectual disability are likely to have prejudiced and stereotypical views of 'intellectual disability', then witnessing such behaviour or having a short 'uncomfortable' encounter with Dan may confirm the prejudice rather than challenge it.

Clegg (2006) asserts that the growth of tolerance and acceptance will not happen by condemning or ignoring people who react 'negatively' to 'others' who appear to be 'a bit too different'. Acknowledging this 'disconcerting interactional space' is a step on the way to working out how to deal with it. This will not always be easy. How, for example, should the staff on the tram have responded to the passenger who went and sat at the other end of the carriage? Was it their role to pursue the man the length of the carriage in order to share some ideas about people with intellectual disability with the aim of changing his way of relating to Joseph?

Limited control and influence

Many of the goals that are subsumed by 'inclusion' are an attempt to shape and control public attitudes towards people with disabilities. They also aim to enhance the role played by members of the general public in supporting them. As we have made clear, the goal of *building inclusive communities* requires the expansion of service-users' informal personal relationships. This is a social engineering project that will require the penetration of official institutions into people's private lives. Frank Furedi (2004) terms this 'the colonization of people's informal lives' and he makes the important point that the policies of social inclusion have not been a response to popular demand.

If we exclude the employees of human services, non-disabled people have not demanded that people with disabilities have access to sports centres, cinemas, cafés or supermarkets. Nor have they lobbied for close relationships with people with intellectual disabilities. There is unlikely to be a public outcry from non-disabled people if everyone does not have a close relationship with a person with intellectual disability (Clement 2006).

These issues create a difficult and confusing context in which to facilitate the use of natural supports. Direct support staff are being asked to influence the attitudes and behaviour of non-disabled people, typically in settings where they have little or no control, and in a context at the very limit, or beyond, of their legitimate sphere of influence. The fact that some people are successful in this endeavour is testament to their persistence, resilience and skills.

The research findings of James Gardner and Deborah Curran (2005) suggest that organisations are less successful at facilitating outcomes that are not under their direct control, but rather depend upon supports and services from multiple sources within the community. These include those outcomes related to choices about where and with whom people with intellectual disabilities live with, where they work and the interactions they have with members of the community. How much easier it is for a direct support staff to plan and organise a group trip to the beach at Ocean Grove than it is to concern him or herself with facilitating a meaningful relationship between Franco and a member of the urban orienteering group. It should be no surprise that human service employees are drawn to undertake activities that are within their immediate control.

Concluding remarks

We have highlighted a number of factors that can lead to people with intellectual disabilities having *community presence* and *community participation*, but have implied that those leading to *community presence* are more numerous and have greater strength.

The label of 'intellectual disability' has significant consequences for people in the related social category. Despite the rhetoric of 'inclusion' we still build special environments for people with intellectual disabilities. Human service employees look to forge relationships with other individuals with this label, ensuring that people spend much of their time in the company of people with intellectual disabilities and paid staff. This leaves little time to build relationships with non-disabled people.

At the same time, staff are being asked to build natural supports in a confused broader social context. The goal of 'inclusion' is itself not clear, and staff have little influence over the actions of non-disabled people. People with disabilities call for inclusion but also choose to self-segregate. Processes that exacerbate the social exclusion of people with intellectual disabilities, and processes that improve their inclusion, operate simultaneously.

In part, this helps to explain why there has been less progress towards the goal of 'inclusion' in the last 30 years that we might have hoped. The outcome of 'inclusion' is still an imagined society. As a broad social policy goal, which reflects what society and its people ought to be like, it still holds the promise of a 'better' society.

Issues for consideration

- How can you achieve a better balance between service-based and natural supports for the people you support?

- Scrutinise the activities that people are doing: where are they doing them, who are they doing them with and how are they doing them?

- How can you enlarge people's social networks, particularly by engaging new people who are not known to everyone in the existing network?

- How can you change the composition of people's social networks, specifically by bringing non-disabled people into them?

- How can you change the quality of service-users' relationships with non-disabled people, so that some are characterised by familiarity and friendship?

- Do service-users go to places where they can meet the same non-disabled people routinely, where social interaction is high, so that the non-disabled people can have direct experience of people with intellectual disabilities?

- How can you help people to gain familiarity with one another so that they can make a decision about whether they want to spend time with each other?

- Can you help staff to focus on the difficulties non-disabled people experience when they first encounter somebody with significant disabilities?

- Do direct support staff understand that part of their role is to expand the social networks of people with intellectual disabilities to include relationships with non-disabled people?

- Do direct support staff have the knowledge and skills they need to provide support to people with intellectual disabilities in a way that looks beyond service-based supports towards informal or natural supports? In particular, provide some clarity about the goal of 'inclusion', and support people to deal with the tensions inherent within it.

Notes

1   Intimacy does not necessarily have a sexual connotation here. It has more to do with close-ness and familiarity. In their discussion of intimacy, the King's Fund Centre write, 'We share confidences with some people more than with others. Some of our ties and connections involve a lot of trust' (1988, p.3). Intimacy was one of four qualities they identified as being related to the strength of people's 'ties and connections'. The others were time, intensity and reciprocity.

2   We are indebted to Joanne Martin's (2002) discussion of organisational boundaries in devel-oping our thinking about the nature of boundaries.

3   The distinction is sometimes made between public and private space. Our own homes epito-mise the notion of private space: places that are said to be relatively free from state regula-tions and pressures to adhere to publicly accepted standards of morality (Honderich 1995). This distinction reveals a further way in which group homes are different from 'ordinary homes', as they are more subject to laws, regulations and the authority of others, in compari-son to our own homes.

4   These outings are similar in nature to the group activities from another group home that we discussed in relation to Figure 4.3, where the likely outcome is *community presence*.

5   This is based on the philosophical distinction between the realm of 'necessity' and the realm of 'freedom' (see Honderich 1995).

Chapter 7

Practice Leadership

Introduction

The activities of every employee in a human service organisation should contribute to high-quality outcomes being achieved for the service-users. Yet, when it
comes to group homes, the house supervisor is often perceived as shouldering a
disproportionate responsibility for achieving these outcomes. Not only is she
typically seen as being the key figure in achieving the outcomes we have discussed (creating a home; enabling the residents to have highly individualised
lifestyles; making sure that they are engaged in meaningful activities and experience both *community presence* and *community participation*), but also in the 'quality
of life' domains we have not considered explicitly. This perception is reflected in
the view of a former house supervisor, now a middle-manager:

I believe the house supervisor's role is the key role in [our supported
accommodation service]… It's the most important role. If you look at your
direct care staff, house supervisor and the team manager, I think the house
supervisor counts for 50 per cent of it, 25 per cent direct care staff and the
team manager even less. It's the most important role.

In the organisation where we did our research the house supervisor's job
description states that it is their duty to 'Manage a component of a residential
programme providing direct care services to clients' (DHS 2002a). As an adjunct
to the ethnographic and action research projects discussed so far, we also undertook some semi-structured interviews with an *extreme sample* (Miles and

Huberman 1994) of highly performing house supervisors and more senior managers in order to explore the house supervisor's role in more depth (Clement and Bigby 2007). Most of the quotations in this chapter, and the one that follows, are from those interviews.

This house supervisor's account of her initial experiences at a group home illustrates the scale of the challenges facing some house supervisors and the tenacity required to address them.

When I got here I honest to God, I nearly had a nervous breakdown thinking that a place with so much resources and so much attention could be run so badly. It just tore at my heart, it tore at my spirit. I think I didn't sleep for six months. A couple of times I was nearly suspended from duties 'cos I said, 'No, that's not going to happen any more.' And the staff they'd go, 'Well, no, this is how it's always happened.' [I said,] 'No, which part of "No" don't you understand? If it happens again you'll be on conduct, you will be on conduct, it's not acceptable, just not acceptable.' The office would come down because I was bullying [staff]. And a couple of times I was pulled out for bullying. I had to stop the bullies, had to stop the bullies. I think I was just trying to manage, but you know, when you've got somebody standing over the top of you telling you how it's going to be, and it's a great big man, really I like to stand up and go, 'No!' That can be perceived as bullying, you see. Now they, with their tail between their legs, go to the office and say, 'This is how she treated me,' I sit there and laugh and go, 'Well this is the full story, he's put in the complaint, I now have to respond to it.' I understand all of that, but that's the way it was here, it was a house of blood and bruise, it was just disgusting. It was disgusting. The last knife incident happened because the staff member had done sleepover, they've gotten up and they were cooking themselves bacon and eggs for breakfast. The client came out and gone, 'Ooh, that smells delicious, can I have some?' 'Nup, shut up,' was the actual response. 'You're having Weetbix, you know that's all you're allowed to have.' 'I don't want Weetbix, can't I just have one egg? Why can't I just have one egg? One egg can't be bad for me.' 'Shut up, you know the answer to that question.' So [the resident] picked up the knife that [the staff had] been cutting up their breakfast with and it all happened. I don't believe that she intended to hurt; I believe that she was just bloody over it. But that's the way it was.

It is not our intention to ignore the significance of adequate resources and organisational structures; however, this chapter adopts a more individualised perspective, focusing on the role of the house supervisor. The importance of organisational context is considered in the chapter that follows.

We begin by outlining the knowledge, skills, abilities and orientations (Dipboye, Smith and Howell 1994) required by house supervisors to manage a group home, before discussing the notion of 'practice leadership', a term that has been around for a number of years, but has gained greater currency in intellectual disability services in the twenty-first century. We focus on practice leadership because it is increasingly identified as a concept that will achieve the high-quality outcomes that human service organisations aspire to. In doing so, we put forward some ideas about this inadequately defined term.

The competencies required of house supervisors

Although there are some useful books on managing in human service organisations in general (Brody 1993; Jackson and Donovan 1999; Tropman 2006), and residential services in particular (Burton 1998; Henderson and Atkinson 2003; Seden and Reynolds 2003), Jane Gifford (2006) concluded from her review of the literature that house supervisors' work and experiences have largely been overlooked within the research arena. Of the published research, the work carried out at the University of Minnesota underscores the aforementioned strong link between the house supervisor's management role and service quality. Drawing on a number of studies, Amy Hewitt and Sheryl Larson concluded, 'We are now beginning to appreciate that for direct support professionals, it is the frontline supervisor who defines the job, provides the training, mediates the stresses, creates the culture, helps people find the personally satisfying rewards of direct support work, and establishes a well-functioning work environment' (2005, p.133). Hewitt et al. (2004) encouraged other organisations to review a list of 142 house supervisor competencies, which had emerged from their research (Hewitt et al. 1998).[1] Table 7.1 shows one outcome of a validation study we undertook in Victoria (Clement and Bigby 2007). Although we did not alter their basic organising structure of 14 domains, some of the original competencies were deleted, new ones added, and every statement was reworded to reflect the local context.

Table 7.1 Competency areas for DHS house supervisors (adapted from Hewitt et al. 1998)

Competency area	Definition
1. Enhancing staff relations	House supervisors enhance staff relations by using effective communication skills, encouraging growth and self-development, facilitating teamwork, employing conflict resolution skills and providing adequate supports to staff.
2. Providing direct support	House supervisors provide direct supports to residents and role model such supports to direct support staff by assisting with living skills, communicating and interacting with residents, facilitating community inclusion, maintaining an appropriate physical environment, providing transportation, maintaining finances, developing behaviour support plans and demonstrating the importance of residents becoming active citizens in their neighbourhoods and local communities.
3. Building inclusive communities and supporting residents' networks	House supervisors facilitate and support the development and maintenance of resident support networks through outreach to family members, community members and professionals and through coordination of personal planning sessions in collaboration with the individual served.
4. Support planning and monitoring	House supervisors oversee support planning and monitoring by planning and developing individual goals and outcomes with residents, coordinating and participating in support network meetings, monitoring, documenting and reporting progress toward meeting outcomes, and communicating with other service organisations.
5. Managing staff	House supervisors participate in processes to hire new staff, provide professional development and supervision, facilitate team work and staff meetings, delegate tasks and responsibilities, encourage effective communication, defuse crises/conflicts between staff, and in conjunction with his/her manager respond to grievances and offer, monitor and review fixed-term contracts.
6. Leading training and staff development activities	House supervisors coordinate and participate in direct support staff training by orienting new staff, ensure that staff attend training sessions, document staff participation in training events and support ongoing staff development.

7. Promoting public relations	House supervisors promote public relations by educating community members about people with intellectual disabilities, advocate for the rights and responsibilities of people with intellectual disabilities, contribute to in-service promotional materials and accept students on educational placements.
8. Maintaining homes, vehicles and property	House supervisors coordinate and participate in maintaining homes, vehicles and personal property in proper order.
9. Protecting health and safety	House supervisors ensure that residents are safe and living healthy lives by monitoring safety issues, coordinating, monitoring and documenting medical supports, practising appropriate emergency procedures, responding to emergencies and promoting residents' rights regarding health and safety issues. As the home is also a workplace, house supervisors ensure that the house is a safe and healthy workplace for staff, contractors and visitors.
10. Managing financial activities	House supervisors ensure financial responsibility by managing the Client Expenditure Recording System (CERS), supporting residents in the management of their finances; reviewing, managing and implementing household budgets; arranging payment for specific bills; and completing audits of household and resident finances.
11. Rostering and payroll	House supervisors ensure direct support professionals are rostered, paid and receive time off when requested.
12. Coordinating weekday daytime supports	House supervisors monitor residents' involvement in external activities (e.g. day programmes) and/or ensure that schedules are created for residents who are 'at home' on weekdays that are based on their individual preferences and needs.
13. Coordinating policies, procedures and rule compliance	House supervisors understand and implement current State rules and regulations, the Department of Human Services' policies and practices and ensure that individual rights are protected.
14. Office work	House supervisors communicate effectively in writing and via the telephone, complete various office tasks and utilise the computer effectively for word processing, developing spread sheets and managing databases.

Inherent in the competencies is the knowledge, skills and abilities required to be a successful house supervisor. We do not have space to list the entire 141 competencies that we ended up with, but given their breadth and depth, it is perhaps no surprise that Hewitt and Larson (2005) claimed that the house supervisor's position is one of the most complex and difficult jobs in the field of community human services.[2]

More recently, Larson *et al.* (2007) have validated their competencies nationally, i.e. in the USA, which resulted in five items being dropped from their 'national competency listing'. It seems to be the case that wherever the group home, whether it is in Melbourne, Miami or Minneapolis, and, one might suspect, Manchester, the job of the house supervisor has much in common. That is, the job of house supervisor is underpinned by core competencies, which are transferable from one group home to another.

Although the house supervisor's role is underpinned by core competencies, the fact that changes were made in Victoria to the original list illustrates that there are likely to be specific variations between organisations. Tasks that are performed in some organisations are not in others. A major difference between the North American competencies and 'Victorian' competencies is the extent to which house supervisors are responsible for the recruitment of direct support staff. A number of competency statements relating to recruitment, advertising, background checks and health assessments were not undertaken by the Department of Human Services' house supervisors.[3] This is why the national competency statements must be tailored to a specific organisation.

Specific knowledge in every group home

Whilst we believe that the house supervisor competencies are transferable from one group home to another, we want to emphasise an important way in which group homes differ from one another, which may require house supervisors to have additional, more specific KSAOs. This adds to the challenge of establishing and maintaining high-quality services. In particular, we want to highlight the variability in the residents' personal characteristics and the challenges this creates for managing services. Human beings may share a common humanity, but we also have immense individual differences. This is reflected in the 'personalisation' agenda that we discussed in Chapter 4. As a consequence, a house supervisor (and a staff team) may need very specific KSAOs to effectively support an individual. This may, for example, be related to additional impairments, specific health issues or the presence of challenging behaviour. In one group home a house supervisor may need specific knowledge about

Prader–Willi syndrome, diabetes and self-injurious behaviour but in another may need to know about Auslan[4] and schizophrenia. And, of course, an overarching theme of this book is that people need specific KSAOs to work with people with severe and profound intellectual disabilities.

Such is the variation between people with intellectual differences that some competency statements may not appear to transfer very readily between settings. There is, therefore, a need to think through what the competencies mean in different group homes. For example, if a competent house supervisor seeks opinions from residents when recruiting new staff, then what does this mean for a house supervisor working with people with profound intellectual disabilities? For one of the authors, residents were always involved in the recruitment process for new staff in the group homes he managed, regardless of their level of intellectual disability. People with mild or moderate intellectual disabilities could meaningfully be part of a formal interview panel, whereas residents with severe or profound intellectual disabilities met and interacted with applicants in their home.

Are people with severe or profound intellectual disabilities harder to support?

It is perhaps understandable, although not very helpful, and possibly not even true, to suggest that some group homes are 'easier' to work in than others, although this perception exists. Often this notion of 'ease' is attributed to the residents' personal characteristics. One manager said:

We do have some more attractive houses where residents are quite capable and it's fun, whereas we have some others that are quite 'heavy' in nature because of the resident group and the support needs, or challenging in other ways, but they're probably less attractive to staff.

Possibly more people find it 'easier' to support people with mild intellectual disabilities. However, we are fortunate that direct support staff are differently motivated. Whilst working with people with challenging behaviour does not suit everyone, some staff enjoy the challenge. Others prefer the greater proportion of personal care that accompanies supporting people with severe or profound impairments. Making sure that there is a good 'fit' between the residents and the staff who support them is a key recruitment issue.

Every group home has its challenges, and if a house supervisor takes on board the aspirations of contemporary social policy, then achieving the related goals makes every setting equally hard. Working with people with mild intellectual disabilities is 'easier' if one's sights are set low. An 'easy house' is probably only a group home where staff believe that they can 'take it easy'. Really listening to the aspirations of people with mild intellectual disabilities who live in group homes undermines this service model; hence the promotion of 'supported living' we discussed in Chapter 1. One would expect to see higher levels of choice and decision-making by people with mild intellectual disabilities and some real inroads in achieving valued roles in the community. Often those choices and valued roles can be hard to realise. Typical aspirations about where and who to live with, whether to have a sexual relationship, to get married, to have children or get a job are not easily achieved for people with mild intellectual disabilities.

House supervisor 'orientations': Passion and vocation

Identifying house supervisor competencies through a job analysis is the first step in deciding what to look for in recruiting to the position. Although it is easier to determine the knowledge, skills and abilities (KSAs) necessary to achieve these competencies, it is harder to specify the specific temperaments or attitudes that are needed in the job. Dipboye *et al.* (1994) label these 'orientations'.[5] Having the 'right' temperament or attitude to work with people with intellectual disabilities is generally thought to be important to human service organisations (see Emerson, Hastings and McGill 1994). The importance placed on a house supervisor's personal 'orientation' to the job is summed up by this house supervisor, who told us, 'It's all of [those competencies] but I think the actual attitude of the house supervisor is the important thing.'

Some findings about desirable 'orientations' emerged from interviews we conducted with house supervisors, two of which we labelled as 'passion' and 'vocation'. The passion that the respondents had for working directly with people with intellectual disabilities is clearly embedded in the interview transcripts.

I still feel that I have a lot to contribute in this area. I don't think there's been a day [in 20 years] that I've been unhappy to go to work. Every shift, if there was one thing that I can make even the smallest difference with them that day, that might be assisting someone to have an excellent shower, the best shower, or supporting them to mow the lawn because that's something that a person really wants to do, if I achieve something every day, then I feel like I'm making some improvement, or supporting or assisting the person that I'm with, then that's really exciting to me.

The same house supervisor described working with people with intellectual disabilities as a 'vocation'.

I have a problem with some people looking at it as a job that anybody could [do], that it's an unskilled job, that you don't require skills to do it. Anybody working with other people needs to be incredibly skilled, and consciously want to keep learning from other people around them, from the people they support, and getting more information. It seems to be a dirty word to say it's a 'vocation' to work with other people. I think we get hung up with language sometimes that you're not allowed to say it's a vocation to want to support people with intellectual, physical or sensory disabilities. You have to be fairly passionate about wanting to work with people, to be doing the job.

This passion was directed towards making a positive difference in the residents' lives.

I've been given the job of overseeing four individuals' lives, and my God I'm going to do it to the best of my ability, with or without [the help of the organisation]. I'm going to do it. I take that role very, very, very seriously.

For some people, working with the residents was a positive counterbalance to what this house supervisor saw as less attractive aspects of the role.

I like [being a house supervisor] because you're with the clients. There's a lot of people who do the job because of the rewards you get from working with clients. They are a lovely diversion from the other crap we have to do. There's a lot of stuff we have to do that's mundane and boring, you know, paperwork. So, it's lovely to be able to put all of that away and spend time with them and do music, race around the block with them, walk around the park. That's a lovely way to be able to spend some time with someone, and you're paid to do that. We're paid to be able to assist them to be able to pick up a cup on their own. If you can see them take those little steps, that's why we do all the other 'crap' for want of a better word. I enjoy the job because I do enjoy working with the clients.

Other house supervisors were more content with the balance of tasks.

What attracts me to supervising is I've got the best of both worlds. I've got client contact, so I'm working with clients. I've also got my admin, so I enjoy that. It's not good when you have staffing issues. I like the variety. I can be on a bus and go for a country trip and have this wonderful day out, and then the next day I'm doing paperwork. I've got the best of both worlds.

As we suggested above, these orientations emerged from the interviews we conducted to validate the house supervisor competencies. We would recommend that, given the scepticism we reported from direct support staff about paperwork, a positive orientation from house supervisors towards paperwork is more desirable than seeing it as mundane or boring. Further research is necessary to obtain a more comprehensive list of orientations that might be useful in recruiting suitable house supervisors.

Practice leadership

It is likely that a number of the house supervisor competencies fall under the rubric of 'practice leadership'. This is a concept that is increasingly being flagged as an important aspect of the house supervisor's role. As a phrase, it appears as an undefined term in some earlier writing of Jim Mansell and his colleagues (Mansell 1996; Mansell, Hughes and McGill 1994). In more recent publications about Active Support it has started to be written about as a more defined concept:

> Managers stop spending almost all of their time in the office doing paperwork, problem-solving on the telephone or in meetings. Now they become 'practice-leaders' teaching, guiding and leading their staff in providing person-centred active support to the people they serve. This means they spend most of their time with their staff, coaching them to provide good support. (Mansell *et al.* 2004, p.123)

The suggestion that (first-line) managers spend 'almost all of their time in the office doing paperwork' is probably rhetorical; reflecting the belief that house supervisors spend a disproportionate amount of time doing activities that are not the most important work for someone in their position.

Although the house supervisors in our research had significant administrative responsibilities, a structured diary that 12 house supervisors kept of their work activities revealed that 40 per cent of their recorded activities related to providing direct support to the residents. House supervisors spend a significant amount of their time working directly with residents inside and outside of a group home, although some incumbents might have got the balance wrong.

You've got to be out and about [interacting with residents]. I suppose the one thing that concerns me is sometimes when we get casuals or new staff coming in and saying, 'Well, who's the supervisor here? It couldn't possibly be you, you're out here with everybody and you're not in the office with the door shut.' Surely that's not still something that's going on in the houses? But it would appear that perhaps to some degree it is.

This house supervisor's 'turn of phrase' to describe the practice of house supervisors who spend too much time in the office is apposite.

I think one of the important things for house supervisors [is] not to be seen as the office gopher. I tell the staff I've got to mop the floor every morning otherwise I have a bad day, which is total crap, but what it is about is that I do the same job that every other person [does]. It's not that Alfred sits in the office and plays with the computer all day, but I spend time with the residents, I do things with the residents. I went to the pictures last night with the residents, but I do what I expect the staff to do. I have got [special] jobs and administration tasks as well, but that's not all I do. I'm part of the actual goings on of the house. I think that's very important because staff respond better to managers who are seen as part of the process, rather than separate to the process. You set the standard too. If staff see you cleaning they're going to be more likely to be wanting to clean the house, rather than saying, 'Well hang on, I'm vacuuming the floors at the moment, while that lazy bugger's sitting there on eBay!' So I think that's very important, you set your standards, and people model themselves on what they see you do. They see you talking and chatting with residents, they say, 'Oh it's the proper way to behave,' so they also do that.

The point that Mansell and his colleagues are making is that high levels of meaningful engagement cannot be achieved from the seclusion of the office, but by watching the practice of direct support staff and guiding them towards acceptable performance. Rather than being a manager who has no direct engagement in practice, what Causer and Exworthy (1999) term a *non-practising managing professional*, the house supervisor is a *practising managing professional*, i.e. someone who has some direct engagement in 'professional' practice and the primary responsibility for the management of the day-to-day work of direct support staff. Although house supervisors do not necessarily have a professional qualification, they need to be a person who performs their role to a high level of competence.

Reynolds applies the term *practice-led management* to the front-line manager's position, where the demands of practice situations need to be kept in focus. She writes:

> These links between practice and management are very important in considering the role of the frontline manager. Whatever the layers and length of lines of accountability and management in an organisation, the frontline manager is the closest person in the managerial hierarchy to the delivery of the service or practice… It gives the frontline manager a unique perspective on the needs of service users, the responses they receive and the extent to which responses meet needs…the frontline manager is in touch with the action 'at the sharp end', and this carries particular responsibilities. (2003, p.7)

This house supervisor agrees that being in touch with the action at the sharp end is integral to her role:

When someone says to me 'Such and such a person is doing this', I have an understanding of what they're talking about because I have been involved and I can see it. Being removed from that, when someone's talking to me about an issue or an event that's happened, I'm only going on what my experiences have been in the past, because I haven't been in that environment for a period of time. So I don't know the individual's likes, dislikes, how they cope with changes, stress, all that stuff. So being removed from the hands-on [role] means that I don't have a full understanding of what's going on. In order to be able to give people advice and support, how am I going to do that if I'm not there, still in touch with what the people need, to have an understanding of what their needs are? For me it's always been, if you're removed from it, if you've been sitting behind a desk, then how can you give advice or lead by example? If someone says 'Oh, I've got a problem with such and such', you could try giving them suggestions but I think you can do a better job when you're actually in there and you haven't been removed from it, still being involved with it and still picking up things... If someone comes in and says 'Oh, the task's too hard for me', well I'm thinking, 'I've been doing that task'... I know from experience, because I'm doing that task as well. I think that's important. If you do the task and you're involved, then you can actually make a proper judgement. If you're sitting a little bit away from where the action's happening, then personally I don't think you make a proper judgement.

Regardless of whether practice leadership or practice-led management is the better term (see Clement and Bigby 2007), the important point here is that house supervisors have a key role in supporting the effective performance of the direct support staff.[6] Our aim in this chapter is to concentrate on making clearer the meaning of these related terms.

Perceptions of practice leadership

It seems likely that practice leadership will establish itself as a recognised term, as it already has some currency in the extant literature, and is being more actively promoted. However, it was not a term that had percolated down to the mid-level managers and house supervisors that we interviewed. In general, we found that incumbents spoke about their job with little reference to theoretical frameworks, but expressed 'practitioner knowledge' (Pawson et al. 2003), offering explanations about practice leadership in language that was more familiar to them. We have linked their words to 'tried and tested' frameworks but see our respondents' spoken words as a useful way of explicating the concept of practice leadership. A manager said:

I actually haven't heard of [practice leadership] before, until you've mentioned it now. I would assume that it's a role modelling term; the expectation is that house supervisors are going to be good role models for the CRU [group home] staff that work within their team. It's not really a term that I've heard before.

Two house supervisors, both unfamiliar with the term, similarly described it in terms of (role) modelling.

I've no idea what [practice leadership] means. It means I'm trying to practise being a leader! [Laughs.] I honestly don't know what that would mean. I suppose that I lead by the practice that I work? Modelling is the thing that we do all the time. Being a new person in this house, with the old staff, they'll say, 'Oh you can't do that.' [Yet] the guys [residents] would respond to what I did instantly. And I'd go, 'Why can't I do that?' If you don't model it then they're not going to understand that it's going to work. And if you model it and it doesn't work, well that's fine; you go off and try something else. It's just the way I've always appeared to do it.

I haven't heard [the job of house supervisor described in practice leadership] terms, but that's a given... I am the house supervisor. It's in everything I do. I emanate...I sweat 'supervisor'. I see myself as the role model in everything I do, always. Even role modelling being relaxed. Even role modelling, 'Take it easy, this rule we can bend, you don't have to follow every rule that strictly.' Trying to role model every aspect.

Implicit in these quotations is an important element of practice leadership, that house supervisors must consciously and deliberately demonstrate ways of behaving for staff (and residents) so that they learn that this is the way that they are expected to behave.

There are a number of different ways that house supervisors can act as a role model. This house supervisor talked about how she could role model in a relatively informal way, identifying a time when she could show a staff member how to complete a teaching programme.

I think you do [practice leadership] without even knowing you're doing it. Some people will look at a programme and it's daunting. 'Oh I don't know how to do a programme; I don't know how to do a cooking programme.' So you're going to say, 'Well this is what you need to do. Look, I'm on with you on Tuesday night, this is how it is.' It is a lot of role playing. I don't think it's so formal, I think it's more visual. It's a lot of things that you know through your own time here. I don't know if it's so much leadership, I think it's more role modelling and communicating effectively with information. I don't know if I'd walk about thinking I'm a leader.

Demonstrating practice leadership 'without even knowing you're doing it' suggests that this house supervisor has practised this 'ability' so much that it has become 'second nature'. This is a useful reminder that learning is a process and that people go through various stages when learning a new ability, behaviour or skill. 'Doing something without even knowing you're doing it' evokes *unconscious competence*, the end stage in the 'conscious competence learning model' (Boag 1998).

A recurring proposition was that house supervisors would not ask people to do something that they would not do themselves, i.e. they model everything. Being involved in everything in this way sets the 'tone' for the direct care staff.

The basic premise is, 'I'm there.' I take on all roles. If there's muck to be cleaned up, I'm there cleaning it up, because I have to set the standard. I have to set the expectation. Many a time I'll be in the toilet cleaning up the muck, dry retching, leaving the room and laughing, 'It's okay.' It's not a pleasant job, no one should think it's a pleasant job, because it's just not. That is the reality of the situation, the real side to it.

In a similar vein this house supervisor talked about 'practising what you preach'.

Well the way I would look at [practice leadership] is it's just a matter of practising what you preach. If you're talking about Positive Behaviour Support then you've got to carry that out. I've heard through casuals and staff that have worked at other houses about supervisors who will say, 'You've got to do this, you've got to do that,' but they don't do it themselves. In my opinion leadership is: if you want your staff to do something then model it, work the same way. That's what I try to do here anyway.

Respondents highlighted the importance of being 'visible' to staff. Direct support staff cannot informally pick up on good practice if they do not witness it.

Practice leadership [is] just what you do in the everyday sort of thing. It's the way you communicate, the way you talk to someone. Say I was addressing one of the guys. If there's staff around, that's going to impact on how they're going to talk to [the residents]. How I address that person, the wording, and my tone of voice. If I show respect and dignity, [the staff are] going to do the same. So practice leadership would be doing that, where you lead by example. It's like role modelling, what you do, then other people will tend to do the same, like having them involved in making choices. My staff go 'You know this person can't talk', or 'This person just likes to sit there, so I'll decide what they're going to have.' It's saying, 'How about we put something in front of them and let's see if they give some sort of indication.' Just by doing that then staff tend to follow that later on and do the same thing.

Implicit in this quotation is a distinction between a more passive and active form of role modelling. The former is suggested in the first half of the quotation, where the hope is that the staff member will somehow pick up on what she sees, whereas the second half points to an active intervention. The house supervisor indicated that she was aware of what was happening in the house, listened to what the staff members were saying and as a consequence gave some guidance or instruction. These are key elements of coaching (Stone 1998), which is nicely portrayed in this example.

I walked into the bathroom a couple of weeks ago and there's a staff assisting one of our clients to dress themselves. 'Don't do that,' just quietly, 'Don't do that.' And she looked and she thought, 'Oh!' This resident knew exactly what she was doing 'cos she looked at me and smiled. I took the clothes off the staff member and I said, 'Put that on. What do you think you're doing? You expect us to work?' She's laughing, and she dressed herself and that staff member was absolutely amazed.

Although 'coaching' appeared less frequently as a spontaneous term in the interview transcripts, respondents did use it or recognised it as a term that they could attach to their behaviour. Coaching is a form of on-the-job training, which Stone (1998) describes as a process by which employees obtain the knowledge, skills and abilities to become effective in their jobs. Although similar or even synonymous with the active role modelling described above, making clear to staff what they should do and how they should do it through the coaching process is another aspect of practice leadership.

Unfortunately, as we suggested in Chapter 5, staff (and residents) can learn to behave in unwanted ways by exactly the same process. Work groups can exert social pressure on individual employees to behave in inappropriate ways. This house supervisor underscores the key point, that it is house supervisors, not direct support staff, who must have the primary practice leadership responsibility, which is why house supervisors must retain a significant practice role.

If you're not out being an example of [good practice] every day then who is leading the staff? What are they seeing every day? What's being reinforced, the staff member who is really prescriptive and really directive? So [the residents] just go, 'All right, I know this is familiar, so this is what's routine.' A new staff comes in, 'Well that works. I've never worked in a house before, you yell and you're really loud, and then [the residents] just all do what they're supposed to do.'

House supervisors recognised that being a role model meant that they needed to be competent. Maintaining a high standard placed a good deal of responsibility on them to be 'perfect' all the time.

You need to be good at what you're doing, skilled in all aspects of what you're doing, and needing to be able to correct or direct your staff in their practice; role modelling good practice yourself. Fitting in that role, as well as doing the office role, is a big task.

An interesting extension of the research by Larson *et al.* (2007) was asking respondents to identify the point in time at which a house supervisor needs to be proficient at each of the competencies they identified. Seventy-five per cent or more of the respondents reported that house supervisors needed to be competent in 66 skills (just over 45 per cent of the total number) within 30 days of starting a new position, including 27 (just under 20 per cent of the total number) in which house supervisors needed to be competent at the time of hire. Although this has implications for recruitment, training, support and mentoring, it also highlights the significant number of competencies that a house supervisor must possess very quickly if a well-functioning work environment is to be established.

Low levels of coaching

The passive form of role modelling relies on house supervisors' practices being seen by other staff members and the active form, which hereafter we refer to as coaching, on having the time to show or model practice in a more formal way. Even though house supervisors spent a significant amount of time directly supporting residents, the way that support was organised meant that only a small proportion of a house supervisor's practice was likely to be witnessed by other staff members. In the morning a house supervisor may be supporting a person to have the 'best' shower, but this was unlikely to be seen by another staff member who would have been helping another resident to shower, get dressed or eat breakfast. Or later in the day the house supervisor may be supporting a resident to make a cake, whilst a second staff member is out picking up the residents from a day programme. Although such modelling is important, expecting staff to pick up good practice in this way represents a 'wishful thinking' or weaker approach to delivering quality services. A stronger intervention, through coaching, is going to be more effective, although it was little reported in the house supervisors' structured diaries.

Fewer than 0.25 per cent of the total number of activities recorded by house supervisors in their structured diaries were coded under the 'role modelling' competency ('modelling, teaching and coaching direct support personnel in the most effective approaches to achieve the direct support competencies'). In the next chapter we argue that the low levels of coaching we observed were related to the organisation's formal structures. If the majority of a house supervisor's support hours are needed to directly support residents, rather than being supernumerary, then opportunities to coach staff are severely constrained.

Modes of supervision

So far, the literature we have cited, and the house supervisors we have quoted, have used words like coaching, guiding, instructing and modelling to describe the actions of house supervisors. Rather than being a new concept, this suggests that practice leadership is more likely to be a currently favoured overarching term that embraces a number of 'tried and tested' management techniques, mastery of which has eluded a significant number of human service managers over the years. LaVigna *et al.* claim that:

> Although human service supervisors, managers, and administrators tend to blame low wages, bad attitudes, lack of skills, poor communication, insufficient resources, and other factors outside their control for inconsistency and poor quality in the services provided, the real culprit seems to be *poor management practice.* (1994, p.xiv)

We want to add another well-known management concept to the above list, the concept of 'supervising' or 'supervision'. Table 7.2 shows that 'supervision' can be provided in different ways. Drawing on the work of Ford and Hargreaves (1991), we make the distinction between *formal* and *informal supervision* and *planned* and *impromptu supervision*, in order to differentiate between three modes of supervision.[7]

Table 7.2 Three modes of supervision (adapted from Ford and Hargreaves 1991)

Planned supervision	Formal	Planned meetings on an individual or group basis; with an agreed agenda and methods for reaching objectives. Such meetings can be arranged for a limited or indefinite period of time, for general or specific purposes.
		Agreements are reached between individuals and members of the group to give help, advice, constructive criticism and other forms of feedback, while working with clients or carrying out the service tasks. These agreements are made in advance, according to predetermined objectives and made subject to monitoring and regular review.
Impromptu supervision	Formal	Unplanned discussions and consultations on an individual or group basis, where the agenda has to be agreed on the spot; often when an unforeseen crisis or problem has arisen. However, some space and time is created away from service-delivery to work on the problem.
	Informal	Supervision is tacitly given while individuals are working with clients or engaged in service-delivery tasks. It may take the form of help, advice, constructive criticism or offered through demonstration and example. This activity may become the focus of discussion in a more formal context, but first occurs as unplanned activity because of needs and circumstances.

We gave examples of *impromptu informal supervision* earlier. The house supervisor who came across a staff member dressing a resident, and intervened to demonstrate that if supported differently the resident could dress herself, is one such example from the quotations. More often than not, an incident such as this would be discussed in a *planned formal supervision* meeting. The specific incident, for example, might generate into a broader discussion about teaching adaptive behaviours to all the residents as a core principle of the group home's 'model of support' and could be recorded as a work objective for the employee.

In human service organisations 'supervision' is often understood in a narrow way, referring to such structured meetings between a manager and a 'subordinate'. The relevant grouping in Table 7.2 expands this notion of *planned formal supervision* to include formalised ways of observing direct support staff whilst they are working with people with intellectual disabilities, with the aims of monitoring practice, providing feedback and giving any coaching that may be necessary.

This type of supervision was not represented in our interview data, nor witnessed in any of our fieldwork, with one very specific exception, which we discussed in Chapter 5. This represents a significant gap in the house supervisors' repertoire of interventions. We suggested that direct observation of staff practice could be observed more formally on a regular basis in the same way that the staff experience interactive training (Toogood 2008; Totsika *et al.* 2008a).

Observing staff practice in this way is not a new management approach. Jan Porterfield's (1987) under-acknowledged *Positive Monitoring*, for example, was a well-defined approach to help house supervisors structure the way in which they supervise. It contains six components, two of which mirror elements of *interactive training* and the form of *planned formal supervision* we are discussing here:

- Defining the aims of the service.

- Specifying clearly what staff should do to achieve service aims.

- Helping staff to work in the specified way.

- *Regularly watching staff work and looking at other records and other aspects of the service.*

- *Giving specific feedback to staff on their work and listening to staff comments and suggestions.*

- Reviewing individual job performance.

(Porterfield 1987, p.14, emphasis added)

The Active Support literature, in particular, attaches a great deal of importance to managers watching staff work and then providing feedback on their performance. Yet, as Stancliffe *et al.* point out, there is no published research that has reported on 'the amount of time that managers spend in providing practice leadership by observing and coaching staff in [Active Support]' (2008, p.208). Nor is there any specific research data that exists on whether this approach effects engagement in the short or long term. Sandy Toogood cautions that, 'Despite the power of observation, modelling and feedback, these techniques do not in themselves guarantee the adoption, maintenance or generalisation of new behaviours by staff' (2008, p.216).

Although we think the data we have presented in this chapter has gone some way towards illustrating what is meant by practice leadership, we believe that it is a concept that has been inadequately theorised, and is currently 'trapped' in the Active Support literature. If practice leadership is to become a useful term it is important that it is not operationalised too narrowly. It is more than 'on-the-job coaching' for the successful implementation of Active Support training. Neither will it be of use as either a sensitising or analytic concept if it refers to everything a house supervisor does or says.

A more comprehensive understanding of practice leadership is likely to encompass all the modes of supervision in Table 7.2. Having discussed one form of *planned formal supervision* in detail, we now turn our attention to the remaining modes of supervision, giving particular weight to *planned formal supervision meetings*, which have long been recognised as an important forum in human service organisations (Sines 1992).

PLANNED FORMAL SUPERVISION MEETINGS

As we stated earlier, 'supervision' in human service organisations is commonly understood as referring to a structured meeting between a manager and a 'subordinate'. These meetings are another forum where practice leadership can be exercised. Amongst other things, *planned formal supervision meetings* are a space for reviewing how staff are doing, keeping direct support staff 'in touch' with the goals of the service, and reinforcing the organisation's values (Mansell *et al.* 2004). These aims are also suggested by Brigid Proctor's (1998) framework for clinical supervision, which sets out three supervision functions:

- *Formative* – provides a framework and process for reflective learning

- *Normative* – maintaining and developing practice to agreed standards

- *Restorative* – offers opportunities for 'letting off steam' and exploring feelings.

Good supervision meetings should maintain a balance between the three domains. In many human service organisations, *planned formal supervision meetings* are often weakly implemented. An earlier study acknowledged that employees in the organisation where we conducted our research had insufficient supervision, and that the supervision people did receive was not always appropriate (DHS 2005a). This resulted in the development of the *Professional Development and Supervision Policy and Practice Guidelines* (DHS 2005b).

Our data revealed wide-ranging attitudes towards supervision and accounts of variable practice. The house supervisors' structured diaries revealed that less than 1 per cent of their recorded activities related to the conduct of formal supervision meetings. On average house supervisors were spending just over 20 minutes each week on this activity. As the average number of direct support staff in a group home was seven, this is about three minutes for each staff member per week.

David Sines (1992) argues that formal supervision processes should be backed up by strong policies and procedures. This house supervisor recognised the value of supervision as a management tool, but also the personal benefits of receiving supervision. Her comments suggest that it is her personal commitment to the supervision process, rather than a strongly embedded policy, that ensures supervision meetings take place for the staff she manages.

I think I'd probably be one of the few house supervisors that I know that would definitely complete monthly individual supervision. I think there's a couple of reasons for that, the first one is time. A lot of people don't feel that they have the time. The second one is that the Department rolled out the *Professional Development* [*and Supervision Policy and Practice Guidelines*], a different type of supervision, maybe 18 months ago. I thought it was quite a good idea and it would be an effective tool, sadly there was no follow-up on it. I think a lot of supervisors became confused and thought, 'Well, am I supposed to be doing the old one, or the new one?' There's been no follow-up, or training or input, so that as a consequence they're really not doing much at all. It's certainly been my experience and observation that if you don't have as close to monthly supervision that a lot of things for the people you're supporting are not going to get done and there's the increase of staff conflict because you're not giving the person that individual time to discuss the issues with you, to thrash it out, to debrief and then look at some strategies you can put into place to keep everybody happy. I'm a very strong advocate of supervision and if I've missed my supervision with my manager, I will constantly request it.

The next house supervisor is less committed to formal supervision meetings and her response reinforces the claim that the supervision policy had not been embedded into everyday practice. Her comments additionally reveal a degree of confusion about the different 'performance management' policies.

I try to do [formal supervision monthly]. I don't do it that often, 'cos we're all very close here and we talk, so I usually know if there's something wrong. That's one of my weaknesses; I need to do it more often in that sense. It's always the same thing; I sit there, 'Have you got any issues?' 'No.' They'll come to me straight away if they've got a problem with something. It probably depends on your house and your supervisor. There was confusion about different [management tools and processes]; if you've got a discipline problem then you don't do it in PDS [professional development and supervision meetings] and I think supervisors were getting really confused about the different processes. Then there's workplace action plans for people who have underperformance issues. It would be nice if they brought out a folder, with it all outlined perfectly. I think supervisors were bringing up performance issues in PDS and they're not meant to bring it up in PDS, that's supposed to be a positive chat about how you're going with work and what development need they have.

As well as suggesting that some house supervisors are confused about the purpose of *planned formal supervision meetings* and how different polices relate to one another, this house supervisor appears to privilege other modes of supervision, suggestive of the remaining supervision mode, *impromptu formal supervision*, where the agenda is agreed on the spot when a staff member comes with an 'issue'.

Some house supervisors saw formal supervision meetings as only being necessary when an employee's performance was poor, which ignores the formative and restorative functions of supervision.

I don't actually do [formal supervision] unless I have performance issues. [Then] I do triplicate formal supervision. Otherwise usually per shift I take a staff person and we sit down and chat, that can be over a cigarette and coffee, that can be in the staff room, it depends on the direction. I give direction. So it could be a new skill that I want them to take on, or it could be that we're going to discuss ideology, and their personality as part of the team. And that has to be done in a quiet area where we're all very chummy over a cup of coffee. Is that formal? I consider it to be formal. I consider every single time that I talk with staff member to be formal, because I am.

This house supervisor is also describing *impromptu formal supervision*, making some space away from service-delivery to discuss a topic that has arisen on the spot. A more familiar example is a house supervisor taking a staff member who has been assaulted by a resident to a quiet space to discuss the incident. There is, of course, merit in such impromptu discussions, but major management processes, such as managing poor performance, performance-related pay, appraisal, personal development, identifying training needs and so on, require documented evidence, which typically results from formal structured meetings.

Reluctance to document issues may stem from direct support staff's perceptions of this process.

I've had people say to me, 'I don't want you to write it down. What if someone opens up the filing cabinet and sees it?' It'll be something little like, 'I want to move, I need a change, but you can't tell anyone, I don't want anyone to know.' Yet, if I was working on shift they'd tell me about that. People are more inclined to be open when they're not sitting there with a piece of paper and a pen. It was having to change the attitude about it, that it wasn't a negative thing, it was all also about, 'Look, you've done this really well, but what portfolio[8] would you like that you're in charge of?' I've got to work on that and how I deliver it. It carries a bit of a negative thing, but it was drummed from higher management, you must do it. I was hesitant. I have started. I'm still new at it. I've had people say, 'This is a wank, I don't want to sit here and talk to you like this. I've just told you all this yesterday, why am I going to sit down and write it down? This is stupid.' We did have to change the culture of it all.

Planned formal supervision meetings will be perceived by direct support staff as being a place where employees get 'told off', if this is their dominant function. The practice of the earlier house supervisor who used formal meetings solely to manage poor performance would perpetuate this impression in the setting where she manages. This house supervisor had begun to change the negative perception of supervision.

We use the term 'supervision' now, not in the negative sense any more. It's a good opportunity to say, 'This is what's working well, this is what you're doing well.' I try and do it once a month and I try not to make it too formal because it scares the crap out of people. It varies a little bit because sometimes you get people going off on holidays, but I try [to make it monthly]. I think they're getting [to a place where they value it] and it's getting people comfortable talking. That's a bit of a skill, to get people to the point where they can sit down and say, 'Oh yes, I was doing this but I didn't like doing that.' You've got to get them to where you can have those real conversations. It's not just you sitting there telling people a list of jobs they've got to do for the next month. It's more about how you're going with this, to move it to that point.

If *planned formal supervision meetings* are carried out consistently well, with a balanced agenda that highlights the things employees are doing well, in addition to areas for improvement, then staff are more likely to see it as a valued activity. This is equally true of formal observation and feedback of staff practice. With regard to interactive training, Totsika *et al.* (2008b) reported that the most frequently reported difficultly was 'being observed', but staff also reported that having someone observe the way they work was helpful. Direct support staff will come to accept that tacit supervision, formal supervision meetings and observation and feedback are 'the way things are done around here', when they become routine practices.

NEGATIVE FEEDBACK – A NECESSARY PART OF SUPERVISION?

The words and practices of some house supervisors revealed a degree of confusion that existed in relation to the organisation's relevant policy documents, which had tried to separate out 'performance management and discipline' issues from 'professional development and supervision'. This seemed to us to be artificial, confusing and ultimately unhelpful to house supervisors whose *raison d'être* is to influence staff performance. Reid, Parsons and Green use supervision and management interchangeably to refer to:

> applications within human service settings that are designed to impact staff performance. When considered in this light, the job of a human service manager or supervisor consists of two main functions: (a) to take specific action to *change* the day-to-day work performance of staff when such performance is problematic or less than optimal; and (b) to take specific action to *maintain* the routine work activities of staff when their performance is appropriate and acceptable. Hence, the supervisor should be considered a behavior change agent, with staff-behavior the first-level focus of the supervisor's behavior change practices, and client welfare the second-level focus. (1989, p.16)

Managing staff members cannot always be a positive experience, nor are supervision meetings a cosy place to chat. Performance management is embedded in the supervisory process, and should focus on things that people do well but *also* on things that they need to improve. Inadequate feedback to poor performers is one reason why some direct support staff do not engage in desired practices. Without a focus on the things that direct care staff need to improve, they may be left thinking that they are performing satisfactorily and therefore they have no reason to change (Fournies 1988). Clements and Zarkowska write that:

> One school of thought suggests that negative feedback should never be used – the focus should be entirely upon positive feedback for positive behaviours. Whilst this raises an interesting philosophical discussion there is a serious practical problem in negative behaviours going unremarked. This is that negative behaviours may be strengthened by
>
> • Repetition – the more they are done the more they are likely to be done ('habit')
> • Reward – the behaviours themselves may achieve positive results for the staff which if not checked will strengthen the behaviours. (1994, pp.172–3)

Although organisations tend to have a separate disciplinary procedure, issues of discipline cannot entirely be removed from *planned formal supervision meetings*. Documented regular discussion, planning, setting of objectives and review are processes that will help to keep direct care staff out of the formal disciplinary processes or make sure that there is a seamless transition between them. One of the first places to address the performance of direct care staff who are not meeting the minimum requirements of their role ought to be *planned formal supervision*. This will inevitably require negative feedback.

Practice leadership: The group context

In this final subsection we consider the importance of teamwork in group homes and some ideas about leadership, before highlighting the house or team meeting as a key setting where house supervisors can exercise practice leadership.

Many of the examples we have presented have been interactions between a house supervisor and an individual staff member. Yet, it is obvious to anyone who has worked in a group home that delivering high-quality services relies on teamwork, and in earlier chapters we have highlighted the group dimension as an important facet of such settings. Staff members who are attempting to teach a resident a new skill or reduce the frequency of challenging behaviour know that consistency is vital. Teaching a person with severe intellectual disability to feed himself is unlikely to be successful if six staff members are using six different approaches. A reduction in the frequency of a self-injurious behaviour is unlikely if every member of staff is left to respond to a resident poking his own eyeball in their own idiosyncratic ways. House supervisors were quick to highlight the creative strength of teamwork.

You need a team that will follow through. The key to alleviating a lot of issues is a consistent approach. When you've got a consistent team, who at a house meeting say 'This is a great idea, let's go with it', and everyone adopts the same approach, it will work. All you need is one person to go 'Nup, that's wrong', and try and sabotage a project, [and] the clients are affected.

You have to build a team so everyone trusts each other, can rely on each other. If you don't have a good team you won't have a good house. It doesn't matter what sort of clients you've got, if you haven't got a good team, you won't have a good house.

As this house supervisor makes clear, a dysfunctional or underperforming staff group impacts on the residents' 'quality of life'.

If the team isn't working properly, [then] it is a resident issue. Then the residents aren't getting the care that they should be getting. They're not getting the environment and the atmosphere that they should be getting.

Practice leadership therefore also needs to be considered in a group context, where the notion of leadership comes to the fore. Unfortunately, leadership is not an easy concept to define and it has been understood in different ways (Bryman 1996). Contemporary understandings posit that anyone in a team can exercise leadership (Francis and Young 1992) but, as the manager of a group home, the house supervisor is the person most likely to fulfil this role and create the climate where direct support staff can take on a leadership role.

A house supervisor therefore needs the knowledge and understanding that underpins teamwork and leadership. Space constraints do not allow us the luxury of providing a thorough overview of the literature related to these concepts. However, they are embedded in the house supervisor competencies (Table 7.1), and the onus is on the organisation to develop the competence of house supervisors in these areas.

An important idea is that there is not one 'best style' of management, but that an appropriate style will depend upon the house supervisor, the specific group home, the direct support staff and the task to be completed. This is known as a contingency or situational leadership (Blanchard, Zigarmi and Zigarmi 1986; Tannenbaum and Schmidt 1958). This house supervisor highlights the importance of inviting staff to contribute to a discussion before making a decision, which is part of a democratic leadership style (White and Lippit 1953).

> I think when staff have the opportunity to be able to bring something and they're passionate about what they're doing, they do it well. I'm not a supervisor that goes, 'I think we should do this.' It's always at a house meeting, 'What ideas do we have? How can we do this? How can we do that?' And then everyone contributes. And if someone feels confident enough to say, 'Look, I've been thinking such and such, I want to get [a resident] involved with this, what do you think?' 'Oh right, that sounds great to me.'

The democratic style is underpinned by the belief that involving people generates greater commitment and energy from a group of people. In certain circumstances, situational leadership decrees that an autocratic leadership style will be appropriate, as these house supervisors imply:

> I do have to make decisions that some people may not like, but that's part of my job. But if you empower people to have ownership or be a part of the decision-making process, then they're going to be a part of moving forward as well.

> You need to take [staff] opinions on and don't always make decisions by yourself, because nine times out of ten you might have missed a little piece. If I have a major decision that's going to affect all of my residents and my staff...with the staff I take on board what they're saying. If it's a sensible enough plan of action, and it's completely different to what I thought and their action's better, I take their actions. But only if it's a better action. There've been times when they've all gone, 'No I'm not doing that,' and I go, 'Too bad, you're completely wrong, this is what we're doing.'

Newer approaches to leadership have been referred to as 'transformational leadership', 'charismatic leadership' and 'visionary leadership'. According to Bryman these labels conceptualise a leader as, 'Someone who defines organizational reality through the articulation of a vision which is a reflection of how he or she defines an organization's mission and the values which will support it' (1996, p.280).

In the main, managers at a senior level will already have defined what the future should look like, drawing on policy documents like *Valuing People* (Department of Health 2001) and the *State Disability Plan* (DHS 2002b) or frameworks like the Five Accomplishments (O'Brien 1987). Rather than develop a new vision, it is the job of house supervisors and middle managers to establish a 'model of support' that is congruent with the service's values and policy. In the absence of clear policy statements this will involve translating abstract concepts into meaningful and relevant guidance for working with people with severe and profound intellectual disabilities.

As well as providing a useful metaphor for the house supervisor's role, the quotation below reflects sophisticated ideas about leadership; that house supervisors have a role in constructing organisational 'reality' in the heads and minds of direct support staff (see Morgan 1997).

One of the more difficult roles as a house supervisor is manoeuvring staff ideology and ideas... As a supervisor it's hard because I need to construct a future and then I need to enrol everybody to be part of that future, clients and staff all working towards that future. As a supervisor, if I don't recognise that role, then we flounder. I often use the analogy of 'captain of the ship'. I can't get from Australia to South America unless I have a good crew. If they're sitting around having cigarettes all day long, when the good wind comes we're going to miss it, we're going to flounder around. You have to have a captain, you have to have a crew; you can't have one without the other. Who is more important? A boat won't function without both, so both are important, but someone has to make the tough decision. It's the way that you go about doing that.

It may be necessary to challenge employees' understanding of their role and current ways of doing things, by pushing staff's conceptual territory. This involves introducing new ideas, concepts and options that they must deal with (Schein 1999). The house supervisor below explains that she had to challenge people's understanding when she took over the management of a group home.

[Changing the culture is] slow and steady, 'cos [the staff have] all been here for quite a while. It's like, 'Well, we've done that for the past ten years,' and I've said, 'Well, I'm sorry, you've done it wrong for the past ten years. This is the way that it needs to be done. It's policy, so it needs to be followed.' It's not negotiable with certain things. A perfect example is when I came here. One of the residents went bowling on a Sunday, and he'd been doing it for years. It was one of my first Sundays here and the person wanted to sleep in that Sunday. The staff member said they have to go to bowling and I said, 'Well, why do they have to go to bowling?' 'Because it says that he goes to bowling on a Sunday.' I said, 'But why does he go to bowling? Is it relaxation? Is it a job?' It'd be different if he was getting paid. And she said, 'Oh, recreation.' I said, 'Well, is there any reason if he doesn't want to go to bowling that he has to go to bowling?' So things like that have changed. In the end he gave it up and he's now doing ten-pin bowling through the Special Olympics, which is once a month. He makes his own way there and he loves it. Whereas he was going there and only a couple of people were showing up, or nobody was showing up and he'd have to go and bowl on his own. That was the culture that I was breaking through; it says that this person does this on this date, this person mops the floor on this date, this person does this on this date, does his washing at this time, but if he wants to go to the movies, can't he do his washing tomorrow?

House supervisors have the difficult task of building effective teams. Francis and Young (1992) see the commitment to teamwork as a distinctive management style, which requires the house supervisor to develop the resources of the group. It is important that the staff team should not just be perceived as the names that appear on the staffing roster. This manager recognised that the importance of teamwork extended to the organisational structures beyond the group home. She sees herself as being part of the group home staff team:

[House supervisors] have to be able to relate to us in 'management' too. There's too much of 'them and us'. I try and break that down with my house supervisors. I very much see myself as part of their team and they know I see myself as a leader of that team. I'm very much a part of it and we communicate quite well. I think you have to have a commitment to the rights of people with disabilities. There's no point in being there if you haven't got that because you're not going to be able to show that to the team. They're going to be guided by whatever you do, so you've got to have those skills and leadership. You've got to be able to lead. I've seen many a bad house supervisor that I don't think was competent; their staff have come in new and gone that way as well, because they've seen them as their leader and they've followed. You've got to present yourself well, you've got to have the rights of the client, you've got to be able to work with the policies. My big thing's the team, that you're working as a team, and not as individuals.

The house supervisor's most valuable forum for demonstrating a commitment to teamwork is a house meeting. It is a key forum for enhancing staff relations, canvassing opinions, communicating information, and a place where house supervisors can exercise practice leadership. As we discussed in Chapter 5, it is also a forum where external managers can be seen to be part of 'the team'.

Facilitating house meetings accounted for 3 per cent of the activities recorded by house supervisors in their structured diaries, about 70 minutes in a week. Mansell *et al.* (1987) and Sines (1992) suggest the need for a weekly meeting. A weekly two-hour house meeting, plus 30 minutes for preparation and one hour to write minutes, would account for 10 per cent of our house supervisors' time.

All of the focal houses had a monthly meeting scheduled on the roster. Many of the meetings we observed were relatively poorly managed, which meant that the potential to realise many of the benefits we described above were untapped. Running effective meetings is a teachable, learnable skill (Video Arts 1976) but, more often than not, without training, the practice of running meetings does not improve with experience, and new staff members in a group home merely pick up and repeat others' bad habits. Once again, the onus is on the organisation to provide house supervisors with the training and coaching necessary to run effective meetings.

Concluding remarks

Given that house supervisors are responsible for the management of the day-to-day work of direct support staff, then attaching the concept of practice leadership to the house supervisor's position seems useful. It sends a strong message to house supervisors that they have a key role in shaping the work performance of direct support staff.

Practice leadership was not, however, a term familiar to most of the house supervisors and managers whom we interviewed. This will change over time if it is used in everyday speech and gets developed into a tighter concept. At present it is a term most commonly associated with the Active Support literature, but should be applied more broadly. House supervisors and managers were able to explicate the concept of practice leadership using everyday speech. We linked their terms to more recognised managerial language and theoretical frameworks. Practice leadership was initially described by using commonplace phrases, such as 'modelling' and 'leading by example'. We added in words like coaching, directing and instructing, prior to describing some supervisory frameworks (see Table 7.3).

Table 7.3 Conceptions of practice leadership

What practice leaders do

Making clear to staff what they should do and how they should do it

'Leading by example'; 'Practising what you preach'; 'Only asking staff to do things that they would do themselves'

How practice leadership is exercised

Active role modelling, coaching or on-the-job training[9]

'Consciously and deliberately demonstrating ways of behaving for staff'; 'Offering advice, constructive criticism, feedback, guidance, help and instruction'

Forums for practice leadership

Planned formal supervision

Impromptu formal supervision

Impromptu informal supervision

House meetings

Orientations of practice leaders

Passionate about the job and the delivery of excellent support

Commitment to teamwork

Practice leadership seems to have a number of important dimensions. First, it is enacted in interactions between a house supervisor and one other person, most likely a resident or an employee. House supervisors' practice needs to be competent and it must be seen by direct support staff. Practice leaders actively, consciously and deliberately make clear to direct support staff what they should do and how they should do it. Being passionate about working directly with people with intellectual disabilities seems to be an important orientation for house supervisors.

Second, practice leadership has a group dimension. Practice leaders have an orientation to 'teamwork', a knowledge and understanding of management, and the ability to translate policy into meaningful guidance for direct support staff.

They can use different management styles and must have time to discuss and demonstrate good practice, which happens in both informal and formal spaces. House supervisors need to be skilled at, and employ, all three modes of supervision that we have discussed. Planned formal supervision, impromptu formal supervision and impromptu informal supervision are three ways in which house supervisors can exercise practice leadership and manage the performance of direct support staff.

The relatively poor outcomes we have discussed in previous chapters can, in part, be attributed to weak practice leadership. Without a clear understanding of key concepts like 'homeliness' and 'building inclusive communities' house supervisors could not make it clear to direct support staff what they should do. Thus we described an emphasis on meeting basic needs, low levels of meaningful engagement, a group orientation to providing support, prominence given to *community presence* and weak implementation of ameliorating processes such as Active Support, keyworking, planning and 'supervision'.

This brings us to a third important dimension of practice leadership, the broader organisational context. Although implicit throughout the chapter, the organisational context was consciously pushed towards the background as we adopted a more individualised perspective in regard to the house supervisor's role. Practice leadership is bolstered by organisational structures and resources. We have highlighted 'supervision' at length, and staff meetings to a lesser extent, because they are recognised as foundational management structures. In order for house supervisors to exercise their role, to engage in practice leadership, resources must be allocated and organisational structures must be in place. If they are not, as we shall show in the next chapter, even a competent house supervisor may struggle to enable high-quality outcomes.

Issues for consideration

- Is it worth validating the house supervisor national competency statements for your organisation? This will help to: clarify what you expect house supervisors to do, recruit people to the role and provide adequate training and development.

- What specific knowledge, skills and abilities are required in each group home?

- How are house supervisors spending their time? Get house supervisors to keep a structured diary for one month, so that they can review how they are spending their time.

- What can you do to promote the notion of practice leadership, particularly through the three modes of supervision?

- Does the organisation have robust policies and procedures in regard to the supervision and management of staff?

- What are you doing to develop the strong teams necessary for achieving high-quality services?

- Are the meetings you run of a high quality?

Notes

1   Although the use of competency-based models is widespread, they have their critics (Hyland 1993; Lum 1999). Two key criticisms that we want to briefly address here are that there is no agreed definition of 'competence' and that some approaches focus on what people 'do', thereby marginalising what they 'know'. Hewitt *et al.* (1998, 2004) do not provide a definition of how they are using 'competence', but we suggest that their approach is closest to an 'outcome model', which defines and describes what a person in a particular job role is expected to achieve (Boag 1998).

   The more complex a competency, the more important it is for a person to know why he or she should behave in a particular way, i.e. *knowledge* and *understanding* are important. Given the complexity of the house supervisor's position, underpinning knowledge is essential. Hewitt *et al.* (1998) go some way towards addressing this requirement by identifying performance indicators for each competency, some of which involve the need to assess knowledge and understanding.

2   The full list of competencies is available on request from the authors at www.latrobe.edu.au/ socialwork. The Minnesotan competencies should also be available from the Research and Training Center on Community Living at the University of Minnesota: www.rtc.umn.edu/main.

3   Interestingly, the house supervisors whom we interviewed were unequivocal in their view that they would like a bigger say in hiring the staff they have to manage. They suggested that their particular insights into the attitudes and skills needed to work with specific residents would result in a better 'fit', and their intimate knowledge of the staff team would result in a more balanced team with a better skill mix.

4   Auslan is the language of the deaf community of Australia.

5   Some competency approaches include 'values' as competencies. Whilst Hewitt *et al.* (1998) generally steered clear of doing this in writing their competency statements, they went to great lengths to stress that contemporary community-based services are based on certain values and that their competency statements reflect these values.

6   The notions of management and leadership are often used interchangeably. We don't think that this is good practice. Although discussions about the relationship between leadership and management are characterised by heated disagreements, we think there are useful distinctions to be made between the terms at the extreme ends of the management/leadership divide (Jackson and Donovan 1999). House supervisors will engage in both management and leadership activities. However, the activities undertaken by house supervisors that we have described are essentially management activities. Undertaking 'supervision', coaching and facilitating meetings are all management activities. House supervisors look to their

senior managers to provide leadership (Rogers and Reynolds 2003); they must implement policies and procedures. Practice leadership is essentially 'good management' and therefore 'management' more accurately describes what house supervisors do, although 'practice management' does not seem to have the same 'appeal' as practice leadership.

7   Ford and Hargreaves (1991) used similar dimensions to distinguish between four modes of supervision. Their notion of *planned informal supervision* seems like an oxymoron, in that anything that is planned has a degree of formality about it. The way that they described *planned informal supervision* fits more comfortably as another way of providing *planned formal supervision*.

8   Some group homes created portfolios, areas of responsibility for direct support staff, such as fire safety, the ordering and storage of medication and so on.

9   We contrasted active role modelling with passive role modelling, which we described as hoping that staff will pick up good practices by serendipitously observing house supervisors' practices. Although house supervisors should always perform appropriately, we understand practice leadership as an active intervention, i.e. they must do specific things at specific times to influence the performance of direct support staff.

Chapter 8

The Organisational Context

Introduction

In the previous chapter we consciously adopted a more individualistic perspective in discussing the link between the house supervisor's management role and service quality. Unfortunately, a good house supervisor is merely one requirement for establishing and maintaining a quality service in a group home. We also need to pay attention to the organisational context in which people are managing (Henderson and Atkinson 2003). As Burton writes, 'It is rare for the manager of the Home…to be sufficiently determined (and lucky) to resist the management failures of the organisation which runs the Home' (1998, p.xv). In this chapter we emphasise the book's much stronger orientation: the need to understand how an organisational system functions as a whole, including its relationships with the immediate environment (e.g. interactions with other human service organisations, families, labour unions, Government agencies) and the broader general environment (Morgan 1997).

Implicit in our writing is that many of the issues that we have discussed, and the weaker outcomes we have described, are a consequence of the way in which the actual residential service was 'designed' and/or 'put into practice'. This is consistent with a model which suggests that service structures and processes mediate service outcomes (Felce *et al.* 1998).

Achieving 'ordinary life' outcomes for service-users must be led from the top (Ashbaugh 2008) and, in this regard, senior managers, i.e. the chief executive officer, heads of functional departments and so on, bear the leadership and management responsibilities. These managers fashion 'formal practices' so that employees fulfil their role requirements (Tsoukas 1994).

Formal practices have been the subject of much organisational research. Table 8.1 lists the four types of formal practices listed by Joanne Martin (2002) that we will refer to in this chapter.

Table 8.1 Formal organisational practices (adapted from Martin 2002)

Organisational structure	The way in which an organisation is put together. Depicted in an organisational chart, with the relevant job descriptions and reporting relationships. Other aspects of the structure relate to how the organisation is differentiated, often divided into functional departments and geographical areas.
Technology and tasks	What employees are required to do to produce whatever goods or services the organisation offers. Active Support, for example, is a way of producing high levels of 'meaningful engagement'.
Rules and procedures	A standard to which behaviour is expected to conform. Larger organisations tend to have handbooks of rules and procedures. Some of the examples we refer to in this chapter are the *Professional Development and Supervision Policy and Practice Guidelines* (DHS 2005b), hiring decisions and the construction of staff rosters.
Financial controls	Accounting procedures, pay and benefit allocations, budgeting procedures. For example, the Client Expenditure Record System.

Formal practices are evident in the following quotation from Judith Jenkins and her colleagues, writing about the lessons from an early group home demonstration project.

> Behind the 'ordinary life' of the people in the home lies a strong system of planning the day, creating learning opportunities and recording results together with a behavioural framework taught to staff both 'on the job', at weekly staff meetings, and at in-service training sessions. (1987, p.264)

Managers generally pay a lot of attention to formal practices, because they are an area that they can more easily control (Martin 2002). Managers establish a practice framework, by codifying organisational values, setting goals, writing job descriptions and providing policies and practice guidance. Employees are socialised into the organisation through a formal induction process, in-service training and so on. We like to think of this focus on the actions of senior managers as an 'upstream' orientation, after this story, related by Gerard Egan and Michael Cowan:

A person walking alongside a river sees someone drowning. This person jumps in, pulls the victim out, and begins artificial respiration. While this is going on, another person calls for help; the rescuer jumps into the water again and pulls the new victim out. This process repeats itself several times until the rescuer gets up and walks away from the scene. A bystander approaches and asks in surprise where he is going, to which the rescuer replies 'I'm going upstream to find out who's pushing all these people in and see if I can stop it!' (1979, pp.3–4)

Rather than looking at the behaviour of direct support staff and house supervisors out of context, we focus on how formal practices influence the outcomes in a group home. A central idea is that decisions made 'upstream' impacted on the practices and outcomes we have described. This includes practices that originated way upstream, beyond the boundaries of the organisation, such as the allocation of public finances to intellectual disability services in Australia and the creation of Victorian social policies. In this first part of the chapter we show how organisational structures can create barriers for house supervisors, and argue that this is likely to lead to poorer management practices. In the second half we draw together a number of issues related to the implementation of organisational rules and procedures, which are linked to the overarching goal of realising 'an ordinary life'. Throughout the chapter we refer to a number of *informal practices,* which often highlight inconsistencies between what actually happens and what formal practices require (Martin 2002). Finally, we suggest that a characteristic of community-based services is that they endow staff working in group homes with enough autonomy to undermine the goal of realising high-quality outcomes.

Organisational structures that lead to weaker practice leadership

In the previous chapter we noted that the house supervisors' structured diaries revealed few activities that could be coded as being either to do with facilitating staff meetings or both types of *planned formal supervision,* i.e. formal meetings and structured observation and feedback. About 4 per cent of the house supervisors' time was spent on these key activities. Was this because they chose not to do these things, or were there significant barriers to achieving them?

Individual house supervisors obviously have a degree of autonomy to prioritise their work tasks, and some may choose to concentrate on tasks that others judge to be of lesser importance. However, the views of house supervisors that follow suggest that they faced both resource and structural constraints in regard to the key managerial systems we have highlighted.

Variability in the allocation of resources for house meetings

The Department of Human Services in Victoria manages over 500 group homes, which are divided into separate administrative regions. This gives each region a degree of autonomy and flexibility. Without a common standard for the provision of house meetings, regions allocated resources for scheduled house meetings variably. In one region, each group home had a scheduled house meeting every two months, and a degree of flexibility to schedule additional meetings if necessary, as this manager explains.

> Our staff meetings within the region, they're bi-monthly. Certainly the ones that I had, we did a lot of work on the residents' programmes in those meetings. We also had ones that were just specific to one client whereas the staff meetings tended to cover all of the residents in the house, plus any other house issues. We had more specific ones if the need arose. There are houses that have them more frequently, and there are times within certain houses that you require them to be more frequent, in terms of say behaviour and you're developing new plans and you need to train all the staff. But typically we've got the six a year and we have other training opportunities, lots of the mandatory training stuff as well.

In another region, this group home had a meeting every four weeks.

> We have a [rostered house meeting] and it's the third Wednesday of every month. We have some permanent casuals[1] and they are encouraged [to attend]. If you work here for a couple of months to have the house running effectively they need to know what our thinking is. It makes it an easier job for the casuals themselves. They know where everyone's coming from, they know what the expectations are, they know that we've got some special ideas on how to treat different clients, everybody knows we all work in the same manner. It makes for more positive outcome for the clients. You can't do it with one doing it one way and then one doing it another way.

Another group home within the same region did not have a meeting formally scheduled on the roster. In order for the staff to meet, it was necessary to rely on the staff team's goodwill.

We don't have a rostered meeting, which is a bit of an issue, because the staff have to come in on their time off. We do use time-in-lieu, but staff have families and so it is difficult to get everybody together at the same time. I try to have one every month. We were going to have one this afternoon, it has been cancelled because a couple of people can't come now, so there's no point in having it. This one's a big one, there's lots of decisions that need to be made, so I'm going to have to reschedule it to a time where everyone can attend, otherwise it defeats the purpose of having a staff meeting and working together... It's very hard to do your job properly without having [a rostered house meeting where everyone attends].

If a house meeting is formally rostered for the entire staff team to attend, it becomes part of their working week. This sets the expectation that people must attend. Without this, employee goodwill may only stretch so far.

I've said it to management so I'm happy to say it to you, if I was on my day off and you asked me to come in and give up three and a half hours of my day, even if I was being paid, and it was in the middle of the day between eleven and four, then that's ruined my whole day and I may consider not to come... I think you can ask people to be dedicated but only to a point. In the end they go, 'I do my job, I am dedicated while I'm there but I have a life outside of my work.'

Where there were rostered house meetings, the entire staff group were not always scheduled to attend. In the focal houses, the part-time staff were excluded. This meant that up to one third of the staff group were not included at this forum for information sharing, problem solving or decision making. This makes it much harder for the group to develop into a team, and creates 'extra' work for the house supervisor if she attempts to involve the missing staff members in these important processes. The advantages of having the entire team present are self-evident.

[The house meeting] is rostered in [for everyone to attend], that's very important. The problem is, if you don't roster it in, people don't turn up. That's when your team breaks down. The meeting is one of the most important aspects, because that's where you can bring all your concerns. If we've got an issue with our client's autistic behaviours, [which] are always changing, then as a team we'll go, 'Look, I've tried this, I've tried this, I've tried that, that worked, that didn't' and then we come up with a plan. That's really important.

As we have stated before, one of the earlier group home demonstration projects had weekly house meetings (Felce 1989). A well-run weekly staff meeting, organised at a time that is convenient to the residents' schedule,[2] requires a commitment of resources that are often limited. Our own experience suggests that a house meeting every eight weeks is not frequent enough, and may contribute little to improving resident outcomes. Organisations may, as one of the respondents suggested, have a 'reserve' budget that enables meetings to be scheduled on an 'as needed' basis, i.e. to develop new behaviour management plans, develop a new staff team and so on.

Constraints in having planned formal supervision meetings

If the house supervisor's job is as complex and difficult as is suggested (Hewitt and Larson 2005), then it is perhaps no surprise that some house supervisors described their job as 'undoable' in the time they have available. In such circumstances, a house supervisor may have to make some tough decisions about what tasks to prioritise.

The job is undoable within the time constraints and I had to lower my standards quite a bit, and not be so proud about my job. I've shifted my focus, because I'm very driven to be very organised from an administrative standpoint. I've had to realise that I just can't achieve that level within here [the office], but out there is where I get my satisfaction and I have to really remember that's what it's about. These days it's hard to get me in the office, because I do get most of my satisfaction out of working with direct care, just because this part of it is so overwhelming. When you think about it, it's two jobs in one.

This house supervisor chose to prioritise *planned formal supervision meetings* over other tasks.

> I see [planned formal supervision meetings] as something that's crucial, along with the staff meetings. One of the most crucial things in my job is the communication side of it with my staff. If I don't do the regular monthly supervision, things end up, it's just awful, it can really snowball certain things. It's a really good opportunity to have a one-to-one chat. I know that some supervisors don't, but I make it a priority. And consequently I think that's probably why I don't have a great deal of time to do any other things.

Rather than time constraints, this house supervisor was constrained by the way in which the roster created unequal opportunities for the supervision of the staff. She also highlights an important principle, which is that, as far as possible, time for *planned formal supervision meetings* should happen when staff are not required to support the residents.

> [The roster allows the space for formal supervision] with certain staff, and it doesn't with other staff, because we've got staff that start at two-thirty, but the clients would come [home] and there you are, sitting there. The staff are like, 'Well I'm on direct care now.' For them it was a pain. 'Are we done?' They'd sit down for ten [minutes]. 'Are we done? Is that it? I've got nothing to say.'

For other house supervisors there is no designated time for supervision on the roster for any staff. In such circumstances, as with attendance at house meetings, if supervision meetings are to take place they rely on employee goodwill.

> There's no time in the roster for supervision. There is no non-contact hours[3] for the staff... If I come in when another staff member's on, I'm travelling all the way from home in the middle of the day, asking them to come in early as well, on my day off to do supervision. Or, I'm asking them to come in on my day on, on their day off, or come in early, interrupting their day. They can take it as [time-in-lieu] but they don't get paid for that, and I don't get paid for that. That's not good enough. Why should staff have to do that?

Human service organisations tend to benefit from 'organisational citizenship behaviour': cooperative and helpful behaviour that goes beyond people's formal roles (Organ and Ryan 1995). Employees are often willing to swap shifts, work additional hours for short periods or come in when there are special occasions, but this is unsustainable in the long term and unreasonable when a job has become so onerous that nobody could do it in the time available. The house supervisors' structured diaries revealed that 9 out of 16 respondents reported working in excess of their rostered hours. In Gifford's (2006) study, residential managers recorded working excess hours on one of every three shifts.[4] It is very easy to erode the employee goodwill that is necessary for the smooth running of an organisation.

Constraints in observing direct support staff practices and giving feedback

Just as the roster constrained *planned formal supervision meetings*, so house supervisors were limited in administering the other type of *planned formal supervision*: structured observation of staff practices and the provision of feedback; and *impromptu informal supervision*: giving supervision more spontaneously whilst direct support staff are working with residents.

In this business often you don't see the people you're trying to manage. Calista, for example, she struggles with English, but I probably see her twice a week for an hour or two. So there's not a lot of time where you're there to be able to assist or support or give her directions, show her how to do [the paperwork]… She's a part-timer. She works mostly afternoon/night shifts, so she works usually from say two, three, four in the afternoon, through to eight or nine at night. I have very few of those shifts, I usually work seven 'til four-thirty. I run a couple of night shifts but generally seven to four-thirty. So generally by the time I'm finishing work she's just starting, and I'm going through the process of closing down my day. You're not there to manage or to observe her work, observe what she's doing, observe how she's doing it, so in that sense [the roster] doesn't work for me. I have a certain sense about her work but I don't really witness it that often. To do that means special trips in. I have to work extra hours just to do that sort of observation and supervision work.

Some of the weaker management practices that we have highlighted should not therefore be entirely understood as being due to an individual's poor management skills, but as resulting from the organisation's formal practices. Without the opportunity to observe every staff member at work, this house supervisor hopes that good practice will diffuse through the staff team via the staff whom she sees most often.

I've got two staff that I only work with four hours a fortnight. To model for them is really hard, but I feel that if you've modelled enough with the people that I work with on a really regular basis, they then get into the habit of doing that and showing other people what to do.

Another house supervisor falls back on the 'tools' that are available to her, in this instance 'management through the communication book', which she knows is less effective.

I can't get that level of consistency across the whole staff. I suppose that is frustrating. You write in the communication book to convey certain things, and you do become accustomed to reading between the lines, on your days off, piecing together what's occurred and knowing how to coach staff in a non-confrontational way via the daily report book, making very inclusive statements, 'Can we please try and...', not singling people out so much.

In the same way that we described in the previous chapter, this former house supervisor was 'compelled' to rely on *impromptu informal supervision* and only use *planned formal supervision meetings* when there was a significant performance issue. As before, this is likely to lead to, or maintain, the perception that 'supervision' is the place where employees get 'told off'.

[An obstacle to formal supervision is] usually the amount of time that house supervisors have. I had a large staff team, about eight on the team. Two hours of formal supervision would probably take up a fortnight's worth of [my] non-contact time. None of the CRU staff have any non-contact time... So I have to say a lot of supervision was done on the floor, on the job, and it was done informally. As you were going, you'd be saying, 'Well, next time can you try it this way?' The only time I did supervision was when there were performance issues, so it was documented very clearly. I think a lot of people would say the same, there is this expectation from our level that it needs to be done and there is this idea that there is time to do it. I'd like someone to show me how, because it's not realistic.

Rosters: The allocation of staff

In mentioning whether there was a rostered house meeting, rostered *planned formal supervision meetings* or time to meet direct support staff informally, house supervisors were referring to how staff, the biggest item on a group home's budget, are organised. Employees' working hours are allocated via a roster. Given that the way in which staff provide support to the residents has been identified as a key determinant of client-outcomes, then it follows that the allocation of their time and the support they receive is absolutely crucial in developing high-quality services.

There are a number of ways to create staff rosters. In the organisation where we did our research a four-week fixed-roster was utilised. This means that a staff member will work the same hours on the corresponding day of each 28-day cycle. One benefit for employees is that each staff member can work out what day he or she will be working *ad infinitum*. A fixed-roster has a tendency towards staff-centredness. This is acknowledged by the organisation's own *Disability Services Workforce Study* (DHS 2005a), which highlighted the need to improve the utilisation of staff by exploring client-centred rosters and promoting greater staff flexibility.[5]

If staff on a fixed-roster are unwilling to change their scheduled hours or countenance any flexibility, then resident activities may have to fit in with the staff schedule, as this example illustrates.

Two women came to the Christmas party at 96 High Street from another group home. The accompanying staff member was due to finish work at eight o'clock that evening. She left the party with the two women at half-past-seven in order to get back to the group home, so that she could leave at the end of her rostered shift. The women were the last to arrive, ate some food, and were then taken home immediately afterwards.

An organisation one of the authors worked for operated a three-week flexible-roster. As with fixed-rosters, there are rules about the number of days in a row that a person should work, the length of shifts, procedures for requesting 'days off' and so on, but flexible-rosters tend to be more 'client-centred'. Each three-week roster was created to fit in with the service-users' fluid lives. Consequently, each staff member only knew what days he or she was working when the roster was published. Support to residents could be allocated much more flexibly to accommodate doctor's appointments, meetings, leisure activities and so on. In the above instance the staff hours would have been allocated to fit in with the residents' wishes regarding their arrival and departure from the party.

Rules regarding the construction of rosters are determined by a number of 'internal' and 'external' factors, such as the policies of a particular organisation, whether the workforce is unionised, and legislation limiting the length of the working day. Employees in the research organisation were backed by a strong union, which was heavily involved in negotiating the redeployment of staff from the institution (Kew Residential Services) to group homes. This house supervisor's desire to make better use of the available staff hours were hamstrung by agreements that had been reached at more senior levels.

Currently the roster that we have was developed to meet the needs of the staff so they would agree to come and work here when the house opened. We've found [reviewing the rosters] very difficult because we have to include the union from Kew. They have a list of things that they're wanting to be met. There were only two staff here under the Kew EBA [Enterprise Bargaining Agreement], we weren't allowed to touch their hours or their shifts, and those two lines dictated what the rest of the roster did. We were unable to move it, we've attempted about ten times in the last two and a half years. I have a roster developed that I'm just sitting on. For example, one day in the roster we have two full-time staff members on all day, and there's no residents at home, and a third staff member starting at one o'clock. [Those hours] could be used to do a lot of great stuff, but I don't think you need quite that much time, when we could put that in a Friday night, or one other day where we could really support more one-to-one activities. There's lots of examples of that in the roster.

Past agreements had given greater weight to reducing the number of days that people worked, rather than limiting the length of their working day. Whereas most full-time employees might expect to work 20 days in a four-week period, the four full-time employees at 96 High Street worked either 16 or 17 days. Whilst staff have the benefit of extra days 'at home', the residents' 'quality of life' is likely to suffer, because staff members will probably not be able to sustain good practice when their working days are elongated to compensate for fewer days at work.

Another feature of the roster that is incredibly difficult is I've got staff working 13-hour days. And I don't know how you can get an effective work, I can performance-manage as much as I like, but you can't performance-manage fatigue. Thirteen-hour days are a standard. It's just impossible, so you have to be really sensitive with your staff and take all of those sorts of things into consideration. I can't expect 110 per cent out of my staff if they've been working for 13 hours a day. I might get 50 or 40 [per cent] by the end of the day. Those sorts of things have to be taken into consideration as well, I mean, you've got to be realistic.

Figure 8.1 shows the times when house supervisors started their shifts on weekdays and at weekends, which reveals that house supervisors were more likely to start work in the morning. There is a rationale for this, which reflects perceptions about the house supervisor's tasks that are thought to be important.

House supervisors tended to talk about their position as if it had two components: 'working with the residents or administration'; 'hands-on or paperwork'; 'out there or office work'; 'contact or non-contact time'. During the weekdays, when the residents go to day programmes, starting work in the morning allows time for what this house supervisor abbreviates to 'admin'.

The Department gives you admin times, and those times are usually through the day when the ladies are at placement. If you start at seven o'clock in the morning you'll work seven 'til ten-thirty on the floor, showering, feeding and spending time with the ladies and getting them ready for placement. Then whatever else chores that have to be done around the house around 'til about ten or eleven. Then we've got three or four hours to deal with admin. The girls are home again at around about four, and by then you've had enough of admin anyway, so you're happy to go out. You have to be really dedicated in making sure that you do your admin in those hours. There's days when you don't want to do it and there's a million other things that happen and there's a million other meetings you've got to go to, but you've just got to be self-driven I suppose, to make sure that you get it done in those [hours]. What you've missed today you make sure you pick up and do it tomorrow so you don't get behind. I guess it's a bit of time-management.

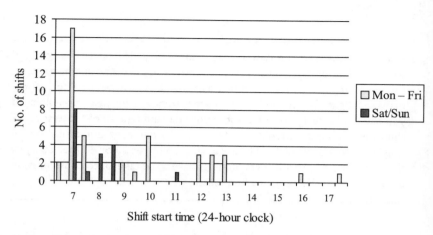

Figure 8.1 Frequency of house supervisor shift start-times on weekdays and at weekends

This arrangement allows the house supervisor to engage in direct support at a busy time of the day and have time for paper-based tasks. For employees who had a sense of how the post has evolved, there was a perception that house supervisors had to deal with an increased amount of paperwork.

> I think the administrative stuff has grown exponentially. When I was a house supervisor my non-contact time was eight hours, and that was low for anyone back then. Even now I think our houses that have got 20 [non-contact] hours are struggling to get through the paperwork that's required of them, the monitoring and the checking and the reporting. So to go from 8 to 20 in six years…in another two or three years I can easily see that average being 25, it's huge.

Jobs are seldom static, and so tasks can be added or removed from the house supervisor's current duties. Changes in the general environment can create changes in the balance of tasks. There is a consensus that the management of risk has become more central to the provision of human services, which is related to a preoccupation with safety in the general environment (Furedi 1997; Green and Sykes 2007).

House supervisors are spending more and more time [identifying and monitoring safety issues within the physical environment]. How they do that takes up a good 30 per cent of their office-based time. I think that it's worthy of highlighting the importance that has in their environment now. Following up investigations for DINMAs,[6] house supervisors need to complete manual handling risk assessments for each task that a resident does. With some houses that's one hundred risk assessments, so it's a huge task. There's Occupational Assault risk assessments. This one [house supervisor competence] undersells the importance that's placed on it now.

If the administrative load for house supervisors has been increased, then it is no surprise that time to complete administration is seen to be important. Employees respond to what their managers emphasise as being important (see Mansell and Elliott 2001). And so, for some people, there may be a tendency to privilege administration over effectively supporting the residents. This manager, for instance, makes a case for increasing the time for administration.

I think house supervisors don't get enough non-contact time... Non-contact hours [for house supervisors] in our region vary a lot. We can have as little as 13 a fortnight in some houses, which by the time you've probably signed your timesheets and you've done your CERS [Client Expenditure Record System] and filled a few shifts and whatever else, that's gone, without doing any of the other stuff, including the supervision which we're supposed to all be doing really regularly... My biggest feedback from this [interview] process would be, you know, 13 hours in a fortnight is not enough, and 20 hours isn't enough in some houses. House supervisors are constantly being given new tools, and new policies and procedures and programmes and so forth, but there's no extra time to be doing that. So I think we need to look at that.

As we argued in the previous chapter, it is important that the house supervisor's position does not mutate into a *non-practising managing professional* (Causer and Exworthy 1999). Without clear guidance about what is important, the competing demands of paper-based tasks and 'hands on' practice may create stress for some individuals.

We're supposed to be client-focused, yet we're supposed to be bloody well documenting everything that's going on with the clients at the same time, and I can't see how you can do that. 'I'm sorry if you want a coffee, but I've really got to do five file notes, an incident report, and fill this shift, tough!' And so as a result what are you going to do? You're going to throw that chair, and I'm going to do another incident report because I couldn't respond to your needs or wants because I've got to do five file notes, an incident report, and…we really do need a little bit more time for the administration side of what we're doing here. Either that or just ditch the administration, one or the other.[7]

The administrative tasks of a house supervisor cannot just be ditched, although some processes might be able to be jettisoned, streamlined or off-loaded either upwards or downwards. There are choices to be made in establishing any job's boundaries, and so in relation to the administrative element, judgements should be made about what tasks house supervisors should do. In any group home it is worth asking:

- Are certain activities consuming a disproportionate amount of the house supervisor's time?

- Are house supervisors doing the most important work for someone in the position?

- What aspects of the job need to be strengthened or weakened?

In our research setting, some house supervisors' workload appeared to be out of balance. This may have been because some individuals had misjudged their priorities. In other cases it may be that their job is 'undoable' in 152 hours a month. For many, the requisite organisational structures were not in place to enable them to be effective house supervisors.

It was beyond the scope of this project to identify the ideal workload for a house supervisor. Any significant changes to people's conditions of service will have to be negotiated with the relevant stakeholders in particular settings. Hewitt and Larson (2005) suggest that house supervisors should do no more than 10–15 hours per week of direct support to maintain the right balance of supervisory and direct support work, although it is not clear how they have arrived at this figure. What was clear in our research setting was that the aspects of the job that are specifically related to practice leadership need to be brought more centre-stage, as they were not prominent enough. This would mean that house supervisors should reduce the amount of time that they spend directly supporting the residents and undertaking administration, in order to create time for the tasks related to practice leadership. This is likely to require a financial injection, but moving towards this arrangement may also be achieved by allocating existing resources differently, in those instances where some staff hours are not used effectively or efficiently.

House supervisors bear a big responsibility for service quality, but we have tried to show that the entire burden should not fall on their shoulders, as this manager underscores.

House supervisors have a role in modelling, teaching and coaching, but I think there's a bit too much reliance placed on a house supervisor's ability to model, teach and coach, and there are not enough other developmental opportunities provided to direct care staff. We always leave it in the hands of the house supervisor to develop staff. They certainly go and get training on mandatory things like first aid and manual handling, but in terms of 'communication with residents' and the broader issues that people would always benefit from tossing around in a room of other people, direct care staff don't get that. I think there's increasingly more pressure on house supervisors to be the one-stop shop for information and support for direct care staff. It's a lot of pressure.

Overloading house supervisors is a sure-fire way to create the perception of an unattractive job, erode goodwill, create burnt-out employees and increase turnover.

Rules and procedures: The importance of clarity

The impact of resources and organisational structures on the house supervisor's position were strongly featured in our data, which we have used to illustrate the importance of understanding organisational context. In the second half of the chapter we develop this theme through a broader discussion of how multiple understandings of rules and procedures shape organisational reality. Throughout the book we have identified the lack of clarity in regard to a number of policy goals, especially in relation to people with severe and profound intellectual disabilities. A lack of clarity can manifest itself in a number of ways, such as ambiguity, conflict and incongruence. If managers in an organisation leave it to 'subordinate' employees to interpret vague policy goals for themselves, then the final meaning of policy rests with them (Becker 2007). In such circumstances employees may believe that they are doing what is required of them. Where policies and procedures are understood and enacted in ways that are not aligned with 'ordinary life' outcomes, this obviously impacts on outcomes for service-users.

It is hard to make any progress towards a goal when there is some uncertainty as to what it is. We showed that ambiguity is present most thoroughly in relation to the goal of *building inclusive communities*. However, we have highlighted and discussed other key concepts that are similarly ambiguous: choice, control, decision-making, independence, friendship, meaningful engagement, 'quality of life', reciprocity, rights and self-determination.

There is evidence to suggest that the greatest influence on how a person actually behaves in an organisation is the 'leadership' of the person's immediate supervisor (Georgiades and Phillimore 1975). When policy is ambiguous, managers can inadvertently communicate messages that are deficient when measured against the 'ordinary life' benchmark. If, for example, a house supervisor understands 'inclusion' as *community presence*, then the practice of an entire staff team may be shaped by that narrow understanding. It is therefore particularly important that house supervisors have a clear understanding of an organisation's policy.

A similar process may be evident when a functional department's perspective of what is important is not aligned with 'an ordinary life'. Within larger organisations some functional departments (e.g. finance or human resources) can act autonomously and fail to consider how other areas will be affected by their agenda (Proehl 2001). This house supervisor was disappointed by a decision made in another part of the organisation:

One thing that I wasn't very happy about is that a couple of years ago they took all of the residents' names off the utility bills. I was very upset about that. So it's now just a generic [bill]. I understand it from an administrative point of view; however, it did fly in the face of being someone's home. Even if [people are] renting the home you'd still have their name on the bill. I was worried about the lack of consultation as well, that it was just done without any consultation. That's depriving someone of a basic right. You can't take somebody's name off a bill without informing them first. I mean we would be outraged if that happened to us.

Financial controls are an important aspect of an organisation's formal practices (Martin 2002). The day-to-day operation of the organisation's Client

Expenditure Record System is a good example of how rules and procedures had a significant impact on how people did their job, particularly because it was backed up by robust monitoring mechanisms.

A long-standing service goal has been to give service-users opportunities to have money in their hands. Amongst other things, this allows them to learn about its function and value; hand over money and receive change in shops so that they can engage with shop assistants; and be seen as contributing members of society. Financial departments put in place procedures to monitor and control expenditure, and in human service organisations they are often motivated to protect public money and the limited resources of people with intellectual disabilities.

We observed staff being trained about the organisation's financial controls. In addition to learning about the formal procedures and the documents they would have to use, the trainer also told the staff a number of stories of employees doing things wrong and getting caught. Stories contain morals for the listeners (Martin 2002). In this particular training session there seemed to be an implicit view that staff are not to be trusted and must therefore be monitored.

The trainer showed the staff a laminated picture, which had a person beating off a large dog with a stick. In the trees a policeman is watching. The auditors were likened to the dog. If the regular monitoring system detected errors, then it was suggested a whole team of people would come to the house to do more thorough and wider searches. They were told that they would receive a six-monthly audit now they were in the community.

One house had gone on holiday recently and a receipt had been submitted for videos. The auditors had phoned the video store to see what videos had been hired. They were deemed not to be 'politically correct'. The staff involved were 'counselled'.

Staff who leave the premises with money that has not been recorded could be charged with 'theft, fraud and misappropriation of funds'. The trainer referred to an employee at [the institution] who had siphoned off money for about two-and-a-half years. The participants were familiar with the story. The system was said to be so tight now that people would be caught after one month, and the amount of money people could take would be negligible. 'Not worth losing your job for.'

A story was told of a staff member who reported a bank card as being stolen, who was subsequently caught on video at Crown Casino withdrawing money from an ATM.

There is a disposal policy for throwing away clients' items. The trainer gave examples of staff behaviour. A staff member says that a CD player got broken by the person's challenging behaviour and that he threw it away. The bin got emptied. The implication of the story is that the CD player is at the staff's home.

A staff member deliberately purchases shoes that are a little large and then buys them off the resident for $20.00.

One of the parents gives you $50.00 to buy something for her son. She's a bit dotty. Next week she says it was $100.00. You're not guilty as it is her word against yours, but you are under suspicion.

Specific staff in the group homes were given debit cards and urged to use electronic payments, which creates a detailed record of expenditure. Not only does this limit opportunities for residents to handle cash, but a climate had been created where staff become reluctant to use money, which is more prone to minor accounting errors. Messages communicated about the operation of the financial system, as well as the formal procedure itself, influences direct support staff's decisions about how to use it, which in turn impacts on outcomes for service-users.

Unless an understanding of 'an ordinary life' is distributed throughout an organisation, the decisions made by people in functional departments that are more removed from service-delivery can negatively impact on the residents' lives. It is therefore important to scrutinise each decision made in the design and implementation of programmes in order to try and ascertain whether the things that people are going to do will produce the outcomes you want (Mansell *et al.* 1987). Although some unintended consequences will inevitably arise, some of the less desirable outcomes we have described could have been anticipated by a more thorough interrogation of aims and objectives, intended future actions, policies and procedures and so on. Nowhere is this more true than in the design of group homes.

The design of services: Architectural features, location, size and staffing

Chapter 3 contained a number of examples of 'upstream' decisions impacting on the practices and outcomes we observed in group homes. We argued that the design of a group home, its décor and furnishings shape what people within those services can see and do (Wolfensberger 1975).

On the one hand, the group homes were equipped with the normal range of domestic equipment to provide the necessary context in which to promote typical patterns of living. But on the other hand, there were some factors that undermined 'ordinary life' aspirations, such as the provision of separate staff amenities that promoted the feel of a 'workplace'. When separate amenities are endorsed by official policy, then it was no surprise that we observed informal practices that made unnecessary distinctions between residents and staff, such as staff mugs, plates and cupboards.

In addition to architectural features, researchers have investigated the impact of a number of other variables, such as the group home's location, group size and staffing (Felce and Perry 1995). Decisions about these issues are usually made upstream.

LOCATION

People with intellectual disabilities have significant constraints regarding the choices available to them about where to live. This is even though the Victorian Government states that, 'as much as possible, people with a disability should be able to choose where they live, with whom and in what type of housing – just like most other members of the Victorian community' (DHS 2002b, p.18).

Principles such as this are typically forced into the background when financial considerations shape what happens in an organisation (Morgan 1997). The dollar may be more important in shaping a decision about where to site a group home, rather than an understanding of how a location can impact on the type of skills that individuals with intellectual disabilities can develop, and how they are perceived by other people (Wolfensberger and Thomas 1983). The availability of community resources, such as shopping options, public services, spiritual centres and recreational facilities, should be a consideration about where to site a group home, as they have implications for 'inclusion' within the local neighbourhood.

Without close proximity to community resources, residents are likely to be dependent on being driven to them, especially when public transport is poor, or people have significant physical impairments. The focal group homes in our research had a minibus, which could accommodate all the residents and the supporting staff. As the design of services shapes what people do, then having a large bus is implicated in the high frequency of group trips that we discussed in Chapters 4 and 6. Group outings may be desirable on occasions, but as a dominant type of outing they are inconsistent with providing more individualised planning and support.

GROUP SIZE AND STAFFING

We have defined a group home as accommodation for between four and six people. This size provides an initial advantage in providing high-quality services over larger residential settings (Felce 1998). Decisions to develop group homes, and how to group people within them, are made upstream. Even within this limited range (four to six residents), the number of residents, their support needs and the number of staff have consequences for the more localised context in which house supervisors are managing.

Having one extra resident increases the workload within a group home significantly. There is one extra Person-Centred Plan to complete, another network of family and service providers to liaise with, extra progress notes to write, another set of individual needs to accommodate within a group context and so on.

Of the 16 house supervisors whom we interviewed, the average house supervisor was responsible for managing about seven staff. In the Larson et al. (2007) study it was just over nine direct support staff. Average figures mask significant differences in the size of staff teams. In our sample, excluding the house supervisor, the smallest staff team was five, and the largest 12. This means that house supervisors in different settings must inevitably be faced with a different balance of tasks and teamwork dynamics to manage.

I have 12 staff so I have 12 different ideas on the one subject. If I don't effectively manage that they start to squabble amongst themselves and they start getting allegiances and alliances with each other and it becomes that survival thing. I think that we don't equip our supervisors with communication skills and styles.

In larger staff teams there is more formal supervision to undertake, more timesheets to complete, more shifts to fill and so on. These houses may have a 'deputy' house supervisor to offset the increased managerial load.

Recruitment

Recruiting suitable people to the direct support role, and keeping them, are often cited as related managerial concerns. The annual turnover rates of staff in these positions can be high. In a North American study the annual turnover rate for direct support staff was just under 40 per cent and for house supervisors just over 24 per cent (Larson et al. 2007). The availability of suitably qualified employees is related to factors in the general environment, such as levels of unemployment, salary levels relative to other available jobs and so on. The absence of available qualified people may lead to an upstream decision to adjust recruitment criteria. Ongoing recruitment issues led this house supervisor to exclaim, 'We're lucky to get a casual to come in and do a shift. I've got seven vacant rows for Pete's sake. We don't care [who we get], so long as it's a body.'

There can be significant differences in the competence levels of employees in the same job. The foundational skills in English literacy, numeracy and basic computer skills that we discussed in Chapter 5 may be absent in some employees.

What I'm finding is in this house in particular is that [the direct support staff are] not into paperwork. They're not as skilled in language, in paperwork tasks; they're not skilled in computer. I don't think any of them are computer-literate at a level where they want to be on the computer. That's a disadvantage for me in terms of the support I've been able to receive from the staff in that sense.

This has significant implications for the level of support that house supervisors have to provide and whether they can delegate tasks to direct support staff. The house supervisor below is significantly advantaged in comparison to the previous one.

There's some things that you can get other staff to do, and that includes the whole admin role. It gives them another insight into what else is going on in the house besides just caring for the ladies. Suzette, for example, looks after the medication cupboard to make sure that all the medications are in, that we have backups if we run out, so that there isn't a time that we run out, that all the prescriptions are up to date. That's a huge responsibility. You can be down the doctor's two or three times a month getting prescriptions and working with the chemist to make sure that everything's right. There's times when the meds come in and the chemist has been busy or they've had a different chemist on and things are packed wrong, so they've all got to be checked. That's quite a big ob, and that's now something that Suzette looks after. I do a lot of the medical appointments, so that you can stay on top of what's going on with the ladies and what they need, but there's a lot of other tests and follow-up things that I don't necessarily have to go to. So I always get the staff involved in that for the same reasons, (a) it helps me, and (b) it keeps them in a loop, it keeps them involved. If they're going to be a part of the ladies' lives, then they need to be able to be a part of all of their lives, not just the nice bits or the mundane bits.

Training

House supervisors and direct support staff need to be proficient in a significant number of competencies at the time of recruitment, and to be competent in the majority within 90 days of hire (Larson *et al.* 2007). Yet very few new direct support staff or house supervisors begin their employment with all the KSAOs they require to be competent employees. Staff training is therefore consistently identified as a key factor in realising 'an ordinary life'. With regard to the house supervisor we have signposted a training curriculum through the house supervisor competencies. We have discussed the importance of specific areas, such as Active Support and keyworking, and highlighted a number of areas in our research context where there seems to be a significant gap between what employees are required to do and actual performance: i.e. facilitating relationships between people with intellectual disabilities and non-disabled people; discovering people's needs and wants; communicating with people with severe and profound disabilities; and displaying medium to long-term planning skills.

However, many of these issues are beyond the training received by most front-line employees, which tends to cover minimum statutory requirements and basic introductory material (Mansell 2005). Training topics send a signal about what is important. The content of an organisation's induction programme and in-service training are influenced by pressures from the general environment and perceptions of what is important in the task environment. Where keeping employees safe is seen as being paramount there is legislation mandating training on Occupational Health and Safety. Where keeping residents safe is an overriding principle, then Fire and Emergency Evacuation Training and First Aid are privileged. Employees tend to have to repeat these courses to maintain competence.

In the Larson *et al.* (2007) study, the average organisation spent 3.7 per cent of their budget on 'training, employee assistance and staff development' activities. In a context where the money available is limited, the training that tends to be given priority will not instil the KSAOs that are necessary to realise the range of 'ordinary life' outcomes. High turnover rates of direct support staff undermine the critical mass of staff needed in each house to achieve these goals.

Weak implementation and gaps in rules and procedures

In addition to suffering from a lack of clarity, there may be weaknesses in implementing rules and procedures, or an absence of organisational policy.

There is an adage that states, 'What gets measured gets done.' Performance monitoring allows an organisation to verify whether it is carrying out its processes as intended and discover if they are achieving the desired outcomes (LaVigna *et al.* 1994). We have highlighted other procedures that were not subject to such rigorous monitoring as the Client Expenditure Record System discussed earlier. For example, we used quotations from house supervisors to suggest that the *Professional Development and Supervision Policy and Practice Guidelines* (DHS 2005b) had not been properly embedded since its release. If *planned formal supervision* had been subject to such rigorous monitoring and review it might have been more strongly implemented. A performance monitoring system would have highlighted the organisation's failings in meeting its 'supervision' objectives. As we suggested in Chapter 1, the problem of weak implementation is a major reason for why poor outcomes are found in many group homes (Mansell 2006).

Sines (1992) identified a number of management systems that are required to reinforce desired practice. We have discussed a number of them, e.g. *planned formal supervision meetings*, house meetings. An additional system is 'staff development and performance review', which we prefer to call *formal performance appraisal.*

Formal appraisal is an important process by which managers can assess employee performance and discuss work issues in a systematic and planned way with the staff they manage (Cole 1988). There are many ways to undertake formal appraisal, but a common way is to have an annual meeting between the line-manager and the 'subordinate' to identify the person's level of job performance, strengths and weaknesses, identify training needs, and establish goals for the coming year. This process is related to the ongoing *planned formal supervision* we have discussed, but different enough for many organisations to have distinct supervision and appraisal processes.

There was no discrete performance appraisal system for employees working in the group homes in the research setting, which we highlight as a procedural gap. A weakness in the organisation's formal practices establishes a context for weaker management. The house supervisor's job could be expanded to encompass this useful process.

The context in which house supervisors are managing

Although group homes can appear to be very similar, digging beneath surface appearances reveals significant differences between houses. There are important individual differences in the people who live in group homes. In one house a resident may have diabetes, whilst in another a person may exhibit self-injurious behaviour. House supervisors must have the skills to deal with variation in the residents' characteristics, which may require some specific training.

Our findings suggest significant variability between settings, which creates an uneven context for managing a group home. There may be as much variation within an organisation as there is between organisations. One group home may have four residents, whilst another may have six. Some houses may have their own transport, others may not. Some houses are sited in locations that have advantages over other settings. The staff team in one house may be comprised of five people, in another it is 12. The staff in one setting may be extremely competent, whilst in another they may have significant weaknesses. Some houses have a rostered house meeting, others do not. Opportunities for *planned formal supervision meetings* may vary from house to house. Some houses have a full staff complement, others have vacant lines, and so on.

The managerial context changes as one examines a specific group home. These are important contextual factors that are likely to be important in explaining the outcomes found in a particular group home. A house supervisor performing competently in one setting could struggle in another where the challenges are overwhelming.

Variation in organisational structures and the allocation of resources is something that is amenable to senior management intervention. The house supervisor's job is difficult enough, without an organisation creating extra barriers to overcome. Senior managers should ensure that, regardless of where house supervisors work, they are operating on a level playing field. This will mean, at a minimum, giving consideration to the issues we have discussed in this chapter.

Concluding remarks

In highlighting 'upstream' responsibilities, we must not overlook 'downstream' ones. As Ashbaugh points out, 'Change is led from the top down and implemented from the bottom up' (2008, p.480). It would therefore be wrong to depict the staff in a group home as casualties of an inadequate system, or as totally compliant to management's will. On the contrary, we have presented them as having a considerable degree of autonomy, sometimes developing informal practices that run counter to what is required to realise 'an ordinary life' for the service's residents.

If direct support staff believe that certain goals are too hard or not practical for the people they support, then their practice is likely to be based on their own beliefs and judgements. Anyone who has worked in residential services for any length of time will have experienced carefully constructed teaching plans and behaviour support plans being undermined by one or a number of staff 'doing their own thing'. A technology like Active Support may generate Activity and Support Plans for staff to follow, but there is enough 'wiggle room' that endows staff with discretionary powers to shape the running of the house and plan leisure activities when they are 'on duty'. Room to manoeuvre allows staff to privilege *community presence* over activities that might lead to *community participation*.

A degree of autonomy is a consequence of the way community-based services are structured. The dispersed nature of the service, i.e. group homes spread over urban and rural Victoria, creates relatively *autonomous work groups* within those settings (Handy 1993). This means that staff groups can create norms and pursue objectives that are incongruent with 'an ordinary life', such as the staff group whose practices resulted in resident disengagement.

As direct support staff practices are often unobserved by house supervisors, individual direct support staff have a significant amount of autonomy to carry out their role independently of what is required by rules and procedures. House supervisors may therefore have little awareness of the day-to-day work of their employees and many direct support staff can be left more or less to their own devices. Their autonomy is exacerbated in settings where direct support staff work with people with severe and profound intellectual disabilities, where feedback to third parties from these 'silent' service-users is unlikely.

In order to realise 'an ordinary life', staff must carry out their role as required. To give this the best chance of happening senior managers must do everything they can to reduce ambiguity. The principle of 'clarity' should extend to every domain, i.e. organisational procedures, operational policies, job descriptions, operational goals, well-defined outcomes and so on. If this is done, then employees who are not performing in the required manner are actively choosing to do so, rather than being guided by visions that they have worked out for themselves. Fournies offers a blunt remedy: 'When it seems clear that a person is wilfully not improving performance, and your coaching discussions fail, terminate the employment' (1988, p.62).

Although clarity about how to achieve 'an ordinary life' is a prerequisite for realising it, we should not assume that 'clarity', together with the right formal practices, automatically give management greater control of front-line practice. It certainly makes it more likely, but the nature of community-based services creates organisations where monitoring and directing the practice of employees is hard. Nonetheless, we need to structure the delivery of support in a way that the evidence suggests is associated with positive outcomes. If this is done, people with severe and profound intellectual disabilities will be best placed to benefit from the inherent opportunities that are found in group homes (Felce *et al.* 1998).

Issues for consideration

- Do your group homes have the necessary resources and organisational structures in place?

- Are resources available for the key managerial systems: *planned formal supervision*, house meetings and performance appraisal?

- Is there a clear link between what employees are expected to do and the organisation's strategic direction? Look for procedural gaps and evaluate how well existing policy is being implemented.

- Are the decisions being made producing the outcomes you want?

- Are staff being allocated in a way that ensures that the best use is being made of their time? Develop flexible, client-centred rosters.

- Do employees in every department understand what is meant by 'an ordinary life' for people with intellectual disabilities? Are their actions aligned with this overarching goal?

Notes

1   Some group homes had ongoing vacancies in their staff teams, which they 'filled' by employing casual employees. A 'permanent casual' referred to someone who worked regularly at the house over a longish period.

2   It is important that consideration should be given to the residents' support needs when scheduling house meetings. Many of the house meetings we observed resulted in residents being left unoccupied for the duration of house meetings. House meetings need to happen in settings where the residents do not make use of a separate day programme. Some thought will need to be given to how meetings can take place and the residents receive support.

3   'Non-contact time' is time not directly supporting the residents.

4   A time-management course is often put forward as the solution for house supervisors who report that they are struggling to manage their time effectively. This is often a good example of 'downstream' thinking. Time-management training may be worthwhile, but the general

focus of such training is on helping the individual rather than examining the organisational context. It may be the case that the organisation is a more appropriate target for intervention.

5   Any roster will be more or less client-centred, or more or less staff-centred. They are not absolute terms, but reflect the degree to which the interests of these different stakeholders have been prioritised. As a 'service-industry', a group home's roster should be skewed towards the client-centred end of the continuum.

6   DINMA is an acronym for Disease Incident Near Miss Accident reports.

7   Mansell (1996) reports that in a home for eight people, there were 72 different types of form or record in use, of which only seven related directly to service-users.

Chapter 9

Final Thoughts

Introduction

Over the last two decades enthusiasm for the group home has waned in some quarters. Peter Kinsella (1993a), an advocate of supported living, acknowledged that people's 'quality of life' improved when they moved from institutions into group homes, but he also asked rhetorically whether people in these settings had the best 'quality of life'. In a similar vein, LaVigna *et al.* wrote:

> No more than 10 or 15 years ago...small group homes were seen as the major alternative for people who had previously lived in state institutions. Today, however, group homes are considered passé. The supported living service model now is seen as more capable of meeting consumer needs and having the potential of providing a better quality of life. In the meantime, some agencies are still wedded to the institutional model, and some are *just getting into* the group home model, not realizing that the train has already left that station. (1994, p.89)

Is a group home the best accommodation for people with severe and profound intellectual disabilities? Perhaps not, although this is a question that must be settled by research. Is it passé? In the sense that some detractors consider the model to be unfashionable, possibly. However, if critics are proposing that the model has been superseded, then the answer is definitely not. In the USA, between 1995 and 2005, the number of people living in group homes increased from 63,431 to 107,118 (Lakin and Stancliffe 2007), a significant rate of growth for a service model that has supposedly had its day (see Figure 1.2). The group home will be one of the range of accommodation options available to people with intellectual disabilities for the foreseeable future.

There are a number of problems with declaring the group home passé. We have argued that limited economic resources will determine that people with severe and profound intellectual disabilities are more likely to live in these settings. If the train has left the station, where does that leave those individuals who are living in group homes? On the platform waiting for the next train to leave? In the minibus on the way to the station? More likely, languishing in a form of accommodation that has been written off by its critics?

Declaring group homes to be passé, if there is little chance that 'better' options will be made available, is demoralising for the organisations that manage them, the staff who work in them and the relatives of the residents who live in them. If group homes are framed as being outmoded, this may have consequences for the resources that are allocated for their upkeep, attracting high-quality staff to work in them and whether they are worth researching.

Although we fully support the political struggle to transform society for all people with intellectual disabilities, the practical task of supporting hundreds of thousands of people with intellectual disabilities in group homes remains an important commitment. In this final chapter we highlight this book's contribution towards this end, and provide a summary of some general points for the future management of group homes as a supplement to the specific questions raised in the separate chapters.

What the book has done

The book has concerned itself with the group home, which we defined as accommodation for between four and six people with intellectual disabilities who require extensive or pervasive paid staff support. We argued that, for a number of pragmatic reasons, the group home will remain part of the intellectual disability service landscape. As such, staff teams must strive to stay true to its original aspirations, the realisation of a number of broad social policy goals that we placed underneath our preferred umbrella term, 'an ordinary life'.

Our findings have underscored a key message from the extant research literature, that the use of small houses equipped with all the paraphernalia for 'ordinary living' is not sufficient to promote 'ordinary lifestyles'. We have highlighted a number of issues that must be addressed if services are to make better progress towards the realisation of 'an ordinary life'. If the vast majority of group homes can consistently achieve good outcomes, this will make the model less open to criticism.

Weak implementation

We drew on the notion of weak implementation to explain why poor outcomes are found in some group homes and illustrated this with examples from our research. We implicitly differentiated between two different 'types' of weak implementation: the first is related to a group home's 'design' and the second to the notion of 'process fidelity' (Rossi *et al.* 2004).

In order for a group home to function in the way that it is meant to, we need to pay attention to its architecture, by which we mean its conceptual structure. All of the prerequisite 'parts' have to be in place. For various reasons, perhaps due to inadequate resources or poor senior management, a group home may be operating without important structures, such as regular staff meetings. In this case, the poor outcomes are a consequence of the way the service is designed. Alternatively, if all the parts are in place, they may not put into practice very well. For example, a technology like Active Support must be well implemented if it is to have the best chance of increasing the levels of the resident engagement in a group home.

Systems theory and complexity

We have adopted and promoted a systemic orientation, i.e. the need to understand how an organisational system functions as a whole. An advantage of taking up this perspective is that it encourages every employee in a human service organisation to understand that they have a responsibility for ensuring quality lifestyles.

In part, the failure to realise good outcomes in group homes can be attributed to poor management practices. We drew attention to the significant role played by the house supervisor, but attributed greater responsibility to managers at more senior levels. We highlighted a number of ways in which senior decision-makers had misjudged, or failed to consider, the impact of their decisions on the group home environment.

Systems theory also cautions us to be prudent in the claims we make about cause–effect relationships, because human service organisations are complex, dynamic environments. As important as a house supervisor is, an incumbent might face significant organisational barriers in fulfilling her role, particularly when inadequate attention is given to the way that the service is resourced or structured.

Each group home can also be conceptualised as a sub-system, with a specific context that we need to understand. For example, group homes differ in the available resources and in staff and residents' characteristics, and these contextual factors will be important in explaining the outcomes found in a particular group home. We also suggested that organisational systems, such as keyworking, may need to be tailored to the particular context in which they are being implemented.

Systems theory also draws our attention to an organisation's relationships with the external environment. We suggested that human service organisations are less successful at facilitating outcomes that are not under their direct control. For instance, some aspects of the goal of *building inclusive communities* require direct support staff to intervene in settings where their sphere of influence is limited.

Severe and profound intellectual disability

We have argued that differences in people's level of intellectual disability have real consequences for how services are delivered. Some of the issues faced by individuals with profound intellectual disabilities are different to those faced by people with mild intellectual disabilities. The greater the level of intellectual disability, the more these issues are to do with the personal restrictions of disability, and hence are less likely to be remedied through the elimination of social barriers.

Although all people with intellectual disabilities are judged by others in terms of this label, this process seems to be extremely strong in regard to people with severe and profound intellectual disabilities. In Victoria, the service-provider Scope used the slogan 'See the person, not the disability' in a series of campaigns to challenge perceptions about people with a disability. It seems to be the case that people find it hard to reduce the significance given to severe and profound intellectual disability.

Social policy goals

Paradoxically, people with severe and profound intellectual disabilities receive little direct mention in the social policy literature. Social policy goals are often written as if their targets are a homogeneous population. We have suggested that this makes them hard to apply to people with severe and profound intellectual disabilities, as a broad goal does not detail the nuanced ways in which meaningful outcomes can vary for subgroups. Without any differentiation in policy documents, many staff working with people with severe and profound intellectual disabilities try to apply commonsense understandings of specific social policy terms, which they may reject as being irrelevant to the people they support.

The importance of what staff 'do' and informal culture

We stressed that outcomes are a consequence of the things that people do. Supporting people with severe or profound intellectual disabilities inevitably means that staff performance is closely linked to the residents' 'quality of life'.

We categorised some of the things direct support staff 'do' as informal practices. Informal practices are not found in any procedural manuals, and this usually means that staff are not doing what they are supposed to be doing. A formal service culture, its working methods and training cannot be simply passed to staff (Felce *et al.* 2002). Staff bring their own agendas to the workplace and are susceptible to influences other than those stemming from the service organisation. Informal practices are more likely to thrive where there are poor management practices.

Competing issues

We have suggested that many of the ideas underpinning social policy goals are not new, and that a number of human service technologies have been around for decades. Variations on the theme of 'inclusion' have shaped service-provision for people with intellectual disabilities for 30 years. Active Support, keyworking and the ideas that underpin practice leadership are all 'tried and tested' techniques. What seems to be an issue is that, over time, management attention shifts to new concerns which undermine the sustainability of good ideas and practices. Suggesting that group homes are passé is a good example of this process. Rather than maintaining a focus on how to make group homes consistently deliver good outcomes, attention shifts to new models like supported living and individualised funding; person-centred planning replaces individual programme planning; and a host of new terms like citizenship, empowerment and personalisation jostle for attention in an over-crowded lexicon.

What we need to do

If people with severe and profound intellectual disabilities are to benefit from the inherent opportunities that are found in group homes, they must be adequately resourced, and the delivery of support must be structured in a way that the evidence suggests is associated with positive outcomes. The attempts to organise important factors into a comprehensive framework remain underdeveloped, and so poses an outstanding task for researchers. Figure 1.6 is one conceptual map which attempts to show the building blocks that need to be in place to establish and maintain high-quality services.

People with severe and profound intellectual disabilities need 'the right support', and direct support staff need to be given the necessary guidance to deliver it. This requires broad social policy goals to be translated into clear statements that detail what each goal means for people with severe and profound intellectual disabilities. These specific statements should be aligned to the overarching goal of 'an ordinary life'. As far as possible, we should avoid introducing new terminology, if it merely serves to replace an existing term. This is confusing and undermines the need to develop a common language.

It is important for senior human service managers to think through every decision related to the initial design of a group home, and then to subject each subsequent alteration or addition to the same degree of scrutiny, in order to ascertain whether these decisions are going to produce the outcomes you want.

Practice leadership needs to be simultaneously promoted and developed. Organisations must make space for reflection and managers must provide regular feedback to staff about their performance, based on observations of staff practices.

Staff need to be recruited who can use, or be trained to use, the essential 'organisational systems'. Supporting people with severe and profound intellectual disabilities to 'get a life' will require support staff to do more than meet those needs that are associated with 'caring for' people. They will also require a broad understanding of 'quality of life', so that good outcomes are realised in the upper levels of Maslow's (1954/1987) 'hierarchy of needs'. This means bringing domains into focus that are often at the periphery of direct support staff's vision and making sure that they have time to work at them. Staff teams should also work to achieve a better balance between individual lifestyles and group activities, with more emphasis needing to be put on the former. Better planning processes should help in this regard.

And finally, there is research to be done that fills in the gaps in our current knowledge. We see the research methods that we have promoted, especially the use of participant observation, as being fruitful in the search to identify support practices that are reliably linked to 'quality of life' outcomes. Participant observation is well suited to investigating the situational factors that operate in a particular group home, the informal service culture, processes at work in a group home and so on.

In recent years, louder calls have been made for evidence-based policymaking and practice. We hope that the research findings presented in this book are both accessible and of use to policymakers and practitioners charged with improving the lives of people with severe and profound intellectual disabilities.

References

Abbott, S. and McConkey, R. (2006) 'The barriers to social inclusion as perceived by people with intellectual disabilities.' *Journal of Intellectual Disabilities 10*, 3, 275–287.

AIHW (2006) *Disability Support Services 2004–05: National Data on Services Provided under the Commonwealth State / Territory Disability Agreement.* Canberra: AIHW.

AIHW (2007) *Australia's Welfare 2007.* Canberra: AIHW.

Allard, M.A. (1996) 'Supported Living Policies and Programmes in the USA.' In J. Mansell and K. Ericsson (eds) *Deinstitutionalization and Community Living: Intellectual Disability Services in Britain, Scandinavia and the USA.* London: Chapman and Hall.

Allen, P., Pahl, J. and Quine, L. (1990) *Care Staff in Transition: The Impact on Staff of Changing Services for People with Mental Handicaps.* London: HMSO.

Alternatives Unlimited Inc. (2008a) *Developmental Disability Services.* Available at www.altrntvs.org/developmental.asp, accessed 22 April 2009.

Alternatives Unlimited Inc. (2008b) *Residential Services.* Available at www.altrntvs.org/developmental_residential_services.asp, accessed 22 April 2009.

Annison, J.E. (2000) 'Towards a clearer understanding of the meaning of "home".' *Journal of Intellectual and Developmental Disability 25*, 4, 251–262.

Anspach, R.R. (1979) 'From stigma to identity politics: Political activism among physically disabled and former mental patients.' *Social Science and Medicine 13A*, 765–773.

Antonak, R.F., Mulick, J.A., Kobe, F.H. and Fielder, C.R. (1995) 'Influence of mental retardation severity and respondent characteristics on self-reported attitudes toward mental retardation and eugenics.' *Journal of Intellectual Disability Research 39*, 4, 316–325.

Ashbaugh, J. (2008) 'Managing system change in human service agencies.' *Intellectual and Developmental Disabilities 46*, 6, 480–483.

Atkinson, D. (1998) 'Living in Residential Care.' In A. Brechin, J. Walmsley, J. Katz and S. Peace (eds) *Care Matters: Concepts, Practice and Research in Health and Social Care.* London: Sage Publications.

Attrill, P. (nd) *Ownership of Our Own Lives Project: A Research Project on How People with an Intellectual Disability Feel about Living in Community Residential Units.* Melbourne: Reinforce Inc.

Bartlett, P. and Wright, D. (eds) (1999) *Outside the Wall of the Asylum: The History of Care in the Community 1750–2000.* London: Athlone Press.

Bauman, Z. (2001) *Community: Seeking Safety in an Insecure World.* Cambridge: Polity Press.

Beadle-Brown, J. (2006) 'Person-centred approaches and quality of life.' *Learning Disability Review 11*, 3, 4–12.

Becker, H.S. (1963) *Outsiders: Studies in the Sociology of Deviance.* New York: Free Press.

Becker, H.S. (2007) *Telling about Society.* Chicago: University of Chicago Press.

Beer, M., Eisenstat, R.A. and Spector, B. (1990) 'Why change programs don't produce change.' *Harvard Business Review* (November–December), 158–166.

Bigby, C. (2007) 'Case Management with People with Intellectual Disabilities: Purpose, Tensions and Challenges.' In C. Bigby, C. Fyffe and E. Ozanne (eds) *Planning and Support for People with Intellectual Disabilities: Issues for Case Managers and Other Professionals.* London: Jessica Kingsley Publishers.

Bigby, C., Clement, T., Mansell, J. and Beadle-Brown, J. (2009) '"It's pretty hard with our ones, they can't talk, the more able bodied can participate": Staff attitudes about the applicability of disability policies to people with severe and profound intellectual disabilities.' *Journal of Intellectual Disability Research 53*, 4, 363–376.

Birenbaum, A. (2009) 'Left behind: Health services and people with severe disabilities.' *Intellectual and Developmental Disabilities 47*, 1, 47–49.

Blanchard, K., Zigarmi, P. and Zigarmi, D. (1986) *Leadership and the One Minute Manager.* London: Willow Books.

Blatt, B., Bogdan, R., Biklen, D. and Taylor, S.J. (1977/1981) 'From institution to community: A conversion model.' In B. Blatt (ed.) *In and Out of Mental Retardation.* Baltimore: University Park Press.

Bloomberg, K. and West, D. (1999) *The Triple C: Checklist of Communication Competencies.* Melbourne: SCIOP/Spastic Society of Victoria.

Blunden, R. and Allen, D. (eds) (1987) *Facing the Challenge: An Ordinary Life for People with Learning Difficulties and Challenging Behaviour.* London: King's Fund Centre.

Boag, G. (1998) *A Complete Guide to Learning Contracts.* Aldershot: Gower.

Braddock, D., Emerson, E., Felce, D. and Stancliffe, R.J. (2001) 'Living circumstances of children and adults with mental retardation or developmental disabilities in the United States, Canada, England and Wales, and Australia.' *Mental Retardation and Developmental Disabilities Research Reviews 7*, 115–121.

Bradshaw, J., McGill, P., Stretton, R., Kelly-Pike, A. *et al.* (2004) 'Implementation and evaluation of active support.' *Journal of Applied Research in Intellectual Disabilities 17*, 139–148.

Brechin, A., Walmsley, J., Katz, J. and Peace, S. (eds) (1998) *Care Matters: Concepts, Practice and Research in Health and Social Care.* London: Sage Publications.

British Psychological Society (2000) *Learning Disability: Definitions and Contexts.* Leicester: British Psychological Society.

Brody, R. (1993) *Effectively Managing Human Service Organizations.* London: Sage Publications.

Brost, M. and Johnson, T. (1982) *Getting to Know You.* Madison: Wisconsin Coalition for Advocacy.

Bryman, A. (1996) 'Leadership in Organizations.' In S.R. Clegg, C. Hardy and W.R. Nord (eds) *Handbook of Organizational Studies.* London: Sage Publications.

Burton, J. (1998) *Managing Residential Care.* London: Routledge.

Castellani, P. J. (2005) *From Snake Pits to Cash Cows: Politics and Public Institutions in New York.* Albany: State University of New York Press.

Causer, G. and Exworthy, M. (1999) 'Professionals as Managers across the Public Sector.' In M. Exworthy and S. Halford (eds) *Professionals and the New Managerialism in the Public Sector.* Buckingham: Open University Press.

Clegg, J. (2006) 'Understanding Intellectually Disabled Clients' Accounts.' In D. Goodley and R. Lawthom (eds) *Disability and Psychology: Critical Introductions and Reflections.* Basingstoke: Palgrave.

Clegg, J. and Lansdall-Welfare, R. (2003) 'Death, disability, and dogma.' *Philosophy, Psychiatry, Psychology 10*, 1, 67–79.

Cleland, C.C. (1979) *The Profoundly Mentally Retarded.* Englewood Cliffs, NJ: Prentice-Hall.

Clement, T. (2006) 'What's the Vision?' In C. Bigby, C. Fyffe and J. Mansell (eds) *From Ideology to Reality: Current Issues in Implementation of Intellectual Disability Policy. Proceedings of the Roundtable on Intellectual Disability Policy.* Bundoora: La Trobe University.

Clement, T. and Bigby, C. (2007) *Making Life Good in the Community: The Importance of Practice Leadership and the Role of the House Supervisor.* Melbourne: Victorian Department of Human Services.

Clement, T. and Bigby, C. (2008) *Making Life Good in the Community: Implementing Person-Centred Active Support in a Group Home for People with Profound Intellectual Disabilities: Issues for House Supervisors and Their Managers.* Melbourne: Victorian Department of Human Services.

Clement, T., Bigby, C. and Warren, S. (2008) *Making Life Good in the Community – Building Inclusive Communities: Facilitating Community Participation for People with Severe Intellectual Disabilities.* Melbourne: Victorian Department of Human Services.

Clements, J. and Zarkowska, E. (1994) *Care Staff Management: A Practitioner's Guide.* Chichester: John Wiley and Sons.

Cole, G.A. (1988) *Personnel Management: Theory and Practice.* London: D.P. Publications Ltd.

College of Direct Support (nd) *Community Support Skill Standards.* Available at www.collegeofdirectsupport.com/CDS50/content/CDSContent/csss.htm, accessed 23 April 2009.

Committee of Enquiry into Mental Handicap Nursing and Care (1979) *A Summary of the Jay Report by Members of the Committee of Enquiry into Mental Handicap Nursing and Care.* London: HMSO.

Creswell, J. (1998) *Qualitative Inquiry and Research Design: Choosing among Five Traditions.* Thousand Oaks, CA: Sage Publications.

Curtis, L. (2007) *Unit Costs of Health and Social Care.* Canterbury: Personal Social Services Research Unit, University of Kent.

Davis, F. (1961) 'Deviance disavowal: The management of strained interaction by the visibly handicapped.' *Social Problems 9,* 2, 120–132.

de Waele, I., van Loon, J., Van Hove, G. and Schalock, R.L. (2005) 'Quality of life versus quality of care: Implications for people and programs.' *Journal of Policy and Practice in Intellectual Disabilities 2,* 3/4, 229–239.

Department of Health (2001) *Valuing People: A New Strategy for Learning Disability for the 21st Century.* Norwich: Stationery Office.

Department of Health (2008a) *An Introduction to Personalisation,* last modified 18 January 2008. Available at www.dh.gov.uk/en/SocialCare/Socialcarereform/Personalisation/DH_080573, accessed 23 April 2009.

Department of Health (2008b) *Transforming Social Care.* Local Authority Circular (DH) (2008) 1. London: Department of Health.

DHS (2002a) 'Job description: DDSO3/(House Supervisor, Community Residential Unit).' Melbourne: State Government of Victoria, Department of Human Services.

DHS (2002b) *Victorian State Disability Plan 2002–2012.* Melbourne: Disability Services Division.

DHS (2005a) *Disability Services Workforce Study.* Melbourne: State Government of Victoria, Department of Human Services.

DHS (2005b) *Professional Development and Supervision Policy and Practice Guidelines.* Melbourne: State Government of Victoria, Department of Human Services.

DHS and Health Services Union of Australia (2002) HACSU Department of Human Services (Intellectual Disability Services Victoria) Kew Residential Services Redevelopment Agreement. Melbourne: State Government of Victoria, Department of Human Services.

Dipboye, R.L., Smith, C.S. and Howell, W.C. (1994) *Understanding Industrial and Organizational Psychology: An Integrated Approach.* Fort Worth, TX: Harcourt Brace College Publishers.

Disability Services Division (2007) *Planning for Individuals: A Resource Kit and Implementation Guide for Disability Service Providers.* Melbourne: State Government of Victoria, Department of Human Services.

Doran, T. (2004) 'Exit Q.' In P. Heuzenroeder (Producer) *Australia: Club Wild* (under the auspices of St Lawrence Community Services Inc).

Dowson, S. (1988) *An Ordinary Day.* London: CMH.

Dowson, S. (1997) 'Empowerment within Services: A Comfortable Delusion.' In P. Ramcharan, G. Roberts, G. Grant and J. Borland (eds) *Empowerment in Everyday Life.* London: Jessica Kingsley Publishers.

Eden, C. and Huxham, C. (1996) 'Action Research for the Study of Organizations.' In S.R. Clegg, C. Hardy and W.R. Nord (eds) *Handbook of Organization Studies.* London: Sage Publications.

Egan, G. and Cowan, M.A. (1979) *People in Systems: A Model for Development in the Human-service Professions and Education.* Monterey, CA: Brooks/Cole Publishing Company.

Egli, M., Feurer, I., Roper, T. and Thompson, T. (2002) 'The role of residential homelikeness in promoting community participation by adults with mental retardation.' *Research in Developmental Disabilities 23,* 179–190.

Ellis, G. (2000) 'Reflective Learning and Supervision.' In L. Cooper and L. Briggs (eds) *Fieldwork in the Human Services: Theory and Practice for Field Educators, Practice Teachers and Supervisors.* St Leonards: Allen and Unwin.

Emerson, E. and Hatton, C. (1994) *Moving Out: The Impact of Relocation from Hospital to Community on the Quality of Life of People with Learning Disabilities.* London: HMSO.

Emerson, E., Hastings, R. and McGill, P. (1994) 'Values, Attitudes and Service Ideology.' In E. Emerson, P. McGill and J. Mansell (eds) *Severe Learning Disabilities and Challenging Behaviour: Designing High Quality Services.* London: Chapman and Hall.

Emerson, E., Malam, S., Davies, I. and Spencer, K. (2005a) *Adults with Learning Difficulties in England 2003/4.* London: Department of Health.

Emerson, E., Robertson, J., Gregory, N., Hatton, C. *et al.* (2001) 'Quality and costs of supported living residences and group homes in the United Kingdom.' *American Journal on Mental Retardation 106,* 5, 401–15.

Emerson, E., Robertson, J., Hatton, C., Knapp, M., Walsh, P.N. and Hallam, A. (2005b) 'Costs and Outcomes of Community Residential Supports in England.' In R.J. Stancliffe and K.C. Lakin (eds) *Costs and Outcomes of Community Services for People with Intellectual Disabilities.* Baltimore: Paul H. Brookes Publishing Co.

Ericsson, K. (1996) 'Housing for the person with intellectual handicap.' In J. Mansell and K. Ericsson (eds) *Deinstitutionalization and Community Living: Intellectual Disability Services in Britain, Scandinavia and the USA.* London: Chapman and Hall.

ERLS Inc. (2006) *A Change of Perspective: A Guide to Accessible and Inclusive Sport and Recreation Opportunities in Your Community.* Melbourne: Eastern Recreation and Leisure Services Inc.

Felce, D. (1989) *The Andover Project: Staffed Housing for Adults with Severe or Profound Mental Handicaps.* Kidderminster: British Institute of Mental Handicap.

Felce, D. (1996) 'Quality of Support for Ordinary Living.' In J. Mansell and K. Ericsson (eds) *Deinstitutionalization and Community Living: Intellectual Disability Services in Britain, Scandinavia and the USA.* London: Chapman and Hall.

Felce, D. (1998) 'The determinants of staff and resident activity in residential services for people with severe intellectual disability: Moving beyond size, building design, location and number of staff.' *Journal of Intellectual and Developmental Disability 23*, 2, 103–119.

Felce, D. and Emerson, E. (2005) 'Costs, Outcomes, and Economies of Scale: Findings from the U.K. Research.' In R.J. Stancliffe and K.C. Lakin (eds) *Costs and Outcomes of Community Services for People with Intellectual Disabilities.* Baltimore: Paul H. Brookes Publishing Co.

Felce, D. and Perry, J. (1995) 'The extent of support for ordinary living provided in staffed housing: The relationship between staffing levels, resident characteristics, staff:resident interactions and resident activity patterns.' *Social Science and Medicine 40*, 6, 799–810.

Felce, D. and Toogood, S. (1988) *Close to Home.* Kidderminster: British Institute of Mental Handicap.

Felce, D., Bowley, C., Baxter, H., Jones, E., Lowe, K. and Emerson, E. (2000) 'The effectiveness of staff support: Evaluating Active Support training using a conditional probability approach.' *Research in Developmental Disabilities 21*, 243–255.

Felce, D., Grant, G., Todd, S., Ramcharan, P. *et al.* (1998) *Towards a Full Life: Researching Policy Innovation for People with Learning Disabilities.* Melbourne: Butterworth Heinemann.

Felce, D., Lowe, K. and Jones, E. (2002) 'Staff activity in supported housing services.' *Journal of Applied Research in Intellectual Disabilities 15*, 4, 388–403.

Felce, D., Perry, J., Romeo, R., Robertson, J. *et al.* (2008) 'Outcomes and costs of community living: Semi-independent living and fully staffed group homes.' *American Journal on Mental Retardation 113*, 2, 87–101.

Felce, D., Smith, J. and Kushlick, A. (1981) 'Evaluation of the Wessex experiment.' *Nursing Times 49*, 2113–2116.

Ferguson, I. (2008) *Reclaiming Social Work: Challenging Neo-liberalism and Promoting Social Justice.* London: Sage Publications.

Finlay, W.M.L. and Lyons, E. (2005) 'Rejecting the label: A social constructionist analysis.' *Mental Retardation 43*, 2, 120–134.

Finlay, W.M.L., Antaki, C. and Walton, C. (2008) 'A manifesto for the use of video in service improvement and staff development in residential services for people with learning disabilities.' *British Journal of Learning Disabilities 36*, 227–231.

Finlay, W.M.L., Antaki, C., Walton, C. and Stribling, P. (2008) 'The dilemma for staff in "playing a game" with a person with profound intellectual disabilities: Empowerment, inclusion and competence in interactional practice.' *Sociology of Health and Illness 30*, 4, 531–549.

Finlay, W.M.L., Walton, C. and Antaki, C. (2008) 'Promoting choice and control in residential services for people with learning disabilities.' *Disability and Society 23*, 4, 349–360.

Fitton, P., O'Brien, C. and Wilson, J. (1995) *Home at Last: How Two Young Women with Profound Intellectual and Multiple Disabilities Achieved Their Own Home.* London: Jessica Kingsley Publishers.

Flynn, R.J. and Aubry, T.D. (1999) 'Integration of Persons with Developmental or Psychiatric Disabilities: Conceptualization and Measurement.' In R.J. Flynn and R.A. Lemay (eds) *A Quarter-century of Normalization and Social Role Valorization: Evolution and Impact.* Ottawa: University of Ottawa Press.

Ford, K. and Hargreaves, S. (1991) *First Line Management: Staff.* Harlow: Longman Group UK.

Fournies, F.F. (1988) *Why Employees Don't Do What They're Supposed to Do and What to Do About It.* Blue Ridge Summit, PA: Liberty Hall Press.

Francis, D. and Young, D. (1992) *Improving Work Groups: A Practical Manual for Team Building.* San Francisco, CA: Jossey-Bass.

Fraser, N. (1996) *Social Justice in the Age of Identity Politics: Redistribution, Recognition, and Participation.* Tanner Lectures on Human Values, Stanford University, 30 April–2 May. Available at www.tannerlectures.utah.edu/lectures/documents/Fraser98.pdf, accessed 23 April 2009.

Freckelton, I. (2005) 'Institutional Death: The Coronial Inquest into the Deaths of Nine Men with Intellectual Disabilities.' In K. Johnson and R. Traustadóttir (eds) *Deinstitutionalization and People with Intellectual Disabilities.* London: Jessica Kingsley Publishers.

Friedman, J. (1999) 'The Hybridization of Roots and the Abhorrence of the Bush.' In M. Featherstone and S. Lash (eds) *Spaces of Culture: City – Nation – World.* London: Sage Publications.

Fryer, R.H. (2006) *Learning for a Change in Healthcare.* London: Department of Health.

Furedi, F. (1997) *Culture of Fear: Risk-taking and the Morality of Low Expectation.* London: Cassell.

Furedi, F. (2004) *Where Have All the Intellectuals Gone? Confronting 21st Century Philistinism.* London: Continuum.

Gardner, J.F. and Curran, D.T. (2005) 'Attainment of personal outcomes by people with developmental disabilities.' *Mental Retardation 43,* 3, 157–174.

Gaskell, E. (1985) *Link-up: An Integrated Leisure Service for Mentally Handicapped Teenagers and Young Adults Living in the Community.* Salford: Barnardo's North West Division.

Georgiades, N.J. and Phillimore, L. (1975) 'The Myth of the Hero-innovator and Alternative Strategies for Organizational Change.' In C.C. Kiernan and F.R. Woodford (eds) *Behaviour Modification with the Severely Retarded.* Amsterdam: Associated Scientific Publishers.

Gershuny, J. (2005) 'Busyness as the badge of honour for the new superordinate working class.' *Working Papers of the Institute for Social and Economic Research,* paper 2005–9. Colchester: University of Essex.

Gibson, G. and Ludwig, E.G. (1968) 'Family structure in a disabled population.' *Journal of Marriage and the Family 30,* 1, 54–63.

Gifford, J.E. (2006) 'A study of the work managers in residential services for people with learning disabilities.' Unpublished PhD in Learning Disabilities, University of Kent, Canterbury.

Gilson, S.F., Tusler, A. and Gill, C. (1997) 'Ethnographic research in disability identity: Self-determination and community.' *Journal of Vocational Rehabilitation 9,* 1–17.

Goffman, E. (1961/1978) *Asylums: Essays on the Social Situation of Mental Patients and Other Inmates.* London: Pelican Books.

Green, D. and Sykes, D. (2007) 'Balancing Rights, Risk and Protection of Adults.' In C. Bigby, C. Fyffe and E. Ozanne (eds) *Planning and Support for People with Intellectual Disabilities: Issues for Case Managers and Other Professionals.* London: Jessica Kingsley Publishers.

Hall, E. (2005) 'The entangled geographies of social exclusion/inclusion for people with learning disabilities.' *Health and Place 11,* 107–115.

Handy, C. (1993) *Understanding Organizations,* 4th edn. London: Penguin.

Haralambos, M. and Holborn, M. (1991) *Sociology: Themes and Perspectives,* 3rd edn. London: Collins Educational.

Hardman, M.L. and Clark, C. (2006) 'Promoting friendship through Best Buddies: A national survey of college program participants.' *Mental Retardation 44,* 1, 56–63.

Hart, E. and Bond, M. (1995) *Action Research for Health and Social Care: A Guide to Practice.* Buckingham: Open University Press.

Hastings, R.P., Remington, B. and Hatton, C. (1995) 'Future directions for research on staff performance in services for people with learning disabilities.' *Mental Handicap Research 8,* 4, 333–339.

Health and Community Services (2005) *IDS Accommodation Services Practice Instruction Manual* (vol. 2). Melbourne: State Government of Victoria, Department of Human Services.

Henderson, J. and Atkinson, D. (eds) (2003) *Managing Care in Context.* London: Routledge/Open University Press.

Hewitt, A.S. and Larson, S.A. (2005) 'Supporting and Training Supervisors.' In S.A. Larson and A.S. Hewitt (eds) *Staff Recruitment, Retention, and Training Strategies for Community Human Services Organizations.* Baltimore: Paul H. Brookes Publishing Co.

Hewitt, A.S., Larson, S., Lakin, K.C., Sauer, J., O'Nell, S. and Sedlezky, L. (2004) 'Role and essential competencies of the frontline supervisors of direct support professionals in community services.' *Mental Retardation 42,* 2, 122–135.

Hewitt, A.S., Larson, S., O'Nell, S., Sauer, J. and Sedlezky, L. (1998) *The Minnesota Frontline Supervisor Competencies and Performance Indicators: A Tool for Agencies Providing Community Services.* Minnesota: Research and Training Center on Community Living – Institute on Community Integration (UAP) and Minnesota Department of Human Services.

Hillery, G.A. (1955) 'Definitions of community: Areas of agreement.' *Rural Sociology 20,* 2, 111–123.

Honderich, T. (ed.) (1995) *The Oxford Companion to Philosophy.* Oxford: Oxford University Press.

Honey, P. and Mumford, A. (1992) *The Manual of Learning Styles.* Maidenhead: Peter Honey Publications.

Hornby, N. (2005) *A Long Way Down.* Camberwell: Penguin Group (Australia).

Howe, J., Horner, R.H. and Newton, J.S. (1998) 'Comparison of supported living and traditional residential services in the state of Oregon.' *Mental Retardation 36,* 1, 1–11.

Hughes, P., Black, A., Kaldor, P., Bellamy, J. and Castle, K. (2007) *Building Stronger Communities.* Sydney: University of New South Wales Press.

Hutchinson, C. (1998) 'Positive Health: A Collective Responsibility.' In P. Lacey and C. Ouvry (eds) *People with Profound and Multiple Learning Disabilities: A Collaborative Approach to Meeting Complex Needs.* London: David Fulton.

Hyland, T. (1993) 'Competence, knowledge and education.' *Journal of Philosophy of Education* 27, 1, 57–68.

Jackson, A.C. and Donovan, F. (1999) *Managing to Survive: Managerial Practice in Not-for-profit Organisations.* Buckingham: Open University Press.

Jenkins, J., Felce, D., Mansell, J., de Kock, U. and Toogood, S. (1987) 'Organising a Residential Service.' In W. Yule and J. Carr (eds) *Behaviour Modification for People with Mental Handicaps.* London: Croom Helm.

Jingree, T. and Finlay, W.M.L. (2008) '"You can't do it…it's theory rather than practice": Staff use of the practice/principle rhetorical device in talk on empowering people with learning disabilities.' *Discourse and Society 19,* 6, 705–726.

Jones, E. and Lowe, K. (2005) 'Empowering Service Users through Active Support.' In P. O'Brien and M. Sullivan (eds) *Allies in Emancipation: Shifting from Providing Service to Being of Support.* Melbourne: Thompson-Dunmore Press.

Jones, E., Felce, D., Lowe, K. and Bowley, C. (2001a) 'Evaluation of the dissemination of active support training and training trainers.' *Journal of Applied Research in Intellectual Disabilities 14,* 79–99.

Jones, E., Felce, D., Lowe, K., Bowley, C. *et al.* (2001b) 'Evaluation of the dissemination of active support training in staffed community residences.' *American Journal on Mental Retardation 106*, 4, 344–358.

Jones, E., Perry, J., Lowe, K., Allen, D., Toogood, S. and Felce, D. (1996a) *Active Support: A Handbook for Planning Daily Activities and Support Arrangements for People with Learning Disabilities* (vol. 3: *Opportunity Plans*). Cardiff: Welsh Centre for Learning Disabilities Applied Research Unit.

Jones, E., Perry, J., Lowe, K., Allen, D., Toogood, S. and Felce, D. (1996b) *Active Support: A Handbook for Planning Daily Activities and Support Arrangements for People with Learning Disabilities* (vol. 1: *Overview*). Cardiff: Welsh Centre for Learning Disabilities Applied Research Unit.

Jones, E., Perry, J., Lowe, K., Felce, D. *et al.* (1999) 'Opportunity and the promotion of activity among adults with severe intellectual disability living in community residences: The impact of training staff in active support.' *Journal of Intellectual Disability Research 43*, 3, 164–178.

Jones, K. (1975) *Opening the Door: A Study of New Policies for the Mentally Handicapped.* London: Routledge and Kegan Paul.

King's Fund Centre (1980) *An Ordinary Life: Comprehensive Locally-based Residential Services for Mentally Handicapped People.* London: King Edward's Hospital Fund.

King's Fund Centre (1984) *An Ordinary Working Life: Vocational Services for People with Mental Handicap.* London: King's Fund Centre.

King's Fund Centre (1988) *Ties and Connections: An Ordinary Community Life for People with Learning Difficulties.* London: King's Fund Centre.

Kinsella, P. (1993a) *Group Homes: An Ordinary Life?* Manchester: National Development Team.

Kinsella, P. (1993b) *Supported Living: A New Paradigm.* Manchester: National Development Team.

Knox, M. (2007) 'A Life Managed or a Lived Life? A Parental View on Case Management.' In C. Bigby, C. Fyffe and E. Ozanne (eds) *Planning and Support for People with Intellectual Disabilities: Issues for Case Managers and Other Professionals.* London: Jessica Kingsley Publishers.

Kozma, A., Mansell, J. and Beadle-Brown, J. (2009) 'Outcomes in different residential settings for people with intellectual disability: A systematic review.' *American Journal on Intellectual and Developmental Disabilities 114*, 3, 193–222.

Kurst-Swanger, K. and Petcosky, J.L. (2003) *Violence in the Home: Multidisciplinary Perspectives.* Oxford: Oxford University Press.

Lakin, K.C. and Stancliffe, R.J. (2007) 'Residential supports for persons with intellectual and developmental disabilities.' *Mental Retardation and Developmental Disabilities Research Reviews 13*, 151–159.

Lakin, K.C., Gardner, J., Larson, S., Wheeler, B. *et al.* (2005) 'Access and Support for Community Lives, Homes, and Social Roles.' In K.C. Lakin and A. Turnbull (eds) *National Goals and Research for People with Intellectual and Developmental Disabilities.* Washington, DC: American Association on Mental Retardation.

Landesman, S. (1988) 'Preventing "Institutionalization" in the Community.' In M.P. Janicki, M. Wyngaardwn Krauss and M.M. Seltzer (eds) *Community Residences for Persons with Developmental Disabilities: Here to Stay.* Baltimore: Paul H Brookes Publishing Co.

Larson, S.A., Doljanac, R., Nord, D.K., Salmi, P., Hewitt, A.S. and O'Nell, S. (2007) *National Validation Study of Competencies for Frontline Supervisors and Direct Support Professionals.*

Minneapolis: University of Minnesota, Research and Training Center on Community Integration.

LaVigna, G.W. (2005) 'A positive behavioural support model for breaking barriers to social and community inclusion.' *Tizard Learning Disability Review 10*, 2, 16–23.

LaVigna, G.W., Willis, T.J., Shaull, J.F., Abedi, M. and Sweitzer, M. (1994) *The Periodic Service Review: A Total Quality Assurance System for Human Services and Education.* Baltimore: Paul H. Brookes Publishing Co.

Lowe, K. and de Paiva, S. (1991) *NIMROD: An Overview. A Summary Report of a 5 Year Research Study of Community Based Service Provision for People with Learning Difficulties.* London: Her Majesty's Stationery Office.

Luckasson, R., Schalock, R.L., Spitalnik, D.M., Spreat, S. *et al.* (eds) (2002) *Mental Retardation: Definition, Classification, and Systems of Supports,* 10th edn. Washington, DC: American Association on Mental Retardation.

Lum, G. (1999) 'Where's the competence in competence-based education and training?' *Journal of Philosophy of Education 33*, 3, 403–418.

Mallinson, I. (1995) *Keyworking: An Examination of a Method of Individualising Care for Older People in Residential Establishments.* Aldershot: Avebury.

Manning, C. (2008) *Bye-bye Charlie: Stories from the Vanishing World of Kew Cottages.* Sydney: University of New South Wales Press.

Mansell, J. (1996) 'Issues in Community Services in Britain.' In J. Mansell and K. Ericsson (eds) *Deinstitutionalization and Community Living: Intellectual Disability Services in Britain, Scandinavia and the USA.* London: Chapman and Hall.

Mansell, J. (2005) 'Deinstitutionalisation and community living: An international perspective.' *Tizard Learning Disability Review 10*, 1, 22–29.

Mansell, J. (2006) 'Deinstitutionalisation and community living: Progress, problems and priorities.' *Journal of Intellectual and Developmental Disabilities 31*, 2, 65–76.

Mansell, J. and Elliott, T. (2001) 'Staff members' prediction of consequences for their work in residential settings.' *American Journal on Mental Retardation 106*, 5, 434–447.

Mansell, J., Beadle-Brown, J., Ashman, B. and Ockenden, J. (2004) *Person-centred Active Support: A Multi-media Training Resource for Staff to Enable Participation, Inclusion and Choice for People with Learning Disabilities.* Brighton: Pavilion Publishing.

Mansell, J., Beadle-Brown, J., Whelton, B., Beckett, C. and Hutchinson, A. (2008) 'Effect of service structure and organization on staff care practices in small community homes for people with intellectual disabilities.' *Journal of Applied Research in Intellectual Disabilities 21*, 5, 398–413.

Mansell, J., Elliott, T., Beadle-Brown, J., Ashman, B. and Macdonald, S. (2002) 'Engagement in meaningful activity and "active support" of people with intellectual disabilities in residential care.' *Research in Developmental Disabilities 23*, 342–352.

Mansell, J., Felce, D. and de Kock, U. (1982) 'Increasing staff ratios in an activity with severely mentally handicapped people.' *British Journal of Mental Subnormality 28*, 97–99.

Mansell, J., Felce, D., Jenkins, J., de Kock, U. and Toogood, S. (1987) *Developing Staffed Housing for People with Mental Handicaps.* Tunbridge Wells: D.J. Costello (Publishers) Ltd.

Mansell, J., Hughes, H. and McGill, P. (1994) 'Maintaining Local Residential Placements.' In E. Emerson, P. McGill and J. Mansell (eds) *Severe Learning Disabilities and Challenging Behaviour: Designing High Quality Services.* London: Chapman and Hall.

Mansell, J., McGill, P. and Emerson, E. (1994) 'Conceptualizing Service Provision.' In E. Emerson, P. McGill and J. Mansell (eds) *Severe Learning Disabilities and Challenging Behaviour: Designing High Quality Services.* London: Chapman and Hall.

Mansell, J., McGill, P. and Emerson, E. (2001) 'Development and evaluation of innovative residential services for people with severe intellectual disability and serious challenging behaviour.' In L.M. Glidden (ed.) *International Review of Research in Mental Retardation 24*, 245–298. New York: Academic Press.

Marquis, R. and Jackson, R. (2000) 'Quality of life and quality of service relationships: Experiences of people with disabilities.' *Disability and Society 15*, 3, 411–425.

Martin, J. (2002) *Organizational Culture: Mapping the Terrain.* London: Sage Publications.

Maslow, A.H. (1954/1987) *Motivation and Personality*, 3rd edn. London: Harper and Row.

McArdle, J. (1998) *Resource Manual for Facilitators in Community Development* (vols I and II). Melbourne: Vista Publications.

McConkey, R. (2005) 'Promoting Friendships and Developing Social Networks.' In G. Grant, P. Goward, M. Richardson and P. Ramcharan (eds) *Learning Disability: A Life Cycle Approach to Valuing People.* Maidenhead: Open University Press.

McCubbery, J. and Fyffe, C. (2006) *Evaluation of Active Support Pilot Project.* Melbourne: Victorian Department of Human Services.

Miles, M.B. and Huberman, A.M. (1994) *Qualitative Data Analysis: A Sourcebook of New Methods*, 2nd edn. London: Sage Publications.

Morgan, G. (1997) *Images of Organization*, 2nd edn. London: Sage Publications.

Mulvany, F., Barron, S. and McConkey, R. (2007) 'Residential provision for adult persons with intellectual disabilities in Ireland.' *Journal of Applied Research in Intellectual Disabilities 20*, 70–76.

Myers, F., Ager, A., Kerr, P. and Myles, S. (1998) 'Outside looking in? Studies of the community integration of people with learning disabilities.' *Disability and Society 13*, 3, 389–413.

Nirje, B. (1969/1976) 'The Normalization Principle.' In R.B. Kugel and A. Shearer (eds) *Changing Patterns in Residential Services for the Mentally Retarded*, rev. edn. Washington, DC: President's Committee on Mental Retardation.

Oakleigh Centre (2006) *Recreation Services.* Available at www.oakleighcentre.org/recreation.htm, accessed 23 April 2009.

O'Brien, J. (1987) 'A Guide to Life-style Planning: Using the Activities Catalog to Integrate Services and Natural Support Systems.' In B. Wilcox and G. Bellamy (eds) *The Activities Catalog: An Alternative Curriculum for Youth and Adults with Severe Disabilities.* Baltimore: Paul H. Brookes Publishing Co.

O'Brien, J. (1994) 'Down stairs that are never your own: Supporting people with developmental disabilities in their own homes.' *Mental Retardation 32*, 1, 1–6.

O'Brien, J. (2005a) 'Out of the Institution Trap.' In K. Johnson and R. Traustadóttir (eds) *Deinstitutionalization and People with Intellectual Disabilities.* London: Jessica Kingsley Publishers.

O'Brien, J. (2005b) 'A turning point in the struggle to replace institutions.' *Tizard Learning Disability Review 10*, 1, 12–17.

O'Brien, J. and Mount, B. (1991) 'Telling New Stories: The Search for Capacity Among People with Severe Handicaps.' In J. O'Brien and C.L. O'Brien (eds) *Framework for Accomplishment: A Workshop for People Developing Better Services.* Lithonia, GA: Responsive Systems Associates.

O'Brien, J. and O'Brien, C.L. (1993) 'Unlikely alliances: Friendships and people with developmental disabilities.' In A.N. Amado (ed.) *Friendships and Community Connections between People with and without Developmental Disabilities.* Baltimore: Paul H. Brookes Publishing Co.

O'Brien, P., Thesing, A. and Capie, A. (2005) 'Supporting People Out of One Institution While Avoiding Another.' In P. O'Brien and M. Sullivan (eds) *Allies in Emancipation: Shifting from Providing Service to Being of Support.* Melbourne: Thompson-Dunmore Press.

Organ, D.W. and Ryan, K. (1995) 'A meta-analytic review of attitudinal and dispositional predictors of organizational citizenship behaviour.' *Personnel Psychology 48,* 775–802.

Osbourne, R. (2002) *Megawords: 200 Terms You Really Need to Know.* London: Sage Publications.

Parmenter, T.R. and Arnold, S.R.C. (2008) *Disability Accommodation and Support Framework Report.* Sydney: Centre for Developmental Disability Studies.

Patton, M.Q. (2008) *Utilization-focused Evaluation,* 4th edn. London: Sage Publications.

Pawlyn, J. and Carnaby, S. (eds) (2009) *Profound Intellectual and Multiple Disabilities: Nursing Complex Needs.* Chichester: Wiley-Blackwell.

Pawson, R., Boaz, A., Grayson, L., Long, A. and Barnes, C. (2003) *Types and Quality of Knowledge in Social Care.* London: Social Care Institute for Excellence.

Peace, S.M. (1998) 'Caring in Place.' In A. Brechin, J. Walmsley, J. Katz and S. Peace (eds) *Care Matters: Concepts, Practice and Research in Health and Social Care.* London: Sage Publications.

Pearce, J. and Smith, S. (2000) *Keyworking.* Brighton: Pavilion Publishing.

Perry, A., Reilly, S., Bloomberg, K. and Johnson, H. (2002) *An Analysis of Needs for People with a Disability who have Complex Communication Needs.* Melbourne: School of Human Communication Sciences, Faculty of Health Sciences, La Trobe University.

Perske, R. (1972) 'The Dignity of Risk.' In W. Wolfensberger (ed.) *The Principle of Normalization in Human Services.* Downsview: NIMR.

Perske, R. (1993) 'Introduction.' In A.N. Amado (ed.) *Friendships and Community Connections between People with and without Developmental Disabilities.* Baltimore: Paul H. Brookes Publishing Co.

Peters, T.J. and Waterman, R.H. (1982) *In Search of Excellence: Lessons from America's Best-run Companies.* New York: HarperCollins.

Porterfield, J. (1987) *Positive Monitoring: A Method of Supporting Staff and Improving Services for People with Learning Disabilities.* Kidderminster: BIMH Publications.

Potts, M. and Fido, R. (1991) *'A Fit Person to be Removed': Personal Accounts of Life in a Mental Deficiency Institution.* Plymouth: Northcote House Publishers.

Proctor, B. (1998) 'Supervision: A Cooperative Exercise in Accountability.' In M. Marken and M. Payne (eds) *Enabling and Ensuring: Supervision in Practice,* 2nd edn. Leicester: National Youth Bureau and Council for Education and Training in Youth and Community Work.

Proehl, R.A. (2001) *Organizational Change in Human Services.* Thousand Oaks, CA: Sage Publications.

Putnam, R.D. (2000) *Bowling Alone: The Collapse and Revival of American Community.* New York: Simon and Schuster.

Putnam, R.D., Feldstein, L. and Cohen, D.J. (2004) *Better Together: Restoring the American Community.* New York: Simon and Schuster.

Ragin, C.C. (1987) *The Comparative Method: Moving Beyond Qualitative and Quantitative Strategies.* Berkeley, CA: University of California Press.

Ramcharan, P. and Richardson, M. (2005) 'Engaging Communities of Interest.' In G. Grant, P. Goward, M. Richardson and P. Ramcharan (eds) *Learning Disability: A Life Cycle Approach to Valuing People.* Maidenhead: Open University Press.

Ramcharan, P., McGrath, M. and Grant, G. (1997) 'Voices and Choices: Mapping Entitlements to Friendships and Community Contacts.' In P. Ramcharan, G. Roberts, G.

Grant and J. Borland (eds) *Empowerment in Everyday Life: Learning Disability.* London: Jessica Kingsley Publishers.

Rapley, M. (2000) 'The Social Construction of Quality of Life: The Interpersonal Production of Well-being Revisited.' In K.D. Keith and R.L. Schalock (eds) *Cross-cultural Perspectives on Quality of Life.* Washington, DC: AAMR.

Raynes, N.V., Wright, K., Shiell, A. and Pettipher, C. (1994) *The Cost and Quality of Community Residential Care.* London: Fulton.

Reid, D.H., Everson, J.M. and Green, C.W. (1999) 'A systematic evaluation of preferences identified through Person-Centred Planning for people with profound multiple disabilities.' *Journal of Applied Behavior Analysis 32,* 4, 467–477.

Reid, D.H., Parsons, M.B. and Green, C.W. (1989) *Staff Management in Human Services: Behavioral Research and Application.* Springfield, IL: Charles C. Thomas.

Reynolds, J. (2003) 'Becoming a Manager: Acting or Reacting?' In J. Seden and J. Reynolds (eds) *Managing Care in Practice.* London: Routledge/Open University Press.

Reynolds, J. and Walmsley, J. (1998) 'Care, Support, or Something Else?' In A. Brechin, J. Walmsley, J. Katz and S. Peace (eds) *Care Matters: Concepts, Practice and Research in Health and Social Care.* London: Sage Publications.

Robertson, A., Frawley, P. and Bigby, C. (2008) *Making Life Good in the Community: When is a House a Home?* Melbourne: Victorian Department of Human Services.

Robertson, J. and Emerson, E. (2007) 'Review of Evaluative Research on Case Management for People with Intellectual Disabilities.' In C. Bigby, C. Fyffe and E. Ozanne (eds) *Planning and Support for People with Intellectual Disabilities: Issues for Case Managers and Other Professionals.* London: Jessica Kingsley Publishers.

Robertson, J., Emerson, E., Gregory, N., Hatton, C. *et al.* (2001) 'Social networks of people with mental retardation in residential settings.' *Mental Retardation 39,* 3, 201–214.

Robertson, J., Emerson, E., Hatton, C., Elliott, J. *et al.* (2005) *The Impact of Person Centred Planning.* Lancaster: Institute for Health Research, Lancaster University.

Robertson, J., Emerson, E., Hatton, C., Elliott, J. *et al.* (2006) 'Longitudinal analysis of the impact and cost of person-centred planning for people with intellectual disabilities in England.' *American Journal on Mental Retardation 111,* 6, 400–416.

Roethlisberger, F.J., Dickson, W.J. and Wright, H.A. (1939/1964) *Management and the Worker: An Account of a Research Program Conducted by the Western Electric Company, Hawthorne Works, Chicago.* Cambridge, MA: Harvard University Press.

Rogers, A. and Reynolds, J. (2003) 'Leadership and Vision.' In J. Seden and J. Reynolds (eds) *Managing Care in Practice.* London: Routledge.

Rose, J. (1993) 'Stress and staff in residential settings: The move from hospital to the community.' *Mental Handicap Research 6,* 4, 312–332.

Rossi, P.H., Lipsey, M.W. and Freeman, H.E. (2004) *Evaluation: A Systematic Approach,* 7th edn. London: Sage Publications.

Sanderson, H., Kennedy, J., Ritchie, P. and Goodwin, G. (2002) *People, Plans and Possibilities: Exploring Person Centred Planning,* 2nd edn. Edinburgh: SHS Ltd.

Schein, E.H. (1999) *Process Consultation Revisited: Building the Helping Relationship.* Sydney: Addison-Wesley Publishing Company.

Schwier, K.M. and Stewart, E.S. (2005) *Breaking Bread, Nourishing Connections – People with and without Disabilities Together at Mealtimes.* Baltimore: Paul H. Brookes Publishing Co.

Scope (Vic) Ltd (2005) *Developing Community Connections at a Local Level.* Melbourne: Scope (Vic) Ltd.

Seden, J. and Reynolds, J. (eds) (2003) *Managing Care in Practice.* London: Routledge/Open University Press.

Simons, K. (1995) *My Home, My Life: Innovative Approaches to Housing and Support for People with Learning Difficulties.* London: Values into Action/The Norah Fry Research Centre.

Simpson, J. and Weiner, E. (eds) (1989) *Oxford English Dictionary,* 2nd edn. Oxford: Oxford University Press.

Sines, D. (1992) 'Managing Services to Assure Quality.' In T. Thompson and P. Mathias (eds) *Standards and Mental Handicap.* London: Baillière Tindall.

Sinson, J.C. (1993) *Group Homes and Community Integration of Developmentally Disabled People: Micro-institutionalisation?* London: Jessica Kingsley Publishers.

Sixsmith, J. (1986) 'The meaning of home: An exploratory study of environmental experience.' *Journal of Environmental Psychology 6,* 4, 281–298.

Smith, M. (2005) 'Foreword: An Appetizer.' In K.M. Schwier and E.S. Stewart (eds) *Breaking Bread, Nourishing Connections – People with and without Disabilities Together at Mealtimes.* Baltimore: Paul H. Brookes Publishing Co.

Smull, M.W. (2002) 'Revisiting Choice.' In J. O'Brien and C.L. O'Brien (eds) *A Little Book about Person Centred Planning.* Toronto: Inclusion Press.

Spradley, J.P. (1980) *Participant Observation.* London: Holt, Rinehart and Winston.

Stancliffe, R.J. (2005) 'Semi-independent Living and Group Homes in Australia.' In R.J. Stancliffe and K.C. Lakin (eds) *Costs and Outcomes of Community Services for People with Intellectual Disabilities.* Baltimore: Paul H. Brookes Publishing Co.

Stancliffe, R. and Keane, S. (2000) 'Outcomes and costs of community living: A matched comparison of group homes and semi-independent living.' *Journal of Intellectual and Developmental Disability 25,* 281-305.

Stancliffe, R.J. and Lakin, K.C. (2005) 'Context and Issues in Research on Expenditures and Outcomes of Community Supports.' In R.J. Stancliffe and K.C. Lakin (eds) *Costs and Outcomes of Community Services for People with Intellectual Disabilities.* Baltimore: Paul H. Brookes Publishing Co.

Stancliffe, R.J., Harman, A.D., Toogood, S. and McVilly, K.R. (2007) 'Australian implementation and evaluation of active support.' *Journal of Applied Research in Intellectual Disabilities 20,* 211–227.

Stancliffe, R.J., Jones, E., Mansell, J. and Lowe, K. (2008) 'Active Support: A critical review and commentary.' *Journal of Intellectual and Developmental Disability 33,* 3, 196–214.

Stone, F.M. (1998) *Coaching, Counseling and Mentoring: How to Choose and Use the Right Technique to Boost Employee Performance.* New York: AMACOM/American Management Association.

Stoner, J.F., Freeman, R.E. and Gilbert, D.R. (1995) *Management,* 6th edn. Englewood Cliffs, NJ: Prentice-Hall International.

Swain, J. and French, S. (1998) 'Normality and Disabling Care.' In A. Brechin, J. Walmsley, J. Katz and S. Peace (eds) *Care Matters: Concepts, Practice and Research in Health and Social Care.* London: Sage Publications.

Sykes, D. (2005) 'Risk and rights: The need to redress the imbalance.' *Journal of Intellectual and Developmental Disability 30,* 3, 185–188.

Tajfel, H. (1978) 'Social categorization, social identity and social comparison.' In H. Tajfel (ed.) *Differentiation between Social Groups: Studies in Social Psychology of Intergroup Relations.* London: Academic Press.

Tannenbaum, A.S. and Schmidt, W.H. (1958) 'How to choose a leadership pattern.' *Harvard Business Review 36* (March–April), 95–101.

Thompson, T., Robinson, J., Dietrich, M., Farris, M. and Sinclair, V. (1996a) 'Architectural features and perceptions of community residences for people with mental retardation.' *American Journal on Mental Retardation 101*, 3, 292–313.

Thompson, T., Robinson, J., Dietrich, M., Farris, M. and Sinclair, V. (1996b) 'Interdependence of architectural features and program variables in community residences for people with mental retardation.' *American Journal on Mental Retardation 101*, 3, 315–327.

Thompson, T., Robinson, J., Graff, M. and Ingenmey, R. (1990) 'Home-like architectural features of residential environments.' *American Journal on Mental Retardation 95*, 3, 328–341.

Todd, S., Evans, G. and Beyer, S. (1990) 'More recognised than known: The social visibility and attachment of people with developmental disabilities.' *Australia and New Zealand Journal of Developmental Disabilities 16*, 207–218.

Toogood, S. (2008) 'Interactive training.' *Journal of Intellectual and Developmental Disability 33*, 3, 215–224.

Tøssebro, J. (2005) 'Reflections on Living Outside: Continuity and Change in the Life of "Outsiders".' In K. Johnson and R. Traustadóttir (eds) *Deinstitutionalization and People with Intellectual Disabilities*. London: Jessica Kingsley Publishers.

Totsika, V., Toogood, S. and Hastings, R. (2008a) 'Active Support: Development, evidence base, and future directions.' *International Review of Research in Mental Retardation 35*, 205–249.

Totsika, V., Toogood, S., Hastings, R. and Nash, S. (2008b) 'Interactive training for active support: Perspectives from staff.' *Journal of Intellectual and Developmental Disability 33*, 3, 225–238.

Towell, D. (1980/1982) 'Foreword – Progress towards "An Ordinary Life".' In King's Fund Centre (ed.) *An Ordinary Life: Comprehensive Locally-based Residential Services for Mentally Handicapped People*. London: King's Fund Centre.

Tracy, E.M. and Abell, N. (1994) 'Social network map: Some further refinements on administration.' *Social Work Research 18*, 1, 56–60.

Tracy, E.M. and Whittaker, J.K. (1990) 'The social network map: Assessing social support in clinical practice.' *Families in Society: The Journal of Contemporary Human Services 71*, 8, 461–470.

Tropman, J.E. (2006) *Supervision and Management in Nonprofits and Human Services*. Peosta, IA: Eddie Bowers Publishing Co.

Tsoukas, H. (1994) 'What is management? An outline of a metatheory.' *British Journal of Management 5*, 289–301.

United Nations (2006) *Convention on the Rights of Persons with Disabilities and Optional Protocol*. Available at www.un.org/disabilities/documents/convention/convoptprot-e.pdf, accessed 23 April 2009.

Victorian Workcover Authority (2005) *Annual Report 2005*. Melbourne: Victorian Workcover Authority.

Video Arts (1976) *Meetings Bloody Meetings* [videotape]. London: Video Arts Ltd.

Walsh, J. (1984) *Friendship Scheme*. Dublin: St Michael's House Research.

Walsh, P.N., Emerson, E., Lobb, C., Hatton *et al.* (2007) *Supported Accommodation Services for People with Intellectual Disabilities: A Review of Models and Instruments Used to Measure Quality of Life in Various Settings*. Dublin: National Disability Authority.

Ward, L. (1992) 'Foreword.' In H. Brown and H. Smith (eds) *Normalisation: The Reader for the Nineties*. London: Routledge.

Ware, J. (2004) 'Ascertaining the views of people with profound and multiple learning disabilities.' *British Journal of Learning Disabilities 32*, 4, 175–179.

Warren, S. (2004/2006) *Activity Learning Log*. Melbourne: Victorian Department of Human Services, Eastern Metropolitan Region.

Wertheimer, A. (1995) *Circles of Support: Building Inclusive Communities*. Mangotsfield: Circles Network UK.

White, R.K. and Lippit, R. (1953) 'Leader Behavior and Member Reaction in Three Social Climates.' In D. Cartwright and A. Zander (eds) *Group Dynamics*. New York: Row, Peterson and Company.

Whittell, B., Ramcharan, P. and Members of People First Cardiff and the Vale (1998) 'Self-advocacy: Speaking up for Ourselves and Each Other.' In L. Ward (ed.) *Innovations in Advocacy and Empowerment for People with Intellectual Disabilities*. Whittle-le-Woods: Lisieux Hall Publications.

Whittington, A. (1993) 'The social networks of people with learning difficulties: Factors influencing networks and a method of promoting network growth.' Unpublished MSc thesis, University of Birmingham.

Williams, P. (1993) 'There's no place like an ordinary home.' *Community Living*, January, 10–11.

Wolcott, H.F. (1994) *Transforming Qualitative Data: Description, Analysis and Interpretation*. London: Sage Publications.

Wolfensberger, W. (1972) *Normalization – The Principle of Normalization in Human Services*. Toronto: National Institute on Mental Retardation.

Wolfensberger, W. (1975) *The Origin and Nature of Our Institutional Models*. Syracuse, NY: Human Policy Press.

Wolfensberger, W. (1983) 'Social role valorization: A proposed new term for the principle of normalization.' *Mental Retardation 21*, 6, 234–239.

Wolfensberger, W. (1998) *A Brief Introduction to Social Role Valorisation: A High-order Concept for Addressing the Plight of Societally Devalued People, and for Structuring Human Services*, 3rd edn. Syracuse, NY: Training Institute for Human Service Planning, Leadership and Change Agentry.

Wolfensberger, W. and Thomas, S. (1983) *Program Analysis of Service Systems Implementation of Normalization Goals (PASSING): Normalization Criteria and Ratings Manual*, 2nd edn. Downsview, Ontario: National Institute on Mental Retardation.

Yazbeck, M., McVilly, K. and Parmenter, T.R. (2004) 'Attitudes toward people with intellectual disabilities.' *Journal of Disability Policy Studies 15*, 2, 97–111.

Zijlstra, R.H.P., Vlaskamp, C. and Buntinx, W.H.E. (2001) 'Direct care staff turnover: An indicator of the quality of life of individuals with profound multiple disabilities.' *European Journal on Mental Disability 22*, 38–55.

Zola, I.K. (1987) 'The politicization of the self-help movement.' *Social Policy 18*, 2, 32–33.

Subject Index

Author Index